National Schism

and Civil Integration

National Schism

and Civil Integration

Mutual Relations between the Israeli Central Government
and the Israeli Arab Palestinian Minority

ALEXANDER BLIGH
and GADI HITMAN

sussex
ACADEMIC
PRESS
Brighton • Portland • Toronto

The right of Alexander Bligh and Gadi Hitman to be identified as Authors of this work has been asserted in accordance with the Copyright, Designs and Patents Act 1988.

2 4 6 8 10 9 7 5 3 1

First published in 2018 by
SUSSEX ACADEMIC PRESS
PO Box 139
Eastbourne BN24 9BP

Distributed in North America by
SUSSEX ACADEMIC PRESS
ISBS Publisher Services
920 NE 58th Ave #300, Portland, OR 97213, USA

British Library Cataloguing in Publication Data
A CIP catalogue record for this book is available from the British Library.

Library of Congress Cataloging-in-Publication Data
Names: Bligh, Alexander, 1949– author. | Hitman, Gadi, author.
Title: National schism and civil integration : mutual relations between the Israeli central government and the Israeli Arab Palestinian minority / Alexander Bligh and Gadi Hitman.
Description: Brighton ; Portland ; Toronto : Sussex Academic Press, [2018] | Includes bibliographical references and index.
Identifiers: LCCN 2017038958 | ISBN 9781845196493 (hbk : alk. paper)
Subjects: LCSH: Palestinian Arabs—Israel—Politics and government. | Palestinian
   Arabs—Israel—History. | Israel—Ethnic relations. | Israel—Politics and government—1993–
Classification: LCC DS113.7 .B55 2018 | DDC 305.80095694—dc23
LC record available at https://lccn.loc.gov/2017038958

MIX
Paper from
responsible sources
FSC
www.fsc.org
FSC® C013056

Typeset and designed by Sussex Academic Press, Brighton & Eastbourne.
Printed by TJ International, Padstow, Cornwall.

Contents

Preface

The relations between majority groups and minorities are a constant subject of research by different disciplines. Since most of the countries in the world are bi-cultural or multi-cultural, many questions arise for historians, sociologists, legal scholars and others that deal with policies adopted towards their minority groups and their place in the public and political domains.[1] One of these questions involves the extent of the private and collective rights that the minority groups have and their ability to preserve their separate cultural identities which often include different languages, religions, traditions and customs. As history has shown in modern times the reality is full of test cases that fashion a different reality from country to country, and this is the outcome of the nature of the regime (democratic, partly democratic, totalitarian, authoritarian and so on).

Since the last decade of the twentieth century international bodies have been trying to deal with the question of the future of minorities throughout the world and this has included efforts made to agree upon a definition of the concept "minority." One definition of a minority group that serves the purposes of this study is "a group whose number of members is lower than the rest of the country's population, is in a non-dominant position and whose members, who are citizens of the country, have different ethnic, religious and linguistic characteristics from those of the rest of the country's population, and who are recognized, even if only by implication, as having the aspiration to preserve their culture, traditions, religion and language."[2]

The existing research literature generally differentiates between three types of minorities, the first being an immigrant group that has, willingly or unwillingly, left its country of origin and settled in or escaped to another country. Sometimes these are work immigrants, sometimes those who are looking for a better quality of life, and sometimes refugees fleeing for their lives. They do not make any territorial claims from their adopted country and are satisfied with demanding basic rights usually in the areas of functional citizenship (identity document, passport, social benefits). Minorities of this type try to preserve the cultural heritage they have brought with them from their places of birth. Examples of this are the Black population that left

Africa and settled in France or the refugees who have fled the Middle East (mainly from Syria) since 2011 after which the area became politically and socially unstable.

The second group is made up of original minorities or natives that are peoples that have been living in territorial regions in which they have, for many years, felt themselves to be the sovereign rulers of the area. Their living space has, however, been conquered by immigrant groups that have chosen to impose a lifestyle, a political routine and a new sovereignty in place of the original-native minority. The outcome of this situation has been that the native minority, that only recently has been master of itself and the territory it has been occupying now finds itself deprived of its status and sovereignty.[3]

The significance of the words original-native is relevant and directly connects up with the third type of minority group. After World War I a document was prepared by the League of Nations entitled "A Protective Regime for Minorities." This document, in line with international law, viewed the minorities as legal entities and classified them as "national minorities," "religious minorities," and "linguistic minorities." The document dealt with the need to provide protection for minorities as human beings and not as citizens or groups that had national longings. In 1995 the European Convention for the Protection of Minorities which discussed the question of national minorities did not succeed in defining them because of the serious differences of opinion among the groups formulating the definition but also, apparently, because of the new reality that had been created in Europe following the flow of Muslims from all over the world to the continent. The Convention declared that the protection of minorities was necessary in order to preserve stability, democratic security and peace in the continent; that the suitable conditions that make it possible for minorities to express their identities, to preserve them and develop them must be created and that the member countries have to act to establish full and effective equality and prevent all forms of discrimination.[4]

This book deals with the complex relationship between Israel, as a Jewish-democratic state, and its Arab minority. The existing academic research on this subject has for many years tried to analyze the mutual relations that exist between the two parties. One of the central keys to understanding these relations is the policy of the State of Israel towards the Arab minority. This issue has become both fascinating and challenging especially because of the fact that the Declaration of Independence of the State of Israel contained a section on "the establishment of Jewish state in the Land of Israel" while at the same time undertaking that the new state would "maintain complete equality, social and political rights for all its citizens regardless of differences in religion, race and sex." Moreover, the declaration called upon the Arab people living in the State of Israel "to preserve the peace and take part in the building of the state on the basis of full citizenship and appropriate representation in all its institutions."[5]

As strange as it may seem, the research literature in its focus upon the policy of the Israeli establishment towards the Arab minority is very small and that which does exist focuses upon the first years after the establishment of the state when the military government was imposed on the Arab minority. In fact the only policy book that exists was signed in 1990, a year which, from a historical point of view, can be defined as a turning point due to the changes that took place in Israel's policy towards the Arab minority.

This study examines a number of key issues on the subject including what the policy lines of the Israeli government towards the Arab minority were from 1990 onwards and follows with the reasons that led to the change that took place in the establishment's policy and how this change was received by the Arab side. On the other side of the equation the study maps the central political and social frameworks in the Arab minority and examines the changes that took place in this group from the 1990s onwards.

Part One analyzes the policy of the Israeli government towards the Arab minority since 1948 from a historical point of view. The analysis is supported by earlier studies and by primary sources such as official documents of the Israeli government, state investigative committees and commissions, newspaper reports in Hebrew and Arabic and the personal diaries of key figures – both Jews and Arabs.

Part Two makes an analysis of the Israeli policy from 1990 until today and is almost completely based upon primary sources that include the official documents of government ministries, reports on subjects connected with the core issues such as religious radicalization among Israeli Arabs, the status of the Bedouins, the involvement of the Arab minority in protest and demonstrations and links to the Palestinian arena. The picture of the Israeli policy that arises is the result of an analysis of the responses made by ministers to the queries asked by members of the Knesset during the 1990s. These responses to queries about a variety of civil subjects such as health, welfare, and local government, the police, religion, culture and sport paint a coherent picture of the new policy that we suggest calling a policy of integration.

Part Three is dedicated to Arab society and the demographic, sociological, employment and social changes it has been undergoing during the last two decades. It includes an analysis of the status of women and their entering the work market, the activities of the civil society in the Arab sector, the attitude of the Arabs towards the initiatives being made about national/civic service, kinds of leisure-time activities of young Arabs and relations with the Israeli establishment.

Finally, the conclusions suggest that a historical examination of the mutual relations between the central government and the Arab minority requires a point of view that is based upon three basic components that will continue to characterize that complex relationship: religion, citizenship and nationalism. A close examination of the developing realities is especially called for since contemporary Israeli is a Jewish and democratic state, which is not prepared to give up its distinctly Jewish character (and thus does not completely include the Arab minority). The Arabs neither can nor want to identify with the Zionist symbols and thus remain hanging suspended between their Palestinian nationality and their Israeli citizenship.

Acknowledgements

My service as Israeli Prime Minister Shamir's deputy advisor and later Advisor on Arab affairs in the late 1980s and early 1990s took me from the ivory tower of academic research into the field and daily interaction with issues hitherto known to me from the literature. For five years I labored to study this ocean-wide topic of Arab affairs, to resolve issues both routine and ordinary, and yet grappling with the need to figure a policy encompassing all strategic dimensions of the topic of the Arab Israeli citizens. They are both Palestinian by their own national choice and Israeli citizens who swore allegiance to their country of residence and are entitled to all rights that go with the term "citizen."

The study presented here started as a course on "Israeli Arabs" at Bar Ilan University, which I taught in 2006. It aspired to put my own conclusions and impressions into academic context and provide the international and the Israeli reader with a thorough study of the mutual relations between the people, the Arab citizens in this case, and the central government. Even though the first couple of years analyzed in this book fall within my government service, the study is by no means a memoir. Quite the contrary. It is an analysis of politics, economics, demographics, and decision making as related to the Israeli Arab population from the perspective of academic norms supplemented by field experience.

This study could not have been carried out without the support both morally and materially of several bodies. The most outstanding among these are Ariel University and Bar Ilan University, through its BESA center led at the time by Prof. Efraim Inbar.

Many thanks to my research assistants who have catered to every request of mine and helped me out with most of the technical details. They included Omer Dostri, Reut Doron, Mor Jamal, and Tamar Cohen most of whom are now in their postgraduate stage.

A word of appreciation is due to my students both at Bar Ilan University and Ariel University who challenged me constantly and also referred me at times to sources that I had missed.

A special thank you goes to my devoted and amazing style editor, Ms. Erica Levin, with whom I have worked for a long time always enjoying her finesse and attitude. Last, but definitely not least, Dr. Gadi Hitman, my former PhD candidate and currently a university faculty member in his own right. This book is his as much as mine. He took upon himself the task to transform a manuscript into an up-to-date book, filling relentlessly the gaps and finally, crossing the t's and dotting the i's. Thank you, Gadi.

PART ONE

The Historical Background

Relations between the government in Israel and the Arab citizens of the country, as a result of complex historical processes, have been both complicated and strained since the State of Israel issued its Declaration of Independence in May 1948. First of all, the Arab minority rejects the fundamental Jewish and democratic ideology of the state with its core principle, agreed upon by the state's majority – that Israel was founded upon Zionist values.[1] Secondly, the Arab population is a native population. In general, original majorities or natives are peoples who have been living in territorial spaces for long periods during which they have considered themselves to be sovereign rulers of those territories. When groups of immigrants take over territories inhabited by native populations, the new rulers establish a new way of life, a new political agenda, and a new sovereignty in place of the original-native population that is now a minority. The native minority then realizes its loss of independence, sovereignty, and status.[2] Such situations usually increase the self-awareness and national demands of minorities.[3]

The Arabic term *Ṣumud* (holding on to the land of the forefathers) has a prime place in the list of priorities of the Arabs in Israel,[4] and from their point of view the state was established upon the ashes of their people and at the cost of the abandonment of Arab villages.[5] This reality has naturally fed the native group's feelings of frustration and bitterness that arise from its feelings of deprivation over having had its quality of life lowered compared with past conditions and because of its status vis-à-vis the ruling group of immigrants.[6]

Third, the Arab minority in Israel is the outgrowth of a population which in the past was the majority population in the country. As such, the national onus that the Arab citizens – at least the Muslims among them who represent most of the minority population – contains within themselves a heritage, attitudes, and expectations of once again becoming a majority. The consciousness that they are part of the population that represents the religion that is dominant in the Middle East also contributes to this feeling they have and to their dissatisfaction at being defined as a minority.

Fourth, in their eyes, the Arab citizens of Israel became a minority after experiencing a severe defeat in the war and this has been engraved in their collective memory under the term of *"Nakba"*[7] which relates to the day that David Ben-Gurion declared the establishment of the State of Israel and the catastrophe that the Arab population suffered following this declaration. This memory is passed on as part of their heritage to the next generations and, since 1998, when Israel has celebrated the jubilee of its establishment, the Arab minority commemorates the *"Nakba"* every year with a series of remembrance and heritage events.

Fifth, the Arab citizens of Israel see themselves as part of a primary circle of relationship as belonging to the Palestinian People, and at least some Palestinians view Israel as their enemy. In wider circles they are part of the Arab nation. Israel finds itself involved in incompletely resolved conflicts with both of these circles. The determination of one of the leaders of the minority as early as the 1950s that "My country finds itself in a state of war against my people"[8] encapsulates the root of the problem, since on the one hand, the Arab minority in Israel identifies itself with national aspirations of the Palestinians, and on the other hand, it lives in a country that does not allow it any expression of the nationalism that it identifies with.

The above and other factors constitute crucial contributors to the formation of a network of relationships between the government and the Arab minority in Israel. Against this background, a research dialogue has developed whose purpose is to historically examine the government's policies towards the Arab minority since the establishment of the State of Israel and, conversely, the pattern of activities and struggles of the minority population relative to the actions of the government.

One of the basic endeavors that have concerned the many research scholars who deal with the relations between governments and minority groups is the analysis of the policies of the establishment towards such groups. A series of earlier studies has tried to examine the policies of the Israeli government towards the Arab minority since the declaration of the state in 1948. Most of them have pointed out the security component as being the dominant factor that dictates policy approaches, based upon the Israeli establishment constant suspecting revelations of hostility, hatred, or the use of terror by the Arab community against the state. In practice, the policies enacted during the first forty years were based upon security deterrence, with minor attention paid to civil issues and individual rights for minority members as befits a democratic regime. From 1990 onwards a significant change took place in the way the Israeli government related to the Arab minority, which expressed itself in a not inconsiderable number of components, including increased attention being paid, an increased allotment of budgets, efforts made to reduce the gaps, and carrying on a dialogue with the minority's leadership (for a detailed analysis see below).

A series of academic publications have investigated the Israeli government's policy towards the Arab minority since the establishment of the state until the 1980s, and this issue has become both fascinating and challenging – especially since the Declaration of Independence of the State of Israel includes a paragraph about "the establishment of a Jewish state in the Land of Israel," which simultaneously promises that the new state will "maintain complete equality in civil and political rights for all its citizens without difference to religion, race or sex." Moreover, the declaration calls upon the Arab people who are residents of the State of Israel "to be peaceful and to take part in the building of the state on the basis of full and equal citizenship and appropriate representation in all its institutions".[9]

A historic debate broke out among the researchers about whether an orderly and planned policy regarding the minority group had been set in place or not. Ben-Gurion, the first Prime Minister of Israel, set up the general approach and line to be taken, the main points of which were: the Arab minority was a group whose loyalty to the state would always be in doubt and they should be seen as a potential threat to the Zionist character of the country.[10] As a rule Ben-Gurion did not deal with minority issues very much, but when he had to he advocated equality and security with the order changing according to the importance of changing external factors. His advisor, Yehoshua Palmon, explained that the intention was to preserve equality for the minority as far as possible "up to an undefined red line because it might or was likely to change as a result of developments and events that could not be foreseen".[11] Other researchers argue that it was already becoming clear with the Declaration of Independence itself that there was no real possibility of maintaining equality in social and political rights, since the timing of the establishment of the state as well as military circumstances were making it impossible for the Arab people living in the country to answer the call to take part in the building of the new country.[12] These same arguments would, up until today, act as a prism through which the Jewish majority examines its attitude towards the Arab minority. In everything, however, concerning the working of the establishment, especially on the operative level, a change in approach did take place.

Some of the studies that dealt with the subject argued that there was a lot of confusion among the Israeli leadership when it had to form a policy about the Arab Israeli citizens. Other studies claimed that the policy aimed to firmly establish the Jewish state and to exclude the Arab minority from the public-political arena – with the hidden assumption being, at least during the first decade of the state, that this minority would prefer to leave the country of its own free will.[13]

Regarding the academic debate over whether there was a policy that was intentional or confused, or even if there was in fact no ordered policy, we will not discuss the question of whether there was a deliberate decision to create opacity involving the components of the Israeli policy towards the Arab minority. Our argument is that it would be impossible for there to be a situation in which no policy existed, even if the establishment were ignoring the minority group living under its rule. It does not make any difference whether this ignoring on the part of the establishment was intentional or not, because from the moment that relations between the parties is characterized by disengagement or disregard by the establishment, a policy is actually in effect even if it is not declared; from the moment it spontaneously begins it has a life of its own. The expression of such a policy is quickly recognized in the region in all areas of civil and security-involved life.

1
The Formation of a Policy after 1948: Security versus Citizenship

From a historical point of view the policies of the State of Israel towards the Arab minority have two basic components. One of these is the security component, founded upon the traditional view of Arabs as representing a security risk to the country, because they are not part of the Jewish people and because they are identified with the Arab or Palestinian nation and the religion of Islam. The second component is the civil aspect which arises out of the democratic identity of the state which is duty-bound to provide equal rights to all its citizens. The tension between these two components has concerned policy makers in Israel since its beginnings.

One of the first decisions concerning the non-Jewish minority, who had remained in the territory that was taken by the provisional government established after the Declaration of Independence, was that the Arabs who had registered during the first population census taken in November 1948 would be able to participate in the first elections.[14] Decisions were also made providing the Muslims and Christians with everything needed for religious purposes and for Hebrew and Arabic to be Israel's official languages. These decisions were the first practical applications of the contents of the Declaration of Independence. They were the endowment of the basic rights inherent to a democratic regime, but as time passed it became clear that additional collective rights for the Arab minority had not accompanied them.

The state's leaders had to deal with three central questions: What policy needed to be adopted towards the minority that had remained in the country? Should Arab refugees be allowed to return to the territory of the country? How should the lands abandoned by the Arabs be used, and should Jews settle there? These questions, in practice, touched upon three central areas: lands, refugees and the identity of the state apparatus that would deal with them. These questions and others opened up differences of opinion between the decision-makers of this period.

After the United Nations' vote on dividing the country on November 29, 1947, Mapai, the largest Israeli political party during Israel's first years, immediately formed a thirteen man committee whose task was "to clarify the way the Arab workers will relate to the state when it is established."[15] Decisions were made in this forum which was then considered to be far-reaching because of the tendency towards equality that characterized their content. At the beginning of 1948, Pinhas Lavon, a prominent Mapai activist and a member of the Knesset from 1949 to 1961, asserted that the military arm would not be able to solve the political (Arab) question. He estimated that the Arab minority would continue to exist in Israel and that the Jewish People would have to prove itself as the majority group. Lavon proposed two approaches for dealing with the Arab question: the autonomic approach which supported the idea that the state would make it possible for the Arabs to form autonomic institutions of their own that would operate within a state that was being ruled by another national majority; and another approach was the national civic approach according to which equal criteria would apply to all citizens. In each approach Lavon maintained the tendency that supported progress and the civil rights of the Arab minority without delving deeply into the security implications. He believed that the integration of the Arabs into the state would be a test case for the Zionist idea and Jewish ethics.[16]

Lavon was not the only one who advocated equal treatment of the Arabs by the state. In Mapam's party organ as well, it was written that the emerging Jewish state had to prepare plans for dealing with its Arab population.[17] After the Declaration of Independence, Mapam published a public statement which proclaimed that it would "place itself at the head of the campaign to enter into a true covenant with the Arab masses in the State of Israel and work towards full equality for all citizens."[18] Bekhor Shalom Shitrit, the Minister for Minority Affairs during 1948–1949, advocated a humane approach towards the non-Jewish population and felt not only that his main role was to preserve the rights of the minorities but also that he could play a central role in determining the policy towards them.[19] He did not manage to implement his policy, since in July 1949 Ben-Gurion decided to close the Ministry for Minority Affairs and to leave the treatment of the Arab minority in the hands of the military government. One possible explanation for this decision is that the military–security approach was supposed to make the implementation of the policy of land appropriation and the settlement of Jews (immigrants) over a widespread geographical distribution on these lands significantly easier. The young country's leadership thought such steps would strengthen national security.

Opposing this approach was the camp, led by Ben-Gurion, which looked at the issue from a security point of view. This camp saw the Arab minority that had remained in the territory of the State of Israel as a real threat to the existence of the state because it was part of the Arab nation that was living in the countries bordering on Israel. Yitzhak Ben Zvi, for example, wrote that: "The goal of the Arabs was to gain control of the country in clear contradiction of the UN decision . . . it was their intention to finish the work of Hitler . . . when the Arab governments find the right time to attack Israel they will have a fifth column here."[20] Ultimately, Prime Minister Ben-Gurion set out the principles for the approach to be taken towards this population and it was his hawkish conception that formed the Israeli government's policy towards the Arab citizens.

2
The Establishment of the Military Government

Overall, the question of the status of the Arab minority, except for the need to deal with concrete and potential security threats, was not a matter of concern for the Israeli establishment during the first two decades of statehood. One of the historical findings that supports this argument is the fact that between 1948 and 1967 the government only held three discussions that related to the situation of the Arab minority: in February 1952, with Decision 249 that equalized the wages earned by Arabs and Jews; in 1954, with the government's decision to hold local elections for the City of Nazareth; and in 1958, with the government's decision to introduce a program for the economic rehabilitation of the Arabs in Israel.

The upshot was that the really important decisions affecting the lives of the Arab minority were not made, as is the general case in a democratic regime, through discussions carried on by the executive authority, i.e., the government. This authorized Ben-Gurion's decision to impose a military government on the Arab population in order to guarantee stronger supervision. The establishment of the military government and its areas of activity, as well as the public and parliamentary controversy over the need for it, is worth deeper analysis; this apparatus was a central, if not the only instrument, used to apply the establishment's policy towards the Arab minority up until the end of the 1960s.

The regulation for the order of governance and law, adopted by the Provisional State Council, stated that the Minister of Defense was authorized to appoint military commanders (governors) for specific areas. In the first stage military governments were introduced into the Galilee and the Negev, except for the Jewish settlements in these areas. The rationale for this, among other things, involved the argument that most of their villages were close to the country's borders with Arab countries, creating a risk that the shared national identity would translate into hostile acts carried out against the country and its citizens. In answer to this threat it was decided to impose security supervision over the population that was defined as hostile; and it was understood that it would have been better had they not been present at all within the area of the State of Israel. An officer named Kidron wrote to Ben-Gurion and the minister in charge of the minorities, in the name of the head of the intelligence services, that allowing freedom of movement to Arabs would prevent the government from exercising any supervision over them.[21] The apprehension expressed about the Arab minority was so great that a decision was taken to prohibit meetings from taking place between Arabs and international representatives. The Military Governor of the conquered territories (the areas under military government) issued an order to his people not to permit direct discussion to take place between the Arab citizens and the representatives of the Red Cross, unless there was a representative of the military government present.[22]

The military government was established in September 1948 and became the operative arm of the government towards the Arab population. It drew its authority from the emergency defense regulations (1945) recognized as legal by the Provisional Government Council. Its first commander was General Elimelech Avner, and it was in fact a military unit within the IDF which was established in the Central Command, but whose activities were also subject to the commanders of the Northern, Central and Southern Commands. Because of the varied activities of the military government in civil matters as well it was, at the same time, also subject to the Military Affairs Department of the Defense Ministry. As time passed, the military government widened the areas of its activities to involve clearly civil issues; it was the body that carried out the government's instructions regarding the Arab sector, and the people in its apparatus were active in political, social and economic affairs. One example of many regarding this can be found in the meeting held between Rehav^cam Amir, the Galilee

Military Governor, and Arab notables from his area in which he informed them that the military government had prepared a program for improving the areas of health, agriculture and education.[23]

The basic goal of the military government was to provide immediate answers to the problems that arose concerning everything that touched upon the Arab minority in the country. In the eyes of the country's leaders under Ben-Gurion, it was a natural step to place the treatment of this issue in the hands of the military and a few civilian experts. The characteristics of this government were an expression of its "military" title – it was security oriented despite being involved in civilian issues. Palmon explained that the decision to establish a military government was to maintain order and provide basic services to the Arab population. In a letter he sent to the military governors, Palmon asked them to explain to the Arab population that the military government was established for their benefit and added that Arab notables had expressed the hope that its presence would continue.[24]

The military government and its activities in the field were a constant subject of public controversy, and between 1949 and 1956 the government appointed four committees of investigation into the question of how necessary the military government was for carrying out the government's policy towards the Arab minority. These are important for any discussion about the establishment's policy towards the Arab minority, because they reflected the political and public atmosphere in Israel during the years in which the state was trying to solidify its existence and was maintaining as fair a relationship with the minority as possible.

The first committee was appointed in March 1949 following a difference of opinion between the military government and the Ministry for the Minorities headed by Minister Shitrit, who supported a more lenient policy towards the Arab minority. General Elimelech headed the committee and presented recommendations to continue with the activities of the military government. The second investigative committee consisted of one man who was close to Ben-Gurion, Shaul Avigur, who in the first half of 1950 was asked to examine the issue of the military government following the reservations raised to the Prime Minister due to political factors. After he had carried out an investigation and visited the field, Avigur presented a recommendation (April 26, 1950) that stated that the military government was essential because it touched upon the most sensitive areas of the State of Israel.[25] As a whole, the letter was security oriented and provided no recommendations concerning civilian areas of life of the Arab minority that might have improved its status in a democratic country.

The third investigative committee was convened in October 1952 after Ben-Gurion turned to Pinhas Lavon, who was at that time a minister without portfolio, and instructed him to examine the quality of the military government's activities. His conclusions, which were presented on November 12, 1952, were critical and among other things, described the military government's personnel as being of low quality. Lavon noted cases of corruption, declared that the military government had not succeeded in establishing an effective administration and also reported many cases of damage being done for no purpose. Accordingly he recommended that handling of the Arab minority be split into two: the army would retain the treatment of security matters and an accompanying civilian apparatus would be established to take care of all the civilian issues that affected the Arab minority.[26] Lavon did not suggest canceling the military government, and his proposal for structural reform was not accepted.

The fourth committee was appointed in December 1955 following continual public criticism and a sense of uneasiness in establishment circles, and was headed by Yohanan Ratner who was the first national commander of the Hagana organization. The committee was active throughout January and February 1956, and it recommended leaving the military government as it was, justifying this by arguing that the Arab states were taking into account that the Israeli Arabs would assist them if war broke out between them and Israel. It also asserted that the Arab population was not loyal to the state and represented "a real danger because of their shared interests with the Arab countries beyond the border."[27] Another argument that the committee presented was based on the assessment that if there were no military government, the country would be witnessing a wave of refugees trying to return to their homes. Accordingly, in the view of the members of the committee, the military government's goals should be: to act as a deterrent to hostile activities such as infiltration and contact with the enemy; to act as a coordinating link between various factors dealing with security; to prevent the mass flow of refugees wanting to return and settle in Israel; to declare certain areas as closed areas; to act as the operative arm for surveillance; to assist the settlement project; and to act as an aid to failing immigrant settlements in matters of security.[28] The spirit of the committee's recommendations illustrates that its members viewed the military government as having at least one role involving civilian issues; this touched upon the strengthening of Jewish settlement in Israel. The central innovation of the work of the Ratner Committee was in its work method as, for the first time, it opened the discussions of the appointed committee investigating the military government to the Arab minority and allowed that group's representatives to air their ideas and evaluations of the issue being investigated. The Ratner Committee's members heard evidence from 39 Jews and 50 Arabs.

Within the central camp of the government there were also figures who opposed the continued operation of the military government. Yigal Alon, one of the main members of *Ahdut ha-Avoda* party, believed that this mechanism of the military government was one of the factors waking and inflaming the nationalist urges of the Arab population.[29] Isser Harel, who was head of the Secret Service Organization, believed that there was no objective reason for the continued existence of the military government mechanism and that the security arguments were only being used to perpetuate its activities.[30] The course that was ultimately chosen was the continued operation of the military government over the Arab minority, in the spirit of the recommendations made by the various committees of investigation and despite the sharp public criticism.

Several ministers[31] who opposed the conclusions of the Ratner Committee called for the cancellation of the military government. Among the public there were more calls being made to cancel it following the massacre in Kafr Qasem (October 1956), in which 49 of its villagers were killed by gunfire from Border Police while making their way home after the curfew imposed upon the village began, and following the publicity surrounding the trial of those involved in the massacre. During this period, which in fact began after the Sinai Campaign and continued until the 1967 War, there was a great improvement in Israel's economy, with creation of many new places of employment for the Arab minority. Many Jewish employers urgently needed workers and they exerted pressure to allow the Arab minority to more easily get to their workplaces. Between the years 1959 and 1966 there was a dramatic increase in the number of Arabs employed, from 10,000 to 40,000 workers.[32] One of the clear expressions of the process of integration of the Arab minority into the Israeli economy during this period was the Arabs gaining membership in the General Workers Federation in August 1958. Ongoing contact with the Arab minority changed the Jewish population's traditional image of them as enemies of the state and also contributed to the public debate over the need for a military government.

After the harsh events in Nazareth in May 1958, the government had to once again examine whether there was a need for a military government and, despite the violent events, Ben-Gurion favored continuation of the military government.[33] Nonetheless, he was prepared to authorize some easement for the Arab minority during these years, especially for citizens who lived in areas under the jurisdiction of the military government. In this way he sanctioned steps which were in effect the first signs of a long process leading to the cancellation of the military government. During these years, the public discourse about the cancellation of the military government became legitimate and the call to cancel it was no longer labeled an "un-Zionist" demand. Even so, the process was slow and gradual and it continued until the end of 1966.

From the beginning of the 1960s, there was a rise in the intensity of the public struggle against operating the mechanism of the military government and reached the parliamentary arena. In February 1960, a vigorous discussion on the subject was held in the Israeli Parliament (Knesset) when three bills that demanded cancellation of the military government were proposed. What was new in these proposals was that they came from the left wing of the political map (Maki, the Communist party) and the right wing (Herut party). Menahem Begin, a member of the Knesset, expressed himself during the discussion thus: "It is possible to establish an efficient civilian government which will, to the same degree – and even better – guarantee the nation's and the state's demands for security."[34] In the same discussion Tawfik Tubi, in the name of Maki, demanded the cancellation of the military government, arguing that it was harming the democratic character of the State of Israel, while noting the great damage that the mechanism had done to Jewish–Arab relations in the country.

The proposed bills were not passed in a parliamentary vote but this did not blunt the sharpness of the battle. After the elections for the Fifth Knesset (August 1961), the government chose to continue the operation of the military government and, following this decision, the struggle continued in the parliamentary and public arenas as well as in the media. One of the stormiest and bitterest debates over the question of the continued operation of the military government took place in February 1962 in which Member of the Knesset and one of the leaders of Maki, Shmuel Mikunis, claimed that he and other members of his party had witnessed support for cancelling the military government coming from new circles, including approval from the ranks of Mapai.[35] During this discussion members of the Knesset from Mapam (Yaʿakov Hazan), from the Progressive party (Pinhas Rozen), from Herut (Menahem Begin), and from *Ahdut ha-Avoda* party (Yisrael Ben Yehuda) proposed similar bills for the cancellation of the military government. Ben-Gurion responded on behalf of the government to the proposed bills and rejected them, while his speech was frequently interrupted by members of the Knesset from different factions.

Some of the factions in the Knesset were not satisfied with just parliamentary activity and were also active in the public arena. Herut, Mapam, the Liberals, and Ahdut ha-Avoda organized public meetings endorsing cancellation of the military government and were supported by an article in the newspaper *Maʿariv* reporting that there was a majority developing in the Knesset for its cancellation.[36] Ultimately, in a vote that took place on February 20 all the proposed bills calling for the cancellation of the military government were rejected for reasons unconnected to this issue but which involved political compromises about other issues. The government, in its efforts to ensure a majority vote that would guarantee preservation of its present policy continuing the military government, promised to accelerate the implementation of its decision made on December 3, 1961 to increase investment and budgets aimed at improving Arab and Druze villages.[37] Along with this, Ben-Gurion made decisions on a series of additional easements for the Arab minority, including cancellation of night curfews and issuing transit licenses annually instead of on a daily or weekly basis.[38] During the same period the powers of the military government staff were reduced and transferred to the police[39] and the easements introduced in this period, which lasted up until Ben-Gurion's resignation in June 1963, reflected the ongoing, but slow and gradual, change in the government's policy toward the Arab minority.

An accelerated change, even a change in direction, in the government's policy only became clear after the change made in the staff of the Prime Minister's Office in the middle of 1963. Levi Eshkol instituted a more lenient policy in many areas, supported easements for the Arab population and wanted to turn the mechanism of the military government into something that "sees but is not seen." At the same time he believed that for the time being "what is needed is a watchful eye and we should pray that we will never need to make use of it."[40] One of the most significant practical expressions of the change in policy was Eshkol's announcement on October 26, 1963 cancelling the regulation that required the Arab minority to equip themselves with personal licenses for freedom of movement, except for citizens who were a security risk.[41]

After the general elections in 1965, Eshkol, who had been re-elected Prime Minister, announced that it was his intention to find ways to cancel the military government. He based his announcement on an evaluation of the situation that made it clear that "granting easements to the Arab population did not lead it to act violently against the Jewish majority and the state's institutions."[42] On November 8, 1966, Eshkol included an announcement in his speech to the Knesset that beginning on December 1, 1966 the military government would be terminated and that "the tasks that were given to this mechanism would be transferred to the relevant civilian authorities."[43] By doing this, Eshkol, in effect gave the final green light for a change in the government's policy towards the Arab minority and to the cancellation of an apparatus that had directly affected the lives of the Arab population for almost two decades.

The announcement about ending the military government did not bring about a practical change in the government's policy toward the Arab minority. In the two months following Eshkol's announcement (in January 1967), all the powers and authority of the military apparatus were transferred to the police and the general security service, and these bodies enforced the policy of surveillance and rule over the Arab population much more strongly than the military government mechanism had. During the first week of the June 1967 War, the government decided to re-impose the military government over the Arab population because of the fear that this population would want to assist the Arab countries. These military steps were cancelled at the end of June after it became clear beyond all doubt that the Arab population had no operative plans against the state in either the area of terrorism or in cooperating with the Arab armies.

3
Policy About the Refugee Issue

Another area in which a harsh policy was already implemented in the early days of the state with its provisional government was that of the return of the Arab refugees to Israel. As early as June 16, 1948, during a lull in the fighting, the government decided not to allow the return of the refugees to their homes. About a month later, Moshe Sharett, the then Foreign Minister, said that the return of the refugees meant the introduction of a fifth column into territory of the State of Israel or the introduction of explosive material into the framework of the State of Israel.[44] Ben-Gurion, who was grappling with the question of the refugees together with his advisors, argued that the Arabs were themselves guilty of running away and should not be allowed to return since they would act as a fifth column.[45] An inter-ministerial committee that was asked to deal with the question of allowing the refugees to return came to the conclusion in 1953 that such an authorization would be suicide and that it would be impossible for these refugees to constitute a social/ethnic group that would be loyal to the state.[46] The issue of the Arab refugees occupied much attention politically from 1948–1952, partly because of American pressure to examine possibilities for returning them to Israel; in practice, however, no refugees were returned.[47]

The legislature boosted the effort to prevent the return of the refugees, as the Knesset wanted to endow the character of the state with a Jewish identity – a process in fundamental opposition to the rights of the Arab citizens argued for by some of their representatives in the Knesset. The goal of the policy was to establish a solid presence and life for the Jewish population in the state. One of the laws that accomplished this was the Law of the Return which was enacted in 1950 – it imposed a list of conditions upon anyone who wanted to get Israeli citizenship and was not a Jew. The process of receiving citizenship in such a case was long, taking five years to complete.[48] The practical outcome of this law was elimination of any possibility for the refugees to return to their homes. During these years the authorities consistently refused to allow the return of refugees to their villages (a situation that exists even today). Parallel to this, the process of establishing settlements for the Jewish population accelerated while no new settlements were established for the Arab minority.

To the list of laws whose aim was to endow the state with a Jewish character was added the law, legislated in 1949, that made service in the IDF compulsory. This law determined that military service in the IDF was a condition for receiving certain rights, services and benefits. Being "ex-army" was assigned great importance, and anyone who fit that criterion was given a special grant of money, according to a law passed during the 1970s. This grant provided a significant benefit for Jewish families, while Arab households of Arabs, who did not serve in the IDF, lacked this benefit. This policy naturally contributed to an increase in the size of the gap between the populations and to feelings of growing deprivation by the Arab minority which, during these years, lacked the necessary degree of awareness and political maturity to create pressure on the government through protest demonstrations for the improvement of their living conditions. Through this policy regarding grants, the Israeli administration made it clear to the refugees that as a matter of fact they had no way to return home.

4
Different Perceptions Regarding Arab Lands

Another area in which a clear policy was enacted was the central one of land, around which the conflict between the Israeli and the Arab (Palestinian) parties was taking place. From the time that the Zionist idea developed during the 1880s, Jewish activists concentrated their efforts on the acquisition of tracts of land in the Land of Israel and upon increasing Jewish control over them. This outlook was shared by the heads of the state, who moreover believed that the tracts had to be used for the purposes of the immigration of Jews to Israel *(Aliya)*, security, and settlement.[49] Sharett, the Foreign Minister, publicly expressed this position when he said, "We tend towards seeing all the abandoned property as the property of the State of Israel which can do what it wishes to with it."[50] The question of land became one of the most sensitive subjects in the network of relations between the government and the Arab minority after the establishment of the state. Any Arabs who were living in The Land of Israel lost their property, including land, during the 1948/49 War. After the war, the Department for Arab Property,[51] which was attached to the Ministry for Minorities, was established and, parallel to this, the Settlement Department of the Jewish Agency prepared a map of a list of Arab villages that had been abandoned, and recommended the housing of settlement groups of new immigrants in the abandoned places. The recommendations were accompanied by an amendment to the emergency regulations (September 1948) which, among other things, stipulated that the state had the right to temporarily (for an undefined period) take over the property of absentee owners, including lands.

Several procedures were used to take control of the Arab lands, the main one being through legal means as follow:

(1) Lands regulations (acquisition for public purposes) 1943. This regulation permitted the appropriation of lands for public purposes with no need for security explanations. Through this law, lands were appropriated in the villages of Nahef, Biʿne and Dir al-Asad during 1961–1963 in order to establish the city of Karmiel.

(2) 1945 Emergency regulations. Section 125 of the regulations in particular allows the declaration of any place as a "closed area," entry into which is prohibited. These regulations made it possible to prevent the return of residents to previously abandoned villages.

(3) Emergency regulations (abandoned property) 1948 obligated anybody who had possession of abandoned property (including Jews) to register with the police. A regulation governing abandoned territory that authorized the government to issue orders to impose state law over territory that had been abandoned followed in 1948. The appointment of a guardian for the property left behind was linked to this order.

(4) Emergency regulations that were published in 1949 permitted the Minister of Agriculture to appropriate and hold lands that had not been worked for more than a year.

(5) A regulation to order the seizing of land in an emergency 1949 made it possible to appropriate land for the defense of the country,

the security of the people, the protection of essential services, the integration of new immigrants, and the settling of demobilized soldiers and the war wounded.

(6) The "Absentee Property" law 1950 replaced the regulations in this matter and defined an "absentee" as anyone who, on November 29, 1947 – the day the UN voted on the Partition Plan – had property in the territory of the Land of Israel and was not present in the territory on the day that the IDF conquered the area in which he had been residing.

(7) The Land Acquisition Law (Authority for Actions and Restitution 1953) authorized the Minister of Finance to appropriate any land that was not in possession of its owner on April 1, 1952 and was needed for purposes of development, settlement or security.[52]

Another way of taking over Arab owned lands was by declaring the areas closed for security reasons. Prominent examples of this were the villages of Ikrit and Bir'am, from which the villagers fled and were not allowed to return because the area was declared a closed military zone, and "Zone 9" which covers an area of 100,000 dunams in the triangle of the villages Dir Hana, 'Arabeh and Sakhnin.

For the Arab minority the issue of lands is very sensitive and unifying, since land for them is precious, even essential – this sector is based upon agriculture and most of the privately owned land has traditionally belonged to the Arabs. The land is considered a symbolic national value that reflects its Arab ownership; it also is seen to constitute a portion of the Arabs' national rights that they see as having been stolen from them after the war.

Researchers, mainly from the Arab sector, into the phenomenon of the land argue that the land regime and planning by the Israeli government threaten the fabric of the relations between the minority and the majority, because over the years they have brought about a pattern of ethnic-national based deprivation and distress. This is expressed through two aspects: First is the proprietary index, according to which the Arab population feels itself victimized since it derives no benefits as individuals or as a collective from national enterprises being located on its lands. The second index is the administration of the lands by the Jews, which includes arrangements that need to be made for registration of lands, leasing, and planning, along with decisions about areas of jurisdiction. The practical result of this has been that the local Arab councils, when they have asked to broaden their areas of jurisdiction, have faced at best procrastination from the Ministry of the Interior – and refusals in other instances. Such demands have usually been interpreted by the state authorities as a desire by the Arabs to gain control of agricultural lands for the purpose of livelihood.

5
The Intensity of Enforcing the Governmental Policy

The Israeli establishment strongly enforced its policy in all three areas of lands, refugees, and military administration during the first years of the state's existence, and certainly in the eyes of the Arab minority all matters involving the military government included the heavy use of components of force.[53] The military governor was, for all intents and purposes, an all-powerful ruler in the area under his control, and there was no recourse available to criticize him, except by appealing to the Supreme Court of Justice. His authority touched upon many areas of everyday life.

Concerning individual rights, for example, the governor was authorized to prohibit a person from being in any place under his jurisdiction – for instance, 2,700 Arabs were found guilty of committing a security offense which involved moving from one area to another without securing a license. The military governor could also force a person to be under police supervision for a period of up to a year, and was authorized to issue an order to confiscate land and demolish buildings, if it was suspected that weapons or explosive materials were being operated from inside them. In all matters concerning movement and traffic the governor had the authority to impose a curfew, close a thoroughfare, or to prohibit or reduce the use of the right of passage on roads or waterways. He could also issue orders to close areas.

The various military governors powerfully enforced policies of the governments and did not hesitate to demonstrate the strong arm the government could use against the minority population. Many examples of this exist in evidence given by people from the Arab minority who published it, as well as in studies that examined the behavior of the military government. The staff of the military government interfered with campaigns for the Knesset and local council elections, put together lists that were "convenient" for them and suppressed lists that were "problematic." At times they went as far as exiling one or another of the candidates that were not acceptable to them. Yosef Vashitz, a staff member of the Arab Department of Mapam, described the lives of the Arabs in Israel in the following way:

"Freedom of movement was seriously curtailed. One needed a license in order to move about and getting one often involved losing a day's work – and even then one didn't always get it. The same limitations applied to car movement and the movement of goods and this helped those lucky people who had acquired the right to free movement to create a monopoly for themselves. Apart from the regular citizens there were many kinds of Arabs with fewer rights".[54]

Another concrete example of the power of the military government can be seen in a letter written by the Advisor for Arab Affairs, Palmon, to the mayor of Shfarᶜam, Khouri Mansur. The latter sent a letter of congratulations to the Prime Minister on the occasion of Israel's first Independence Day (May 14, 1949), in which he asked him to grant clemency to the residents of his village who had entered Israel illegally. He was answered with an absolute refusal and was informed that anybody who had entered Israel without a permit was breaking the law and would not receive clemency. In a letter that he sent at a later time to the military governor of the Galilee, Palmon instructed him to continue with the campaign to locate infiltrators that had found refuge in Shfarᶜam until all were found.[55]

The intensity of the enforcement is also evident in the descriptions of Arab citizens of Israel who were living in Israel during this period. Ṣabri Jiryis, who later became a prominent activist in the PLO, noted that Regulation 125 of the Defense Regulations was "the most suppressive, annoying and troubling because it demanded a permit that included many limitations of movement."[56] He also emphasized the confusion, disorder and humiliation that the Arabs had to endure under the military government in the following words: "The military police would get onto buses, order the Arabs to get off and examine them thoroughly about their identities." Habib Kaougi, also a member of the minorities who was one of the first people in "*al-Arḍ*" move-ment, accused the government of being responsible for the appropriation of land, for the deportations, for creating unemploy-ment in the Arab sector, for the dismissal of teachers, for changing the voting patterns of the Arabs so that they would vote for the candidates of the ruling party and for intrusion into all areas of life. In another place he wrote: "In some of the cases in which Arabs had to stand in a queue, some of them gave up the ghost just from having to wait so long."[57]

The intense enforcement of the policy was also expressed in the government's use of power to prevent expressions of public protest against the military government. In May 1949 hundreds of people carried out a demonstration in Acre demanding the cancellation of the military government, and that elections are held for the mayor of the town. The government's response was to disperse the demonstrators and arrest several of them. The military governor of the region made it clear that he would not permit Arabs to be involved in politics and admitted that the arrest of several of the demonstrators was in order to instill fear in the hearts of the Arabs."[58]

The area for maneuver that the formulation of the regulations left to the military governors was enormous. In matters of everyday life the military government caused damage to the routine of the Arab citizens in the state, and even after its total cancellation, some believe, the after-effects have not yet disappeared and the reality that the military government dictated is still having an effect on the relations between the parties. Saᶜadi, for example, argues that the influence of the military government upon the Arab minority in Israel continued for at least three more decades after its cancellation and that this was, among other reasons, because this period is painfully engraved in the collective consciousness of the Arab minority. In that period "a foundation was laid through thinking patterns, processes and ideological approaches in everything concerning the relations with the government and the majority and minority."[59]

In matters concerning the issue of the Arab refugees, the government acted to prevent their return to Israel. In the "Hiram" campaign in October 1948, the villages of Ikrit and Birᶜam were conquered without resistance and the residents of both villages were ordered to leave their houses by November 13th for resettlement in new locations, as were the residents of the villages of Nebi Rubin, Tarbikha, Surukh and Almansura, which were in the Western Galilee.[60]

At the beginning of the 1950s the two villages (Ikrit in 1951 and Birᶜam two years later) were demolished, and thus for all intents and purposes, the government blocked the possibility of the residents returning to their original homes. A governmental committee that discussed the request made by the residents of these villages to return to their lands published its decision on September 16, 1953 as follows: The residents of the two villages will not be permitted into their houses and will be rehabilitated in existing villages. The residents of Ikrit will be sent to the villages of Rameh, Shfarᶜam and Mghar and the residents of Birᶜam will be moved to Kafr Jish.[61] The residents of the abandoned village Hamam were settled in Mghar. These cases were not the only ones during these years as the government acted forcefully to disperse the Arab population, while simultaneously continuing the process of deporting hundreds of Arabs who had not left their houses during the war. Thousands more who wanted to return to their homes were not given permission to do so.[62]

On the issue of lands, during these years the government appropriated many tracts of Arab lands for the building of cities for the Jewish immigrants who came to Israel from all over the world. In this way it established a policy that was the complete opposite of what had been practiced during the period of the Ottoman rule and the British Mandate. The principal elements of the policy determined that all the lands throughout the country were national lands "except for lands whose owners can prove their ownership of them according to the strictest interpretation of the law."[63] The direct result of this action was the implementation of a vigorous settlement policy during the early years of the state. By 1967, fifty village style Jewish settlements had been established in the Galilee as well as seven Jewish cities (Kiryat Shmona, Hazor, Shlomi, Migdal ha-Emek, Nazareth Elite,[64] Maʿalot and Karmiel). The Arab public naturally felt deep frustration over the government's policy of land appropriation which, as aforementioned, was based upon a comprehensive network of laws and regulations. In practice, however, up until the middle of the 1970s this frustration was not objected to through political expression.

Table 1 Main components of the government's policy towards the Arab population, 1948–1958

How is it expressed?	Intensity of Implementation	Policy
Law of the Return, prevention of non-Jewish family reunion. Long bureaucratic procedures for non-Jews asking to settle in Israel.	High	Preservation of Jewish character
Legislation of laws and publication of regulations that made extensive land appropriation possible; massive building of Jewish settlements.	High	Lands
Refusal of all requests to return to Israel made by non-Jews who had left the country during the War of Independence.	High	Refugees
Military government that imposed a long list of limitations upon the non-Jewish population.	High	Security

Table 1 presents the central subjects that were on the agenda of the Israeli government after the establishment of the state, and the policy that was implemented in regard to each of these subjects. Each subject that appears in the table represents one component of a policy whose goal was to endow the country with a Jewish character (alongside its democratic character) and, through introducing regulations and legislating laws, to limit the ability of the non-Jewish minority to prevent the realization of this policy. During these years the Israeli government implemented its policies in these areas with great forcefulness in order to ensure the firm establishment of the state and to neutralize potential threats that it believed were emanating from the Arab minority.

6
Main Policy Lines, 1967–1990

After the June 1967 War, whose timing coincided with the cancellation of the military government, certain changes took place in the Israeli government's policy towards the Arab minority. The return of the refugees was still prohibited and the appropriation of land for the building of Jewish settlements continued, but in areas of a civilian character signs of change could be seen. The central change during these years was one of consciousness, while the practical change was controlled and slow. In everything involving security risks the security apparatuses did not hesitate to act with force and determination to thwart such dangers. There are those who call policy that was adopted after the war a policy of "co-existence",[65] because there was a movement towards a reality of a cooperative life between two groups living in the state together – with recognition of the tension existing between the two populations that were different in ethnic identity, nationality and religion.

During these years following June 1967, policy based itself upon two governmental arms: security and civilian. The first left no room for doubt about anything touching upon the need to eliminate security risks from within and from without. Examples include the arrest of Arabs soon after the June 1967 War on suspicion of trying to disturb the peace throughout the country with activities against the war, and the arrest of more than three hundred Arabs who were involved with hostile terrorist activities between 1968 and 1974. The second, the civilian arm, aspired to expand the integration of the Arabs into the framework of the state; this won support from the security arm. Avraham Ahituv, who was the General Security appointee responsible for dealing with the Arab citizens of Israel, recommended that the gates of the government administration be opened to educated Arabs except for tasks that were in sensitive areas. This was suggested based on the assumption that their integration into this framework might reduce the influence of negative ideas upon the educated class, which the General Security Service saw as "the most dangerous of all."[66]

Another expression of this policy was the government's official announcement that it intended to integrate the Arab citizens of Israel into all areas of life, to endow them with full equality, to improve their municipal services, to preserve their unique Arab culture, and to make it possible for the Muslim citizens of the country to make the pilgrimage to the holy city of Mecca in Saudi Arabia. One of the areas in which the government invested in order to create the basic conditions that would make the integration of the Arabs into the life of the country possible was education. Schools were built in every village and even in the central encampments of the Bedouin, veteran teachers were provided with teacher training and in-service refresher courses and the Arab Teachers College, which had been operating in Jaffa and had moved to Haifa, began preparing new teachers. During these years criticism was leveled at the large gaps between Jews and Arabs in the education system, but the enormous growth in the number of Arabs who knew how to read and write during the 1960s showed that the investment in education of the Arab population had proven itself. The investment made by the state in education, as will be shown later, had an influence on the development of a new generation of intellectuals among the Arab citizens whose political consciousness led to the phenomenon of an increase in demands from the 1970s onwards by the Arab minority upon the state – some of which were provocative – as well as to patterns of protest activity that were more violent.

Starting from 1963 the Prime Minister's Office, through the Bureau of the Advisor on Arab Affairs, was active in the Arab villages throughout the country in order to make the Arab citizens feel closer to the state.[67] These activities, which were of a civilian nature, were few and far between, so it was difficult to identify any change in the situation of the Arab citizens. It is possible that one of the reasons for this was the lack of attention being paid by the government to the needs of the Arab minority. Shmuel Toledano, the Advisor on Arab Affairs from 1965 to 1977, later recounted that "It was very difficult to convince the Prime Minister to hold a discussion about the Arab population in Israel."[68]

When analyzed from a historical point of view, one can identify that as early as the beginning of the 1970s senior bureaucrats in the government were pointing out the necessity of strengthening civilian components for the Arab minority. This was proven in part in 1973 when, three months before the outbreak of the October war, an effort was made to examine the results of the policy enacted towards the Arab minority. Toledano presented Prime Minister Golda Meir with a document containing a survey of the Arab minority situation and the influence of the government's policy upon it.[69] Among the conclusions of the document was a recommendation to foster feelings of belonging to the state among the Arabs, and thereby reduce the strong nationalistic feelings of the Arab minority towards the Arab countries. The document warned that Israel might find itself with a difficult problem at the beginning of the 1980s as a result of the significant rise in the number of educated Arabs – these citizens were developing political consciousness and in the future would make dangerous demands of the state.

Parallel to the document discussed above, another historical development took place during these years which was no less important. In 1974 the Committee of the Heads of Local Arab Councils was established and received official recognition from the Prime Minister's Yitzhak Rabin cabinet. This recognition was withdrawn in 1977 with the rise of Begin's government; but in practice the dialogue between the ministerial level and the heads of the local councils continued. This dialogue should not be seen as unimportant, since the Israeli government up till today distinguishes between dialogue with the heads of local councils that deal with civilian issues, and the rift that exists between the government and the Higher Monitoring Committee which is the roof body over all the power groups in the Arab sector.

The immediate result of Toledano's recommendations was to convene an inter-ministerial committee that put together another document containing recommendations for governmental policy towards the Arab minority. The basic assumptions of the document were the need to integrate the two populations; it included references to defined subjects such as education and lands. One of the recommendations was to stop the process of appropriating Arab land and to encourage the migration of Arabs to the larger towns. The document was presented to the government plenum, but no real discussion that could have led to decisions about the Arab minority took place. Even after the document was authorized in 1974 in the framework of a discussion that took place in the Ministerial Committee for Security Affairs, there was a significant gap between the decisions made and their implementation in the field – mainly in the areas that the Arab public saw as being essential, first and foremost being the appropriation of lands that continued up until the events of "Land Day."

The government's failure to deal with the document went beyond the fact that there was no discussion of its contents. During the first half of the 1970s the enforcement in the field of the regulations concerning land appropriation increased, and was carried out in two phases until 1976 (1970–1971, 1975–1976). This was part of a broad process of appropriation which had already been decided upon in 1966 as a result of Levi Eshkol's decision to implement a program for the development of the Galilee district. The goal of the program was to develop the Galilee quickly and included increasing the populations of Safed, Ma'alot, Karmiel and Nazareth. Eshkol's plan was not authorized by the government until ten years later when it decided to appropriate 20,000 dunams in four areas in the Galilee on February 29, 1976. Of these, 4,700 dunams were slated for appropriation in the Nazareth area, 3,600 of which (about 77 percent) were owned by Arabs. In the area of Karmiel, 7,500 dunams were slated, of which 1,900 dunams were Arab owned, and 7,500 dunams all owned by Jews or the state and were slated for appropriation in the area of Safed. Of the total of the 20,000 dunams that the government planned to appropriate, 6,320 dunams were Arab owned (31 percent). The Minister of Finance signed the appropriation orders on March 11, 1976.

7
After "Land Day" 1976: Citizenship or Security?

Following the events of "Land Day" in March 1976 during which six Arabs were killed and dozens injured in serious clashes with the security forces as part of the appropriation of land in the Area of Sakhnin, the government held a discussion about the situation of the Arab minority. The working premise of the discussion was set out by Toledano, the then Advisor on Arab Affairs. According to his approach the issue in question was a test of great complexity for Israeli society. During these years a significant change took place in the way the government's institutions perceived the approach that needed to be taken towards the Arab minority. The main elements of this change were based on understanding the need to prepare policy papers for a large number of their areas of activity and not be satisfied with only security issues which, no matter how important they were, only narrowly reflected the way the government was relating to the minority population.

Toledano was not a lone voice asking for the integration of the Arab minority into the different frameworks offered by the government. Moshe Kol, the Minister of Tourism up until the political upheaval that took place in May 1977, as well as the advisors on Arab affairs, supported the policy of integration. They assumed that the national identity of the Arabs was different from that of the Jewish majority and that this would not change in the future, owing to the significant awakening taking place in this population in all matters concerning their being members of the Palestinian People. Based upon this, from 1976 until the beginning of the 1990s, the policy papers that were written by the various advisors emphasized the civil component of this complicated issue.

Minister Kol proposed a plan whose principle points were the absorption of 1,000 educated Arabs into public service, an improvement in the facilities of education for Arab pupils, putting in order the question of lands, and encouragement of economic enterprises between Jews and Arabs.[70] Following these discussions and suggestions the government made three decisions: to establish a ministerial committee to coordinate its activities vis à vis the Arab minority, to adopt a policy whose purpose was to accelerate the integration of Arabs into the life of the country on the basis of their full and equal citizenship, while respecting their cultural and religious uniqueness, and to establish a Jewish–Arab advisory public council.

All of these decisions were made without consulting representatives of the Arab minority. After the government meeting that took place on May 23, 1976, Prime Minister Rabin had a meeting with representatives of the Committee of the Heads of Local Councils and brought them up-to-date about the decisions that had been made, but in reality these decisions were not implemented. The ministerial committee that had been decided upon was not established, while the public committee met only once. After the work teams for various subjects had been decided upon they were never convened.

After the political upheaval of May 1977, Prof. Moshe Sharon became the Advisor for Arab Affairs and expressed criticism of his predecessors in the role, arguing that since 1948 the state had not managed to establish a desirable model of relations between it and the Arab minority. Sharon adopted the approach that supported the integration of the Arab citizens of Israel into the life of the country, and he chose to present his ideas in an unusual way when he visited the home of one of his Arab students in Shfarᶜam. During this visit he undertook to realize the idea of civil equality for all the country's citizens and even promised to resign from his post if his vision failed to come about. Advisor Sharon believed that it was possible to expect civil loyalty from the Arabs and that there was no chance that they would identify emotionally with the state (and its symbols). Accordingly, he had come to the conclusion that a civil basis was the only basis upon which it was possible to establish the fabric of a shared life together. He even believed that a change would take place in the demographic balance between the Jews and the Arab minority that would be detrimental to the Jewish people, and thought that the demographic forecasts about the reduction of the gap between the majority group and the minority group, along with the growing trend towards Palestinian nationalism, were providing the Arab population with a feeling of power.[71]

Later on he indicated his concern about a possible change in the character of the country when he wrote: "The image of a small minority without any ability to act against a dominant Jewish majority has been changed to a new image of being a large public with much influence that is growing rapidly every year."[72]

Sharon presented two possible ways of expressing loyalty to the state for the Arab citizens: first, being prepared to do national service; second, signing a declaration of loyalty which would be accompanied by appropriate behavior. The ultimate test, in his view, for the Arab citizens of Israel to express civil loyalty to the state would be their voting for the Knesset. He even suggested punishments when he wrote that a violation of loyalty would allow the government to halt the provision of benefits to the Arab sector.[73] In the document he presented to the government, Sharon made a series of recommendations: to allocate enough resources to answer the needs of the Arab minority; to fully enforce the law of compulsory education for girls; to populate the Galilee with Jews and dilute the Arab majority living in the region; to ensure that Arab women could get suitable employment (thus encouraging them to leave the house and thereby also reduce the birth rate); and to introduce the idea of family planning into the Arab sector.

In the area of security Sharon recommended taking a series of steps that would assist in dealing with the phenomenon of radicalization that he had identified in the Arab population, including the first signs of ignoring the law and demonstrating contempt for its representatives: dealing with frustration of any national level Arab organization; cancelling benefits for any Arab who did not display loyalty to the state; frustration over any attempt to establish a cooperative framework between Arab Israeli citizens and Palestinians living in the West Bank and the Gaza Strip; and re-examining of the question of mobilizing Christian Arabs for army service.[74]

On the political level, not much attention was paid to Sharon's position on the government's policy towards the Arab minority. His detailed documents, which included an analysis of the situation of the Arab minority and various recommendations, were not discussed in any governmental framework. Yitzhak Reiter, who during these years was working in the Bureau of the Advisor on Arab Affairs, explained

Sharon's lack of success in the complicated political constellation as the result of a battle over authority between Sharon and then Director-General of the Prime Minister's Office, Eliyahu Ben Elisar, which prevented any possibility of convening meetings between the bodies that were relevant to the issue such as the Knesset and the cabinet.[75]

Binyamin Gur Aryeh, who replaced Sharon as advisor, also advocated an approach that combined the definition of the security threat coming from the Arab minority together with the need to deal with it as is done in democratic countries, while preserving the country's Jewish character. He also understood that there was no way to blur the Palestinian national identity of the Arab citizens and focused his analysis upon the construction of civil loyalty. As was the case with his predecessor, the document he presented included specific details in the area of security as well.

Gur Aryeh defined policy goals for the treatment of the Arab population for the government which included: preventing the Arabs from fighting for national demands; making orderly arrangements for a proper network of relations between the state and its Arab citizens; preventing an escalation of the national conflict within the State of Israel; taking action to return the trust of the Arabs regarding the intentions of the government and integrating them into the various state's institutions; and strengthening moderate factors in the Arab population. His recommendations advocated a policy that supported the integration of the Arab citizens into the state frameworks – including the employment of educated citizens in the civil service, the advancement of the Arab minority's economic situation, making orderly arrangements for dealing with the issue of lands, and the authorization of master plans for the Arab villages.

Gur Aryeh also concluded that there was no reason to be more flexible about security policies and recommended using every legal option to frustrate the phenomenon of subversive activities against the state and attempts to change its Jewish character. A general recommendation about this subject was not enough for him, and he added a series of subjects that he divided into "permitted" and "forbidden." Thus he believed that Arab citizens should be allowed to express ideas about giving up territory for peace and to demand the establishment of a university in Nazareth – but not an Arab university. He believed that the Arab population should be prohibited from questioning the borders of the country, expressing identification with the PLO, making national demands of the government (such as autonomy) and making efforts to change the character of the state.[76]

Gur Aryeh's recommendations, like Sharon's, received little attention from the political echelon and there is no evidence of any effective discussion taking place during the period of his time in office about the treatment of the minority populations in Israel. Yosef Ginat, who was the Advisor for Arab Affairs after the 1984 Knesset elections, attested to the fact that the papers that his predecessor had presented "were not accompanied by deeds."[77]

Despite the preparation of policy papers by the senior bureaucratic staffs, none matured into any form of application. The government did not set out any direction to take, discussions on the subject of the Arab minority did not take place at all during these years, and the result was a reality of differential policies. The various ministries found themselves implementing policies of providing assistance to this population as the realities in the field dictated. Thus, between 1978 and 1981, about 15 million shekels were allocated to connecting Arab villages to the national electricity grid, and between 1976 and 1980, nine hundred new classrooms were built in the Arab sector.[78] Parallel to this, the Welfare Ministry carried out a study which mapped out the needs of the Arab population in the area of public services.[79] The Israeli government's wavering conduct about the formation of a civil policy for the Arab minority continued into the 1980s. In January 1985 a committee to deal with Arab affairs made up of Directors General and headed by Avraham Tamir, the Director-General of the Prime Minister's Office was appointed. Ginat, the new Advisor for Arab affairs, prepared a paper based mainly upon the premise of the previous papers, which stated that this was a population whose national identity was Palestinian and that this should be fully accepted as a given. He concluded that it was impossible to prevent processes of distancing or polarization between Jews and Arabs while there was no solution to the Palestinian question,[80] and he believed that the danger emanating from the Arab Israeli citizens existed in a number of possible scenarios, such as: attempting to change the character of the state; establishing alternative institutions in an autarchic, separatist economy as an alternative to services provided by the state to its citizens; demanding to separate from the state; and undermining the demographic balance between the majority group and the minority group. In a paper he prepared for a discussion in the cabinet, Ginat asserted that the most of the Arab citizens' energy was being directed at increasing their civil rights and that their identification with the Palestinian struggle was mainly emotional.

Based on the above and the security position – reducing potential threats being the goal – Ginat argued that one should not demand full identification with the Zionist goals of the state from the Arab minority, but one should rather demand loyalty to the state and its laws on the level of citizenship. He recommended their integration into various areas of activity operating within the framework of the state, in order to rapidly reduce many of the gaps in different areas of life, such as welfare, education, health, and employment, along with the introduction of national service for the Arab population. He even managed to bring the last subject to a discussion in the cabinet but, as had happened in the past, the ministers decided not to decide. Ezer Weitzman, the minister responsible for the Arab population during this time, explained that the reason for this was simple: "The subject of the Arab citizens of Israel was not an urgent matter for the cabinet or the Prime Minister and so there was no need to make a decision".[81]

In addition to the issue of national service, Ginat also presented a comprehensive policy paper concerning many civil areas such as electricity, water, infrastructures, planning and building, and budgeting and employment. He believed that the Arab villages needed to be converted to render their character similar to that of villages housing Jews. Like his predecessors, he expressed concern over a reality in which the Arab citizens of Israel would want to establish independent environments that would-be alternatives to those of the state. Specifically, he wanted to prevent the establishment of an Arab university, a land fund (like the Jewish National Fund) and political structures that were tied to the umbilical cord of the PLO. Ginat's term in office ended at the beginning of 1987 – without his succeeding in presenting the government with any political document regarding the Arab citizens of Israel that would serve as a platform for discussion and decision-making about everything connected with the way the government should act towards the minority population.

Ginat's successor in the role of Advisor on Arab Affairs, Amos Gilboa, entered office in the first half of 1987 following the change of prime ministers in the rotation government. He asked for assistance from academic factions in producing a policy towards the Arab minority in Israel. This sector presented two alternatives: the first Gilboa described as "constant surveillance," which had been the ongoing practice since 1948, and the other received the title of "pluralism."[82] What was special about the document arose from the recommendation not to ignore the question of forming a policy towards the Arab citizens of Israel and to recognize the reality in which the non-Jewish minority was living. In general, the policy paper was similar in its characteristics to earlier papers, since it included recommendations to gradually integrate the Arab citizens into state institutions, and parallel to that, to reduce the possibility of friction with the Jews by authorizing building for the Arabs in their villages and thus prevent their moving to cities. The paper warned against the phenomenon of separatism developing among the Arab citizens as a result of the prevailing mood among educated Arabs, which might reach the point of demanding political separation. What was new in the document was the identification, for the first time in a political document as far as could be determined, of the threatening existence of the Islamic component among the Arab citizens. The danger, according to the document, was: "After the actualization of national rights the struggle will take on the characteristics of Jihad in the spirit of Islam."[83]

Gilboa also prepared a policy paper. He was aware of the prevailing mood that was characterizing the Arab minority and described it as the exacerbation of their feelings of bitterness and frustration together with the sharpening of their sense of national uniqueness. Gilboa identified the political, organizational, economic and demographic strengths that the Arab minority was developing in order to advance its goals, among which he cited the gradual building of an infrastructure for a separate Israeli Arab autonomy. [84] Side by side with the potential threats, including the demand for autonomy, he pointed out the duty of the country, since it was a democratic regime, to allocate the necessary resources for the needs of the minority population. Like Sofer and Ginat, he anticipated that as long as there was no peace agreement between Israel and the Arab countries it would not be possible to overcome the polarization between the Jews and the Arabs within the territory of the State of Israel.

Gilboa recommended adopting a differential approach to the dissimilar groups that make up the non-Jewish minority. He believed that more attention needed to be paid to the Druze community and then, in descending order, to the Bedouins, the Christians, and finally to the Muslims. He opposed the process that would obligate this population to do national service but supported activities that encouraged young men and women to volunteer for national tasks. Along with this, he defined a number of goals for policy towards the Arab citizens of Israel, such as encouraging the trend towards Israelization through the process of modernization, strengthening the minority population's identification with the state, and preventing the conversion of the minority population into a group that identified with and supported the PLO. These goals would be achieved, he claimed, if the government's policy was based upon the following components: a reduction in the gaps between the Jewish majority and the Arab minority through the appropriate allocation of funds until there was complete equality, the creation of a climate that would make it possible for the Arab minority to feel a sense of belonging to the state, the encouragement of activity that was identified by the government as showing loyalty, and the isolation of political forces that were identified with the PLO.

In civil matters, Gilboa recommended a policy that would, among other things, provide: 1) an answer to the needs for building in the Arab sector by legalizing illegal building and updating the master plans; 2) implementation of a five-year plan to develop municipal services in the Arab sector; 3) activation of a program to develop technological education; and 4) creation of incentives for Arab women wanting to gain higher education and work. The document gave details about the financial costs involved in putting the various enterprises into practice, which added up to the sum of ILS250,000,000.

The Gilboa document was put on the agenda of the cabinet only once; it became irrelevant in a period of political crisis over a matter not connected with the Arab minority – after which Minister Arens, who was responsible for the Arab minority, resigned his post.[85] For all intents and purposes this sealed the fate of the document, as had happened with the policy papers prepared by the previous advisors on Arab affairs. Gilboa himself came to the conclusion that the reason for the lack of interest on the political level about the need to determine a policy towards the Arab minority (except of course in security matters) was "prejudiced ideas that some of the ministers had about the Arab minority".[86]

The 1980s, like the previous decade, were characterized by idiosyncratic policies, with each ministry adopting its policy in civil areas that affected the Arab citizen, according to what the minister at the time decided. During this decade, the government made attempts to deal with urgent civil issues that were raised by the leaders of the Arab public. For example, in November 1982 the Knesset Committee for the Interior discussed the budgetary distress of the Arab local councils, and its members concluded that the Ministry of Finance and the Ministry for the Interior should help by finding the budgets needed for the councils.[87] In the middle of 1984, the Ministry for the Interior made agreements with the heads of seventy Arab villages in the north of the country allotting available and reserved lands for these villages.[88]

After receiving the findings of a professional study that had been ordered by the heads of the Ministry of Housing, the Minister began releasing funds for building units for the Arab population at the beginning of 1984. This was the result of efforts made by the Housing Ministry to reduce the housing shortage in the Arab sector.[89]

During these same two months the Ministry of Industry and Commerce recognized the industrial zone of Shfarᶜam as a Development Zone class B; this decision accelerated the establishment of factories and enterprises, which created places of employment for the village residents. These and other activities in civilian areas were instituted via the offices of Ibrahim Nimr Hussein, the chairman of the Committee of the Heads of the Arab Local Councils.

From a historical point of view, two areas were viewed as crucial by the Israeli establishment when it came to stabilize its relations with the Arab minority. One set of concerns came from the national security constellation. These were based upon a perception of the Arab minority as part of the Arab countries, and thus as a population representing an ongoing threat to the existence of the state. The immediate expression of this was the imposition of the military   government, which the government decided to disband at the end of 1966, but which continued in practical terms until January 1968. The national security constellation also expressed its concerns by understanding that the country had to be settled with as large a number of Jews as possible; a wide-ranging process of land appropriation was carried out, from Arabs among others, in order to build new   settlements.

The second area of concern arose from the civil constellation, in which the government's interest was to focus on the establishment of equality between the country's citizens in the spirit of the Declaration of Independence. This constellation promoted granting citizenship and the basic rights of a democracy, such as the right to vote and to be elected to parliament, along with the preservation of the freedom of religious ritual. In practice, up until the 1990s, Israeli policy concentrated more upon the prevention of security threats (terror and subversion against the country) from the Arab minority and less upon advancing the civil issues.

The policy papers of the various advisors on Arab affairs, who operated out of the Prime Minister's Office, contained recommendations to increase integration of the Arab citizens – but not a single one of the recommendations ever succeeded in eliciting a comprehensive discussion that could have brought about a change in perception that in turn might have led to implementing steps to improve the situation of the Arab citizens.[90] Some of the researchers even pointed out the difficulty of characterizing the official policy, except for the narrow security component that included the prevention of sabotage, terror and subversion – since there were no official documents from which it was possible to draw conclusions about the government's actions towards the Arab minority. Based upon this, they argued that the goal of the Israeli establishment was to form a policy that would guarantee efficient control over the minority for an unlimited period, by strengthening their civil loyalty, negating their institutional autonomy, and blocking the development of a country-wide national leadership.[91] The result of all this was a minimal investment made by the establishment in Arab villages, which would bring welfare to the Arab citizens, and enforcement of increased security, which was the result of a working premise that saw the minority as a threat – not necessarily because of their active involvement in hostile activities.

8
Ways the Arab Minority Deals with Israeli Policy

At the end of 1947, towards the end of the British Mandate, there were two million people living in the area of the Land of Israel, two thirds of whom were Arabs. After the war, in 1948, the Arab population became a minority living under the rule of a Jewish majority in the State of Israel. About two years later, the population of Israel numbered 1.2 million people, 86 percent of whom were Jews. Among those who left were part of the leadership of the Arab sector during the period of the Mandate, including lawyers, doctors, merchants, and landowners.[92] From their status as a community that enjoyed political and economic power, the Arab residents became a minority whose everyday life was determined by the policies of the majority government. The Arab population, certainly its leadership, viewed the country as their homeland throughout history – if only because they had been born on this patch of land. The significance of the Arabs becoming a minority and in this case, an indigenous minority, strengthened their feelings of frustration from their defeat in the war and, as Azmi Bishara put it: "The Arab became a survivor holding onto his land."[93] In most of the cases known in the world, including this case, this type of situation increased the self-awareness of the minority and its national demands. The Arabic concept *Ṣumud*, which means holding on to the fatherland, was at that time and still today high on the list of priorities of the Arabs in Israel.[94]

A second reason for the frustration came from the argument raised by the non-Jewish minority members that the Jewish state was established through the destruction of their people and even at the cost of the Arab villages that were abandoned.[95] Thirdly, the new political-diplomatic situation created a reality in which the non-Jewish minority in the country lives in a Jewish country surrounded by Arab countries whose peoplehood is identical to that of those same minority members. On the basis of the claims about the defeat in war, the loss of ownership of the land, and becoming a minority group, the term *"Nakba"* was engraved into the collective memory of the Arab minority in Israel.

This picture of the situation helps in detailing the image of the Arab leadership during the first years of the state. The leaders of the Arab population were the first to leave the country as early as the spring of 1948, some even earlier – just as had been the case during the flight from the country due the wave of violence from 1936–1939, which had ended well, when those who had fled returned to their homes and their jobs.[96] By the end of the fighting in 1949, the whole political elite had left; following this the organizational structures that had existed during the period of the mandate disappeared, including the Supreme Muslim Council, the Supreme Arab Committee, the political parties, the unions, economic bodies, and youth organizations.[97] Palmon, the Advisor on Arab Affairs to Prime Minister Ben-Gurion, described the situation of the Arab citizens of Israel at the end of the fighting in these words: "In all three areas the residents were left with no food supplies, no police, no courts, no education system, no Mukhtar's (village leaders), no community heads, no religious leaders – without any leadership."[98] Yosef Vashitz, who frequently visited Arab villages, described the Arab minority as "weak and divided, suffering from helplessness and feelings of crisis and experiencing the feeling of disappointment at the leaders who had left the country." In the light of this he added that "the Arab minority has no belief in its ability to act independently and there is an expectation among them that they will receive help from Jews who support them." Member of the Knesset, Rustam Bastuni, a member of Mapam, wrote in the middle of the 1960s: "The Arab citizens of Israel were like sleep-walkers, an ethnic minority, a small part of a state that had just been established, no longer nation."[99]

In such a situation, in which the traditional Arab leaders were fleeing the country, the question needs to be asked as to what kind of leadership model had developed in the Arab sector during those years. The new leadership that developed was made up of people from the following power groups: the first model being "representative" leaders who had made their way into the ranks of Mapai and Mapam and others who had joined satellite parties of the Zionist parties. Among these were, for example, Bastuni, Yusuf Khamis and ᶜAbd el-ᶜAziz Zuᶜbi, who were members of Mapam, and Masᶜad Kassis from the Democratic Party, which was a satellite party of Mapai. These people were close to the government because of their political contacts and personal interests; accordingly, they focused on attempting to establish communication with governmental representatives, in order to improve the situation of the Arab minority. Kassis, for example, had no hesitation about coming out publicly against the Communists in order to win public admiration.

A second kind of leadership among Arab Israeli citizens during this period was national leadership belonging to Maki, the Communist group, which enjoyed the patronage of the Soviet Union. The party became the only political force in the Arab sector except for those Knesset members who had made their way into the Zionist parties. The Arab Knesset members from Maki did not give up their national identities, and they established the Union for the Defense of the Arab Minority's Rights. They wanted to achieve such objectives as security for the Arab sector and integration into the life of the state within existing limitations to enable them to achieve as many of their economic goals as possible. This was the first political expression by a national Arab leadership faction that chose integration rather than separatism.

The third kind of leadership was that known in the literature as traditional leadership, which included the heads of clans and of aristocratic families, the village notables, and priests.[100] This leadership saw itself as bound to the new government and maintained contact with it concerning civil matters in order to improve the situation of the population that had remained in the Arab villages throughout the country. Every time a problem came up in one village or another, they turned for help to the Prime Minister or to other representatives of the government such as ministers or advisors on Arab Affairs. The following examples, all of which have been taken from the files of the Bureau of the Advisor on Arab Affairs and have been stored in the State of Israel Archives, are concrete evidence of the traditional leadership's reliance on the government as well as the moderate tone of the requests.

On June 20, 1951, the Mukhtar of the Arab village of a-Shibli, near the foothills of Mt. Tabor, appealed to Prime Minister David Ben-Gurion, in a letter signed by 26 village notables, to return the lands that had been confiscated to the villagers. The Prime Minister passed the request on to the professionals, who replied, after examining the issue, that there was no reason to return the lands to their owners.[101] The same mukhtar sent another letter to the Prime Minister (October 11, 1953) protesting the way the military government staff was handling things. He stressed in his letter that "the villagers are peace lovers –who have proven since statehood that we only wish to live in peace and friendship with the Jewish workers and farmers." A copy of this letter was sent to the Communist bloc in the Knesset.[102]

Hajla Ibrahim Khouri, a woman resident of the village ʿIlabun, sent a letter in the name of the women of the village to the Prime Minister (February 23, 1949) in which she requested the release of villagers from jail. She pointed out that "the villagers have devoted themselves to the State of Israel in the hope of receiving its patronage." The mukhtar of the village, Faraj Diab Srur, sent a similar letter (December 23, 1949), in which he made it clear that the villagers belonged to the minority that were seeking peace.[103] The Iksal and Zalafa Village Committees protested (April 25, 1961) about the reduction of pasture land and threatened to boycott the upcoming elections.[104]

9
The Pattern of Activities of the Arab Minority 1948–1967

Based upon the characterization of the three different kinds of leadership groups, each of which had a different ideology, the question of what patterns of activity these leading political groups used in facing the government needs to be explored.

The examples that have been presented note that the traditional leadership that acted to minimalize damage held the view that the right way to act was to try and discuss things with the Israeli establishment in the hope that making this effort would prevent additional damage to the status of the Arab population. A deeper analysis shows that direct discussions were not available to other, more institutionalized, leadership factions. Parallel to this, the Arab members of the Knesset made many speeches in which they condemned the military government and demanded its cancellation. They also constantly protested the appropriation of land and against the discrimination against the Arab minority. Rustam Bastuni came out against the military government in a speech he made in December 1951,[105] and Member of the Knesset Tawfiq Tubi, from the Communist Party, did the same in a number of speeches he made and even presented a bill to cancel the military government.[106] He warned, as early as in the first months of the military government, that negating the rights of a national minority would lead to the negation of democracy and freedom for all the country's citizens.

The usual pattern of activity of the Communist branch also characterized the party's publicity for the election campaign, and in preparation for the Third Knesset elections in 1955, they published a platform that focused on social issues. In everything relating to the national level, the heads of the party chose to call for cancellation of the emergency situation which had been in place almost since the state's inception.[107]

Another form of response was sending letters to the military governors requesting relief from the distress of the residents. One such letter was sent by the poet Tawfiq Zayyad, who was a prominent activist in the Communist Party and later a member of the Knesset, to the military governor of the region of Nazareth as a response to his confinement to the region. In his letter he mentions that the injustice was not limited to one nationality or another.[108] Other ways of protesting were sending protest groups to the Knesset,[109] signing petitions calling for the cancellation of the military government,[110] protesting against it in written media,[111] and appealing to the wider public.[112] In this context it is worth taking a moment to look at the essence of the evidence given by Arab citizens who appeared before the Ratner Committee, because the messages they wished to pass on to members of the committee can teach us a lot as well about their methods and feelings during these years.

Member of the Knesset Bastuni tried to convince the members of the committee that the military government not only was not making any contribution to the security of the country but was actually harming it, because it was increasing the hostility of the Arabs towards the state.[113] He tried to strengthen his argument by presenting data that showed that since the introduction of the military government over the Israeli Arab citizens, its people had not succeeded in preventing the phenomena of infiltration and smuggling. Yusuf Khamis, a member of the Knesset from Mapam, argued that there was built-in tension between the military government by its nature and the country's democratic identity. Thus, he claimed, the military government's apparatus was made up of bodies that were operational, legislative, and judicial, which was the opposite of what existed in a democracy that promoted the separation of authorities. In order to make his arguments more concrete, Khamis described to members of the committee the involvement of military government personnel in the election campaign, as a step that was not consistent with the principles of a democratic regime. Elias Kussa, a prominent lawyer and public figure, complained to the Ratner Committee that the military government had only been intended to humiliate and suppress the Arab citizens of Israel and to deprive them of their property. His colleague, the businessman Suheil Kanj, who was a member of the Nazareth City Council and not connected to any political body, claimed that the residents of his city were loyal to the state and that there was no reason to discriminate against them.

Masʿad Kassis, a member of the Knesset representing the Democratic List of the Arab Citizens of Israel, which was a satellite party of Mapai, gave evidence that served as a warning that the military government was strengthening the hand of the opponents of the government, the Communists, because it was providing them with propaganda material against the authorities. His colleague from the same list, Sayf al-Din Zuᶜbi, blamed the government because it was mistaken when it promised the Arabs full equality, and when the realization of these failed, certain phenomena developed among the Arabs which he called "insolence and contempt." He supported the continuation of the military government with certain reforms that would put a stop to the various blunders that had been made.

The characteristics of the Arab leadership contributed to choosing courses of action that included criticism and protests within the framework of the law. The political and diplomatic reality that had been imposed upon it after the War of Independence, prevented over the years any extreme protest that might have spilled over into violence, even when the Arab minority experienced harsh events – as happened in October 1956 when the Sinai Campaign and the massacre in Kafr Qasem took place.

The Arab minority's public reaction to the Sinai Campaign, as reported in the official organ of Maki *al-Ittihad*, included the following characteristics: expression of solidarity with Egypt and condemnation of Israel, France, and Britain because of their decision to attack Egypt; the call to solve the Israeli–Arab conflict through agreements and not war; an appeal to the Security Council of the UN to bring an end to the fighting.[114] Ben-Gurion himself was called upon to comment on the members of the Arab minority during the war period, and he stated that quiet was being maintained throughout the country in both the permanent and nomadic settlements (meaning among the Bedouin clans).[115]

The reaction of the leadership to the massacre in Kafr Qasem was more complicated. Formally, the press censor imposed a full blackout on this extremely serious event, while the government established a committee of inquiry into the circumstances of the events as soon as November 1, two days after the massacre.[116] The first public response to the incident was not made by Prime Minister Ben-Gurion until November 12, in an announcement he made to the Knesset. Two weeks after the event took place the item was published on the front page of *al-Ittihad,* whose headline was that the committee of inquiry recognized that the Border Police were responsible for the crime that had taken place close to the village.[117] In the body of the article they wrote that the committee of inquiry decided to file charges against those involved in the event that the government's announcement did not include any details of the event, and that it had acted to conceal the grave details.

The revelation of the details of the massacre in Kafr Qasem was made possible by the activity of the Communist Party's members of the Knesset, Tubi and Meir Vilner, who managed to get to Kafr Qasem about two weeks after the massacre. Vilner only published the fact of his visit in an article that he wrote forty years later in which he related that when he got to the village with Tubi, he discovered the streets were empty, and after a short time the two of them managed to gain entry into the houses where they heard what had happened there from the villagers.[118] An analysis of what was written in the organ of Maki which at that time was the leading national political force in the Arab minority, does not reveal any calls for protests of the kind that are not legally permitted in a democratic country. Although the newspaper did express direct and severe criticism of the government's behavior both regarding the war in Sinai and the massacre in Kafr Qasem, it simultaneously remained loyal to the party's ideology and continued to call for a solution to the conflict through peaceful means.

At the beginning of 1957, during the first two months after the massacre, a limited attempt was made by the Arab minority to protest the massacre; these two months were characterized by activities which included: sending petitions to the government demanding a public trial and a promise that this would not happen again; holding public meetings in different places such as Acre, Nazareth and Haifa, which were attended by hundreds of Arab citizens, in order to bring them up to date on the details of the grave events in Kafr Qasem; declaring a general strike on January 6, 1957 – the day of the military trial of those suspected of carrying out the massacre of the village's residents.[119] Maki and the residents of Kafr Qasem had a similar response on the first anniversary of the massacre, when a public statement aimed at Israeli public opinion and published in October 1957, expressed grief for the 49 victims of the massacre and made it clear that what those who remained wanted was to live as people who were "free, equal and in peace in our homeland. We will defend this with all our strength."[120] The public statement made it clear that the Israeli government had not learned the lessons of the events in Kafr Qasem and had not cancelled the military government, but was using it to look for new laws that would make the lives of the farmers more difficult – referring mainly to the Arab minority whose main livelihood during these years came from agriculture. Those who composed this public statement chose the channel of dialogue with the Jewish public and appealed to "people of conscience, to members of the Knesset, in order to put an end to the harsh reality of Arab life in the country."

Parallel to this public statement, on the first anniversary of the massacre, events were held that involved gatherings commemorating the victims and public meetings marking the incident.[121] Assembling a large number of people (more than a thousand according to newspaper reports) to participate, among other things, was made possible because of the well-oiled organizational abilities of the Communist Party branches.

If the two events that were significant to the Arab citizens – the establishment of the state and the massacre in Kafr Qasem – provoked dialogue and mild protest, this was not the case with what happened in 1958. During the first half of the year a number of developments took place that changed the local and regional picture somewhat. Just before the celebrations to commemorate the tenth anniversary of the establishment of the State of Israel, security personnel identified a rise in nationalistic feelings of the Arab citizens of Israel. They related this to the influence of political media activities of Egyptian president, Gamal Abd al-Nasser, upon the Arab citizens of Israel. Isser Harel, who at this time was the head of the Mossad, told the Mapai Conference on Arab Affairs that he estimated that "an escalation in the relations between Jews and Arabs in the country" was expected.[122] He even believed that there was a danger of this spilling over into a civil war, based on the increase in signs of irredentism in the Arab population and of external influences affecting this population. In February 1958, a political unification took place in the Arab world, which led to the establishment of a united Arab republic that included Egypt and Syria, with foundations consisting of a shared Arab nationality. In Algeria, the first results of the revolt led by the FLN (The National Liberation Front) against the French government in the country were becoming obvious.

Changes began to take place in the Communist Party, which was the only opposition party to the government during this period – but as early as 1956, during the discussions that took place at the party's 20th annual congress, sharp differences of opinion between the Jewish and Arab members began to appear. Tubi, for example, who met with Arab communists in Syria for the first time, demanded a change in Maki's definition of the 1948 War. It was his view that this was not a war of liberation but a war that was "anti-Arab and unjust".[123] Tubi and his colleague, Emil Habibi, questioned the borders of the State of Israel as they had been established after the war in 1948. Researchers into the party see the 13th Conference which took place in Jaffa (May 2, 9, 1957) as an event where for the first time the Communists publicly used their nationalistic expressions. At this time Habibi coined the concept "the right of the Palestinian people to self-determination" to replace the traditional mantra of "Israel's right to exist." In his speech to the conference, his colleague

Emil Tuma made the point that Israel's retreat to the 1947 cease-fire lines was a necessary condition for the Arab countries to recognize it.[124] In January 1958, the Arab leaders of Maki held a secret meeting, which the party center did not know about, in Habibi's home at which a discussion took place about the possibility of carrying on guerrilla warfare similar to what was being waged by the National Liberation Front in Algeria. In the Hebrew press, reports and articles were already published in February 1958, whose central message was that leading Arab factions in Maki had decided to move on to an active struggle against the establishment in order to improve the lot of the Arab minority.[125] During this period, Habibi carried out a rallying campaign in different Arab villages such as Kafr Qara in the triangle and ʿArabeh in the Galilee, at which he called for lifting the burden of the conquest. He also published articles that called for the actualization of the right to self-determination for Arab citizens of Israel, whom he called "The Palestinian Arab People."[126]

These nationalistic feelings were in fact translated into action at a time that Habibi chose – while he ignored counter-measures taken by the police, who quickly arrested dozens of Maki activists during the month of February 1958, on suspicion of incitement against the government. The Nazareth branch of Maki organized an event on May 1, the Workers' Day, calling on the public to join in the central parade in the city. This mass demonstration was an illegal action even before it began, because before the event the police had banned all signs of protest and only permitted public gatherings. The Nazareth branch, encouraged by Habibi, carried out a demonstration of strength and confrontation with the police "without having received permission from the higher authorities of the party".[127] The event in Nazareth turned into a violent clash between the police and the demonstrators, with the demonstrators throwing stones and damaging police vehicles, the events spilling over to the area of Umm el-Fahem. At the height of the stormy events three hundred people were injured and hundreds of the demonstrators were arrested.[128] Two months later the Arab heads of Maki admitted: "It was a miscalculation to choose violent methods".[129]

On May 26, 1958, the Knesset plenum was asked to discuss the Nazareth riots; the query under discussion was the possible prosecution of the Arab minority members that had been arrested in the disturbances. David Ben-Gurion, the then Prime Minister, who spoke during this discussion, chose to exploit the information that exposed the Maki's preparations for the violent confrontation with the security forces, and he pointed an accusative finger at the Arab leadership by claiming that the disturbances were the result of the work of the agents of a hostile country that was trying to incite some of the citizens against the state – and that this was not only done on May Day but also two days earlier. Ben-Gurion claimed: "Everything began when the Nazareth municipality – which I believe is completely composed of Arabs – decided upon celebrating the tenth anniversary of the state and Maki, which acts as the foreign agent of a neighboring hostile country and trumpeted the praises of the tyrannical ruler of that country, decided to break the law and disturb the festivities".[130] The Maki members of the Knesset, who were present in the Knesset during the discussion, did not express opposition to what Ben-Gurion said and the only one who tried to protest in a half-hearted way was the Jewish member of the Knesset, Esther Vilenska, who argued that it was the police who had acted out of control in Nazareth.[131] Ben-Gurion immediately silenced her and said: "That will be decided in the court".[132]

Even after the event in Nazareth in May 1958 and well into the 1960s the Communist Party continued to be the central political force among the Arab minority in Israel. Its members in the Knesset and its activists outside of the legislature continued to try to get the military government cancelled in ways that the law permitted in a democratic country, in the belief that its cancellation would improve the situation of the Arab population. In the parliamentary arena, the Maki members of the Knesset made proposals to the agenda of the Knesset in order to try and gain a majority among the factions in the house that would lead to the cancellation of the military government. One such proposal was that of Member of the Knesset Tubi who, in a speech to the plenum in 1963, argued that there was nothing real in the easements that were being made for the Arab minority as long as the military government continued to exist. Along with the activity in the parliamentary arena, it became clear during these years that the power of the nationalist branch was increasing in the ranks of the Communists. At the 14th conference of the party (May 31–June 3, 1961), Habibi, Tubi and Şliba Khamis demanded that Maki delete the two words "mutual recognition" from its demand to recognize the national rights of the Palestinian People. Their demand was rejected but there was enough to it to make the nationalist feelings of the Arab members concrete.[133] These feelings were again made public at the beginning of 1962 when Moshe Sneh, who was the head of Maki, published an article in which he attacked Ahmed Ben Bella, the would be president of Algeria, for announcing his readiness to send 100,000 soldiers, if a decision were made to eliminate the State of Israel.[134] Tubi and Habibi came out against Sneh's article and argued that "there is no place to criticize any Arab leader, no matter what he says, because he reflected the spirit of Arab nationalism."[135]

Between 1963 and 1967 the process of "evolution of nationalist feelings" among the Arab members of Maki continued. At this stage they were not channeling this into patterns of violent action; it is possible to analyze this historically in order to try to provide a number of reasons for their avoiding turning to violence: first, the remaining memory of the painful riots that took place in Nazareth in May 1958; second, the force used by the government in order to restore order in Nazareth; third, the internal political crisis taking place in the ranks of Maki which had caused the party to deal mainly with the effort to prevent a split, which eventually did take place in 1965; four, the harsh, uncompromising measures taken by the government against the members of the "al-Arḍ" movement, which had adopted a radical and nationalistic approach against the government and had found themselves outside the law as a political body – while some of its members chose to voluntarily exile themselves from the country and found refuge in the various institutions of the Palestinian Liberation Organization.[136]

From the end of the 1950s up until the Six Day War in June 1967, the first changes started to take place in the political map within the Arab minority in Israel. In July 1958, about two months after the events in Nazareth, Arab activists along with prominent Maki activists formed "The Arab Front," which was in fact the first Arab national organization to be established in Israel. The establishment of the new political body, which only lasted a year, was inspired by the awakening of Arab nationalism in Egypt and Syria and the union they formed. Signs of admiration for Nasser, the then Egyptian president, appeared among Arab students who were studying at the Hebrew University in Jerusalem and who developed political awareness because he had promised them a war to liberate the Arab nation from their oppressors –meaning the countries of the west. Ṣabri Jiryis, who was a student at that time, noted that the ability he had to acquire a higher education and expand his horizons helped him to understand the reality he was living in and claimed that this allowed him to develop and clarify his political ideas.[137]

This brief historical discussion of the brief episode of the "Arab Front" is important because its founders became the founding nucleus of the "*al-Arḍ*" (The Land) group which played a central role in the historical development of political frameworks within the Arab minority in Israel. At the beginning the group was called *Usrat al-Arḍ* (The Land Family) and its members directed their activities along three fronts: the State of Israel whose character and political map it wanted to change through the struggle of a group that was built upon Arabs only; the traditional leadership of the Arab minority which they saw as being out of date and no longer suited to the needs of the day; and the Communist Party which they saw as a bitter political rival that had to be fought against.

The new ideology of the group began to express itself in a practical way as early as October 1959, when from then until January 1960 the group published a newspaper which it constantly used to denigrate the state, its institutions and its leaders. From time to time the publications also included threats aimed at the State of Israel from which they demanded, as they wrote in their organ, that the Arabs be allowed to live and that only then, perhaps, they would make it possible for the Jews to live.[138] The reaction of the government to the conduct of the "*al-Arḍ*" group and its publications was immediate. Salah Baransi, the editor, was charged with publishing an unlicensed newspaper, was found guilty, and was given a suspended sentence. This step taken by the government led the members of "*al-Arḍ*" to look for legal ways to operate; they made a request to open a financial company, but here as well the government demonstrated its power, and the registrar of companies refused their request due to security concerns and for the good of the public. Mansur Kardush, one of the leaders of the group, appealed to the Supreme Court of Justice to permit the registration, which the Supreme Court of Justice allowed, and in the summer of 1962 the company was registered.[139]

The decision made by the Supreme Court of Justice encouraged the members of *al-Arḍ* to expand their activities; they requested a license to publish a newspaper but were denied and their appeal to the Supreme Court was also rejected. Parallel to this, *al-Arḍ* turned to international institutions and the foreign press and, through them, tried to awaken international public opinion to the situation of the Arab minority living in Israel. The next stage of *al-Arḍ*'s activities was its members' attempt to found an Ottoman association (in modern Israeli terms, an NGO), since this was the only legal framework that existed for political parties in Israel. The goal of the registration was to have a registered Arab political party that would be able to operate in the political arena and actualize the platform of *al-Arḍ*, whose aim was to change the nature of the country. The government's reaction to this step was also assertive, and the application was refused. The official in charge of the Haifa Region wrote to Ṣabri Jiryis that *al-Arḍ* had been established in order to do harm to the existence of the State of Israel . . . but that "if, despite the aforementioned, it becomes clear that they are acting as a body then action might be taken against them according to the law."[140] The members of *al-Arḍ* did not give up; once again they appealed to the Supreme Court of Justice – this time the Supreme Court judges chose to demonstrate the power of the Judicial

Authority as one of the arms of the government and adopted an uncompromising approach in their response to the appeal. The Supreme Court analyzed the purpose of *al-Arḍ* and came to the conclusion that it was denying the existence of the State of Israel and the rights of the Jewish People. Three Justices – Landau, Cohen, and Agranat – unanimously ruled that the organization called *al-Arḍ* was not included within the definition of what was democratic in the State of Israel.

After this judgment as well, the *al-Arḍ* activists tried to continue with their activities until ultimately in November 1964 the Minister of Defense used the authority given to him by law to sign the order to outlaw the group. Four of its leaders – Baransi, Kardush, Kaoughi and Jiryis – were arrested for questioning. In 1965, the members of *al-Arḍ* were still trying to register a list to take part in the Knesset elections, but the Central Elections Committee invalidated the list on the basis that it was "the same lady dressed differently."[141] The public preoccupation with the *al-Arḍ* group was not the only subject that the Arab minority had to deal with in its charged relations with the government. During the year after the legal procedures involving the self-declared anti-establishment movement were over, an announcement was made by the Prime Minister cancelling the military government, but this was greeted with apathy in the Arab sector, as described by reports made by officers of the military government.[142] Local and country-wide leadership factors sent congratulatory telegrams to the Prime Minister on making this decision that lowered the curtain on a reality that had continued for eighteen years.

The newspaper of the Communist Party did not deal much with the issue of the military government. During the months before the announcement of the cancellation, the newspaper was dealing with international issues including the war in Vietnam, local issues such as the worsening economic situation that was expressing itself in higher prices, and the municipal elections in Nazareth – and it reacted with disinterest to the official announcement of the cancellation of the military government that was made to the Knesset. Articles in the newspaper called for the immediate removal of authority from the military governors, ceasing the policy of closing territories, and halting the wave of arrests of Arabs who had been place on the "blacklists" of the government.[143] After a while this disinterest was replaced with complaints, because the police and General Security Service personnel were insistently enforcing the policy more strongly than the officers of the military government had done. The annoyance of the public figures of the Arab sector was not channeled into any form of widespread public protest. Because of this they chose to act through Jewish figures who were attentive to their woes.

The Members of the Knesset of Rakah (the communist party), which at that time was the leading political force in the Arab minority, scoffed at the Prime Minister's announcement, since they were convinced that this did not mean the cancellation of the apparatus but its replacement by a civilian mechanism. In a speech he gave to the Knesset plenum, Tawfik Tubi argued that the only change would be that the Arabs in Israel would no longer have contact with military personnel but, from now on, with the police instead. What he was saying was that there was nothing new in the Prime Minister's announcement and that the military government was in fact continuing.[144] The tension between Israel and its neighbors during the first half of 1967, which reached its peak with the Six Day War, was felt by the Arab minority as well. The way that the Arab national leadership (the Communist stream) related to the war and its results needs to be examined in the context of the political changes that were taking place within the Communist Party. In the years before the war, a deep split took place in the ranks of this party, which led to the division of the historic structure of the party into two separate political entities, with Maki remaining the political stronghold of the Jewish members and the other new Communist list (Rakah) becoming the home of the Arab members and some of the Jews such as Meir Vilner. The differences between the views of the members of Maki, led by Moshe Sneh, and the members of Rakah, such as Tubi, Habibi, and others, in regard to the solution of the conflict between the Jewish People and The Palestinian People was the background to this split. Sneh wanted to adopt the line of Soviet involvement in the spirit of the Tashkent Agreement in 1965, which brought about peace between Pakistan and India, while Rakah adopted the line advanced by the president of Egypt, and argued, like Tubi had, that the Israeli policy was making it impossible to get to Tashkent.

During the year that preceded the war, enough public evidence had accumulated to indicate that Rakah had taken on the garb of Arab nationalism even if its ideological core remained communist. The members of Rakah deepened their identification with the pro-Arab policy of the USSR, and in parallel, they ignored the acts of terrorism being carried out by the Syrian army and the PLO, which had been established at the beginning of 1965 as the organization that was leading the Palestinian national struggle. On June 6, 1967, one day after the beginning of the war, the editorial of Rakah's newspaper was devoted to the situation of the Arab citizens of Israel during wartime. The central message of the editorial was that one "should not see this population as hostages but rather as a bridge that can be a connection between Israel and the Arab countries."[145] Throughout all the days of the war and, in fact, till the end of June, the newspaper satisfied itself with informative reporting about what was happening in the field and the diplomatic efforts being made to end the war. Along with this, they prominently featured protests about a wave of arrests carried out by the government (June 23, 30) among the communist activists in order to ensure quiet in the Arab sector.

Rakah placed responsibility on the Israeli government for these events, and the Central Committee of the party asserted that Israel had carried out acts of aggression that had been planned by the United States and Britain. The Knesset discussed the results of the war in a special session in July 1967, and after the statement made by Abba Eban, the Foreign Minister, about the significance of the war, a discussion developed in which Emil Habibi chose to focus his speech upon the need to establish peace in the region. He warned that the results of the war had not solved the basic problems of the State of Israel, had made peace more distant, and had increased the danger of another war. Habibi ended his speech by extending his hand in the hope of peace between the people in Israel and the Arab people. There was no call to the Arab public for violent action and aggression towards the state.[146]

There is no supporting evidence to suggest that there was any influential Arab factor that tried to act violently against the state as an expression of identification with the Arab armies during the fighting. It is possible that it was the rapid decisiveness of the Israeli success with which the campaign ended that made the balance of power between the sides clear and in fact prevented any possibility of choosing a pattern of violent action. It is possible that there was another reason which came from the power of the government over the Arab minority during this time. The re-imposition of a military government over the Arab population with the beginning of the war was accompanied by the arrest of Arab supporters and members of Rakah and *al-Arḍ* on the morning of June 5, 1967 as well as their administrative incarceration until June 20, 1967.[147] The rapid action taken to deal with figures who may have called for violent action significantly reduced the possibility of such a thing disturbing the routine life of the country.

The Arab public, in general, chose to express identification with the State of Israel following the impressive military achievement in the war. In Archive material there are hundreds of letters and signatures of Arab citizens expressing pride in the IDF's victory, and some of the letters contain requests from Arabs to be mobilized into national service.[148] The priest George Hakim, for example, one of the senior leaders of the Christian community and a public figure since the first days of the State, published a proclamation in which he called upon the Christian community to donate blood for the wounded IDF soldiers because of the need to help the country that was fighting for its existence.

10
Patterns of Adaptation Adopted by the Arabs from 1967 to 1990

The period following the June 1967 War was full of changes in the life of the Arab minority in Israel. The removal of the physical barrier between this population and the Arab residents of Judea and Samaria quickly made it possible for them to establish direct contact with each other; this contact between the two populations became routine and included familial, economic, commercial, educational and cultural connections. Young Arabs who were citizens of Israel found themselves studying in educational institutions such as colleges, universities and religious institutions in the West Bank.[149] The influence of political streams that existed in the West Bank quickly began to insinuate itself among the Arab citizens of Israel – one of the clear expressions of this was the relatively high rate of Arab citizens of Israel joining the ranks of the Palestinian terrorist organizations. The leaders of *al-Arḍ*, for example, found themselves being absorbed into the various institutions of the PLO, and in parallel to this, in the period between the June 1967 War and the Yom Kippur War in October 1973, 320 Arab citizens of Israel were put on trial for security offences that ranged from being recruited into organizations that were members of the PLO to carrying out attacks on Jewish concentrations of population.[150]

This reality gradually created a change in the character of the minority's leadership which was no longer the well-known, veteran leadership that was made up of the leaders of the Communist branch and people who had chosen to join the Zionist parties. From the beginning of the 1970s new political frameworks appeared, the first of which was the "Sons of the Village," which had new ideologies and a readiness to choose new patterns of activity, even violence, to be used against the Israeli establishment. This was different from the activity chosen by the veteran leadership vis-à-vis the Israeli government.

The need to adopt new patterns of adaptive activity was not only a result of the opening of the borders with Judea and Samaria and the

Gaza Strip. There was another reason for the feelings of alienation that the Arab minority was experiencing regarding the government's relations with it. Bastuni described the Israeli society after the war as "a society in which two communities were living in Israel: the large Jewish community and the second, smaller one, the Arab community, with actually no sufficient communication between them . . . the spiritual ghetto prevented the integration of the Arabs into the life of the country".[151] His words show that after the war as well, quite a loose contact continued between the two ethnic groups in the country; this phenomenon strengthened the question of national identity for the Arabs after the June 1967 War, especially in the educated circles where people felt alienation from the state.

Bastuni was not the only one. An analysis of publications written by intellectuals and politicians who supported dialogue with the authorities, some of whom showed this by joining Zionist parties, indicates an awakening of national feelings in them as well. One of the prominent motifs that appeared in different publications was the determination that the connection with the West Bank which began after the June 1967 War strengthened the Palestinian nationalist connection for the Arab citizens of Israel and the feeling of their belonging to the Arab world.[152] Muhammad Watad, a leading member of Mapam, wrote that the Arab citizens of Israel were experiencing the phenomenon of returning to their sources and of reconnection with the consciousness of suffering in the Arab countries.[153]

This period at the end of the 1960s and the beginning of the 1970s was an important historical milestone in the development of the political consciousness of the Arab minority in Israel. A number of significant components that regularly turned up in the patterns of thinking and acting of the Arab minority's leadership can be identified, among which were the growing recognition of the gap that existed between economic development and the social-political situation, the awakening of the feelings of Palestinian nationalism, the growing understanding of the gap between their situation as a minority group and that of the majority group, an increasing exposure to propaganda against the State of Israel as it appeared in the media of Arab countries and in the East Jerusalem newspapers,[154] and the growth of a generation of young people among the Arab minority who had been educated towards aspiration and achievement. These processes gradually transformed the situation of the Arab citizens of Israel from one of passivity to political activism. The Communist stream, which was the largest, best oiled and organized political group during these years, adopted an ambiguous position. On the one hand it condemned acts of terrorism carried out by Palestinian organizations against Israeli citizens, while on the other hand, the spokesmen of the party regularly attacked and condemned the conquest. Rakah's patterns of behavior at the end of the 1960s and the beginning of the 1970s were characterized by "the organizing of demonstrations and the signing of petitions in favor of the Palestinian struggle while emphasizing their national narrative."[155]

These ideological developments, especially the one that emphasized the awakening of Palestinian nationalist feelings, were expressed in the field from time to time. This, for example, was the case in September 1970 when Nasser, the president of Egypt, died. His death, which took place at the exact same time as the Black September events in Jordan,[156] led to mourning processions by Arabs, citizens of Israel, in the villages of the triangle and throughout the Galilee. Another development that took place at this time and that contributed to the strengthening of these feelings was the PLO's re-examination of its attitude towards the Arab citizens of Israel. The PLO's traditional approach of ignoring the Arabs living in Israel gave way to an approach that recognized the importance of this population for the Palestinian struggle. A direct and concrete expression of this was given in the announcement that summarized the meeting held by the Palestinian National Council in 1972, which, among other things, stated that "the PNC calls for support for the struggle of the 48 [Israeli] Arabs in order to preserve their national and Arab identity and to strengthen the national solidarity between the masses of our brothers in the areas occupied since 1948, the West Bank, in the Gaza Strip and beyond the occupied homeland".[157] In 1974 the PLO received recognition from the Arab states as the sole representative of the Palestinian People and one year later was granted the status of observer in the United Nations. These developments strengthened the status of the organization and its contacts with the Arab population; Rakah exploited this development to call upon the Israeli government to withdraw from the occupied territories, to recognize the PLO, and to make it possible for the Palestinian People to realize its right to self-determination.

The political expression of these processes were, for the first time, reflected in 1969 with elections that took place in September in the Histadrut, the general federation of workers, and a month later in the general elections for the Seventh Knesset. An analysis of the voting patterns of the Arabs who were members of the Histadrut compared to the patterns of Arabs voting in the elections of the same institution in 1965 shows that the percentage of votes for Rakah increased from 19.8 percent in 1965 to 31.4 percent four years later. In absolute figures the number of voters for the Communist list went up from 5,700 to 11,366. Political commentators have explained Rakah's success in the Histadrut elections as being the result of good organization by the party's branches in the field and of the list's platform that was based on the nationalist component, even though this was an election for the Workers Federation. During the election campaign Rakah argued that the other lists were part of the establishment, which was "a conqueror, imperialist and colonialist in the occupied territories".[158] The choice of a nationalistic line over a communistic one, which included the use of provocative expressions against the Israeli government, in contrast to the moderate language used during the 1950s provided Rakah with the characteristics of an Arab nationalist party. This choice turned out to be effective in light of the list's successes in the elections for the General Workers Federation.

Similar patterns of voting by the Arab citizens of Israel were recorded in the elections for the Seventh Knesset in 1969. The Arab voter was, in fact, faced with two "realistic" alternatives: to vote for the Communist list or to vote for Mapam. The latter chose to take part in the elections in a list united with the Labor Party – which was a step that was exploited by Rakah to accuse it of joining the establishment. This was a clear expression of the centrality of the national narrative in the way it acted against the Israeli government.[159]

An analysis of the votes of the Arab voters shows the following findings:

(a) The general rate of voting for the Arab citizens dropped by 5 percent (from 87 percent to 82 percent), and from this one can see a drop in the "relative participation" of the Arab voters in the general elections.[160] This finding also indicates (albeit partially) that there was a small percentage of voters who chose not to go to the voting booth because of the polarity they felt between their nationalistic Arab feelings (as an Arab collective) and the everyday norms of their private lives.

(b) A sharp drop in the rate of voting for the Zionist parties was recorded in comparison with the 1965 elections (a drop from 21.6 percent to only 14.3 percent).

(c) Rakah, as the only list that was campaigning with a nationalist platform, received 28 percent of the Arab votes as opposed to 23 percent in the 1965 elections.

On the basis of these changes and processes that the Arab citizens of Israel were experiencing after June 1967, it was only a question of time before new political frameworks were established – in a period in which the growth of a new generation of educated people whose political consciousness had increased, was identified. In 1971, political activists got together to establish the Association of Arab Academics, an endeavor that was sharply criticized in the Hebrew press. As a result of differences in opinion among the founders, this attempt at establishing a political body failed. The first actual organization took place in 1972, when a new political framework was established by young academics. The name of this movement was "The Sons of the Country" (in Arabic *Abana al Balad*) which later took root as the "Sons of the Village" movement. This new political movement was headed by an attorney called Muhammad Kaywan, a resident of Umm el-Fahem, where the nucleus of the Sons of the Village developed; its first members were students, past security prisoners who had spent time in Israeli jails, and intellectuals who were defined as revolutionaries.[161]

The ideological line of the Sons of the Village was based upon the following ideas: denial of the sovereignty of the State of Israel over Palestinian territories, unambiguous identification with the PLO, and adoption of the platform of the rejectionist organizations. The movement's platform also included denial of the right of the Jewish People to self-determination, and the need to strive for establishment of a democratic secular state in all the land of Palestine within its pre-1948 borders. The way to realize the goals was to be through an armed Palestinian revolution in which all parts of the Palestinian People would take part – including residents of the West Bank, the Gaza Strip, and the State of Israel. The leaders of the movement displayed the slogan, "*al-khalil mithl al-Jalil*" (Hebron equals to the Galilee), in order to emphasize the shared national identity of the populations on both sides of the Green line.[162]

During the same period of time, and in the shadow of these changes in consciousness and politics, several events that were significant and relevant to the Arab minority took place in the Middle East, the most prominent of which was the Yom Kippur War in October 1973. As was the case with the State of Israel, this war came as a complete surprise to the Arab leadership; even if there were public signs of a possible attack by the Arab side, they did not lead to any response from the Arab leadership up till the outbreak of war. An analysis of the September 1973 issues of *al-Ittihad,* the newspaper of the Communist party, show a preoccupation with entirely different matters, the most central being: the army revolt in Chile, the preparations being made for the Central Conference of the Communist party, the general elections to the Knesset, and the political crisis in the Labor party – which was the ruling party.

Beginning on October 9, *al-Ittihad* continually reported on what was happening in the war and the developments that were taking place on the battlefield. Articles written by the leaders of the Communist party (Habibi and Tubi), with one message – that the bloodshed had to stop – were regularly published. On October 12, Habibi wrote an article entitled "We hope that this tragedy is the last one" and on October 19 Tubi asked "How can we turn this war into the last war in the region?" The solution he proposed consisted of an Israeli withdrawal from the occupied territories and the beginning of discussions until a general peace arrangement could be made. In another article Habibi asked: "Is all the blood we (the Arabs) have shed for peace up till now not enough?"[163] In a meeting held by the youth movement of the Communist party in Tel Aviv (October 27), the next generation of the party was called upon to fight for peace. Throughout the entire war, even after the end of the fighting on October 24, the newspaper did not publish any call by a faction of the leadership of the Arab minority to act with violence, and thereby express identification with the Arab states fighting against the State of Israel.

The feeling in the Arab population in Israel after the war was one of pride and victory by the Arab side. These feelings were also expressed in Arabic literature and poetry. The poet Tawfik Zayyad, one of the leaders of Rakah, wrote a poem entitled "The Great Crossing" (in Arabic: *al-ʿUbur al-kabir*) which was a paean to the Egyptian army, praising its crossing of the Suez Canal and its surprising the IDF.[164] External changes that were perceived as positive from the Arab point of view also contributed to this sense of victory – since the PLO solidified its standing in the international arena, Arafat was asked to give a speech at the UN assembly, and the organization was even accepted into the UN with observer status. In practical terms, this feeling was expressed in the establishment of new institutional political structures; among the bodies that were established after the war was the Committee of Heads of the Arab Local Authorities in 1974, student committees in the universities, and later, bodies that were involved in the issue of land appropriation. During 1974 and 1975, these bodies were already holding many protests and strikes arising from consciousness of the deprivation from which the Arab minority was suffering. The Committee of Heads of the Local Authorities, for example, in the announcement about its foundation, made it clear that its goal was to fight for assurances from the government ministries that there would be equal treatment in all the governing bodies in Israel and that the Arab local authorities would be treated in the same way as the Jewish institutions. Strengthening of the Palestinian identity still did not lead to evidence of group political violence during the Yom Kippur War and in the period that followed it up until the events of (1976). The rate of involvement by Arab Israeli citizens in terrorist activities was also small compared to the six years between the June 1967 War and the Yom Kippur War.[165]

In contrast to the pattern of restrained struggle that included media protest against the war, the struggle against land appropriation took on a more violent character from 1975 onwards with a series of political power factors in the Arab minority – i.e. the veteran Communist stream, the young movement of the "Sons of the Village," and the heads of the local authorities becoming active. In June 1975, The Nazareth branch of Rakah organized a meeting which discussed the ways in which the Arab population could work together to protest the intention of the authorities to carry out a program of widespread land appropriation for the needs of the public. At the end of the meeting the participants decided to take action to mobilize public opinion and to organize a country-wide protest against the new program.[166] This initiative gathered strength during the summer months of 1975 when additional meetings to coordinate action were held in Haifa and Nazareth, in which activists from Rakah, representatives of the student and academic committees, religious leaders, and the heads of Arab local councils took part. At the end of a meeting that took place in Nazareth on August 15 the Committee for the Protection of the Lands published an announcement which claimed that the government intended to appropriate 30,000 dunams of land, of which 17,000 were agricultural lands, mostly Arab.[167] In a follow up meeting that took place two months later (October 18, 1975) in which representatives of the Negev Bedouin were also present – which was a step that gave the struggle the character of being a national struggle of the whole minority, a series of decisions were made to establish a national committee to protect the lands that would work for the cancellation of the expected appropriations, send a delegation of protest to the Knesset, and prepare a document including the claims made by the land owners, to be presented to the Prime Minister.

The establishment of the National Committee for the Protection of the Lands, under the aegis of Rakah, which enjoyed control over the heads of the local authorities, was a very significant step from several points of view. First, a national body that crossed political lines, coordinated and led the protest events against the appropriation of lands was established. Second, the establishment of the committee started a chain reaction in which local committees devoted to the protection of the lands in many Arab villages were established, especially in the Galilee and the triangle. Each local committee operated on the local level to explain the dangers involved in the confiscation of the Arab lands. Third, the establishment of the national committee made it possible for the heads of local councils to continue dealing with municipal matters other than the question of the land appropriation.

The activities of the National Committee for the Protection of the Lands during these months were carried out by the Arab leadership under a cloud of uncertainty about what the intentions of the government were. It was clear that the appropriation of land on a wide scale was imminent, but information about the exact scale was not available and different spokesmen for the government published different figures. The exclusion of Arabs from discussions of the various committees that were dealing with the program for the development of the Galilee also contributed to the vagueness. The extent of uncertainty encouraged the members of the committee to increase their activities and to take more radical steps to protest through the newspaper of the Communist party as well. Its headline on February 17, 1976 was "Five Thousand Warriors"; this referred to a report on the mass demonstration that took place in Sakhnin following information received about the appropriation. On February 21, eight days before the decision of the government, Şliba Khamis, one of the members of the committee, announced that the Arab public would carry out a protest outside the Knesset on Land Day, which would also be a day of strikes and protest in the Arab areas of Israel.[168]

Four weeks before the time designated for the planned appropriation, March 2, the main headline of the *al-Ittihad* warned against "violent reactions to the steps being taken to develop the Galilee which were in fact the Judaization of the Galilee".[169] Four days later, the members of the National Committee for the Protection of the Lands, together with the heads of local councils, decided upon a general strike on March 30. In a public statement that was published in the press and distributed to the whole Arab sector, the members of the committee made it clear that they had decided to turn the day of the implementation of the appropriations into "Land Day." On this day, as written in the public statement, the Arabs would raise their voices in a demand to put a stop to the official policy which had become a threat to their future in the country.[170] In preparation for this day, a well-oiled, organized campaign was set up, including advertisements in the press in Hebrew and an information campaign in the villages persuading the public to come to the areas being appropriated. Another proclamation was distributed on March 11 by the National Committee for the Protection of the Lands, in which the Arab public was called upon to declare a general strike on March 30, 1976 and to make this day Land Day in Israel.[171] Forty heads of local councils opposed the Committee for the Protection of the Lands because of their clear line of opposition to the appropriation of lands, believing that they should be working against the appropriation of lands through negotiations with the government. They sent a letter about this to the Prime Minister and met with ministers and senior civil servants in their effort to cancel the decision. Zaki Diab, the head of the Tamra Local Council, who belonged to the camp that believed in dialogue with the government, warned, "If the moderate camp feels it has been hard done by it will be resentful, and if it is resentful it will act, and if it acts there will be a non-constructive force and then there will be a great danger from the Arab citizens of Israel."[172]

This camp objected to holding a general strike and its supporters held two meetings (March 21, 25) at the end of which they decided not to enforce the strike in their villages. Their main activities were with government entities, but at the same time they did not exert pressure on the National Committee for the Protection of Lands to cancel the strike and prevent the scenario of a serious escalation. There is no source that indicates any attempt made by them as a group or as individuals to act against the National Committee for the Protection of the Lands to prevent the mass protest activities that were planned for March 30. This camp's reasoning derived from concern that if they acted against the National Committee for the Protection of Lands they would be perceived by the wider public as cooperating with the government on the sensitive national matter of lands. On the other hand, the continuation of dialogue with the government in an attempt to prevent the appropriations was perceived to be a legitimate part of their roles as the heads of their villages. It is therefore clear, from a historical analysis, that the position taken by the Arab leadership regarding ways to prevent the appropriations was not uniform.

Leading up to the time set for the appropriations, the number of meetings against the proposed appropriations increased rapidly, as did vehement expressions of opinion. In a meeting that was held in Shfarᶜam on March 27, the National Committee for the Protection of Lands again issued a call to strike in order to defend life, land, and the homeland. The aggressive line taken by the National Committee for the Protection of Lands, – which included representatives of all the leadership factions (Rakah, the students, the heads of local councils) – created a highly charged, explosive atmosphere in the field; the practical expression of this took place on March 29. Arab protestors organized a reception for the representatives of the law who were charged with carrying out the appropriation. On the night of March 29–30 the Israeli security forces who came to the Bet Netofa Valley came into contact with many protesters between the villages of ᶜArabeh and Dir Hana, who were burning tires and throwing stones and tins of burning kerosene at them. The security forces returned fire; one of the protestors was killed as a result. The authorities, in an effort to demonstrate forcefulness, sent reinforcements into the field and imposed a curfew over the whole area.

On the morning of March 30 the residents of the villages of Dir Hana, ᶜArabeh, and Sakhnin violated the curfew that had been imposed on them and gathered together in the main streets where they clashed with the security forces. They rushed the police patrol cars, attacked soldiers and border policemen and threw Molotov cocktails at them. The forces responded with gunfire at the rioters and at the end of the day of fighting six protestors had been killed in addition to the Arab citizen who had been killed the night before.

The events that took place in the region of the three villages quickly spilled over into other areas, and disturbances of the peace and riots were recorded in a series of places such as Buᶜeineh-Nujaidat, Kafr Kana, Mashhad, Turᶜan, Ein Mahel, and other Arab villages in the triangle (Taibe, Kalansawa, Tira and Jaljuliyyah). When these fierce clashes were taking place the members of the National Committee for the Protection of the Lands did not restrain the protestors, and Member of the Knesset, Tawfik Zayyad, who was the Mayor of Nazareth, rejected the call made by the regional head of the Ministry of the Interior to call off the strike.

11
After "Land Day": New Arab Political Structures

The events that took place on "Land Day" left a deep scar on the already highly-charged relations between the Arab minority and the government of Israel. For the first time in twenty years Arab citizens had been shot and killed by the security forces, but from the point of view of the Arab population, their deaths did not take place in a vacuum, since the government's choice to uncompromisingly enforce its decision about the land appropriation was also significant. The state in effect marked the boundary between legitimate protest in a democratic regime and prohibited violence.

The events themselves opened up a new period in terms of how the Arab minority dealt with its disputes with the government, including the patterns of protest over both national and civil issues. There were three central phenomena that characterized this period: First, the political map that had begun to change after the June 1967 War stabilized after "Land Day." During this period the "Sons of the Village," the Students Committee, and the Committee of the Heads of Local Councils began to work together with the Communist party. It was also during this period, at the beginning of 1979, that a new political body, The Progressive National Movement, was established by a group of students who called themselves nationalists. The ideological line of this organization completely identified with the Palestinian struggle in the West Bank and the Gaza Strip, and the strategic action it chose, which was expressed by Ibrahim Nasser, one of the heads of the movement, was to distribute its platform not only among the students but also among the whole Arab public.[173]

The existence of new political structures and their political principles gradually made their way into the consciousness of the Arab public during these years, and the new power groups established themselves in the political arena and wanted to influence the public agenda. The Committee of the Heads of Local Councils, for example, was influenced by the personalities of a number of the heads of councils who wanted to adopt a more activist and militant course of action in their contacts with the authorities. Among these were Jamal Tarabiyya from Sakhnin, Jalal Abu Tuaᶜma from Bakah al-Gharbiyyah, and Ahmad Masalha from Daburiyyah. The more deeply they became involved, the more the committee took on the character of a body that would fight for the rights of the Arab citizens of Israel at all levels of activity, including the national level.[174]

The second phenomenon that attested to a change in the Arab minority during these years was the additional strengthening of the Palestinian nationalist component among the Arab Israeli citizens. The national awakening that had begun at the end of the 1960s gained momentum with their growing confidence based upon the feeling that the Arab side had been victorious in the October 1973 War, and this was supported by the events of "Land Day." There were several clear expressions of this phenomenon, first in the nurturing of the nationalist feeling which braced the political activity, and expressed itself through making more demands from the government on civil issues, along with protest activities in the field. Second, the connection between political factions such as "Sons of the Village" and Rakah, and political elements in the West Bank and the Gaza Strip, became closer after "Land Day". The political power elements among the Israeli Arab citizens were encouraged by Palestinian support in the form of expressions of identification with the activities of "Land Day." The mutual visits made by political groups from both sides of the "Green Line" grew in frequency and importance, and close cooperation developed between the parties. One of the prominent activities that took place from 1977 onwards was the creation of shared volunteer camps for youths from the two populations which took place in Nazareth, Jaffa, and Umm el-Fahem – in which thousands of youths took part and whose content was devoted to the strengthening of the nationalist component in the younger generation. Third, the two populations became closer in the political arena after the Palestinian National Council decided (in April 1977) to strengthen their ties with the anti-Zionist forces in Israel.

The third phenomenon that characterized this important period was the awakening of the Islamic current; this phenomenon can also be attributed to the contacts that were formed between the Israel Arab citizens and the residents of the West Bank and the Gaza Strip. The contact made between the populations not only renewed family and commercial ties but also led to the exchange of religious and nationalist ideas. Religious movements that had been active in the West Bank continuously since 1948 found a new arena for activities after the June 1967 War. Among these movements were "The Muslim Brothers" and charity organizations which sent their people into the Arab villages in Israel where they began to spread Islamic ideas. This component was a kind of innovation for the Arab Israeli citizens, mainly because in these direct meetings they discovered a population that was more religious than that of the Arabs living in Israel, especially the residents of the Gaza Strip.

The practical expressions of these phenomena did not take long to appear, and in February 1978 fifty-five intellectuals who were Arab Israeli citizens signed a public statement that came out against Anwar Sadat, the president of Egypt, which was a response to the fact that the PLO had been ignored in discussions about the Palestinian issue during his historic visit to Israel in November 1977. These intellectuals finished off their public statement with a call to establish an independent Palestinian state.[175] Another expression of the national mood took place in January 1979 with the establishment by Arab students of "The Progressive National Front". They sent a letter to the Palestinian National Council which was being convened in Damascus calling for the adoption of a resolution that supported the continuation of the armed struggle, until their legitimate rights were achieved. At a press conference they made it clear that they did not regret their actions and added that they felt alienated from the State of Israel which they did not see as their home. The event created a storm of criticism from governmental entities that went as far as calling for the expulsion of the Arabs from the country.[176]

The new bodies began to establish their power in the field, and "The Sons of the Village" for instance, took part in the election campaign for the student councils of the Hebrew University in Jerusalem and Haifa University in January 1978 in which they achieved impressive results. Influenced by "Land Day" new young people's associations were established in Dir al-Asad, ᶜArᶜarah, ᶜAra, and Taibe, which adopted an ideology similar to that of the "Sons of the Village" movement – they did not hesitate to publicly express its identification with the Palestinian struggle against Israel. In November 1979 activists from the "Sons of the Village" organized a demonstration in Umm el-Fahem in protest at the arrest of the mayor of Nablus, Bassam Shakᶜa, without interference by the authorities. The new political groups chose to adopt a line of increasing confrontation with the government, and publicly announced that they did not recognize the State of Israel and were not interested in receiving assistance from it or agreement with their deeds. They summed up their arguments with the declaration that they felt "alienated from the state."[177]

The first political attempt to act as a group to advance both the rights of the Palestinian people and of the Arab minority as a whole in Israel was made in the middle of 1980. A group of a hundred public figures, led by the Communists, composed a document that came to be called the "June 6 Document." About five thousand Arab citizens signed the document and it quickly became the magnet that attracted people to the conference called the "Congress of the Masses." During the preparations for the congress position papers were composed which, among other things, declared that the right of the Arabs to be equal citizens in Israel was indisputable. The organizers prepared a list of nine national and civil topics, among which was the demand that the government recognize the Arab citizens of Israel as a national minority. The congress was planned to take place in December 1980 in Nazareth, but its convening was prohibited after the authorities identified its activities as something subversive to the integrity of the state. On December 1, 1980 the Prime Minister, Menachem Begin, who was also the Defense Minister at this time, signed the order which declared the "Nazareth Congress" to be a non-authorized assembly. The government took a series of steps prior to the publication of the order which allowed it to act forcefully against the Arab public and to make it clear that the intention to organize this kind of congress was, for the government, crossing a red line. The forceful steps included removal of student agitators from the university campuses, issuing of confinement orders to some of the activists, and the decision to strengthen the Jewish presence in the Galilee by establishing new settlements. The steps taken by the government were accompanied by a public relations campaign which exploited the Rakah spokesman's call to identify with the PLO to present the organizers of the congress as Palestinian nationalists who were identifying with the goals of the organization.

The next attempt to further the rights of the Arab minority took place at the end of 1980 when representatives of "Sons of the Village," "al-Anṣar" (which was a group of people who had quit the "Sons of the Village"), and other independent activists such as Mansur Kardush, gathered together in Umm el-Fahem and formulated a political document, most of which dealt with the Palestinian problem and ways to solve it. The document came to be called the "Umm el-Fahem Charter" and included the following principles: the Palestinian problem is the very heart of the dispute between the National Liberation Movement and the Zionist camp; the main solution depended upon the right of return for the Palestinian refugees, the granting of self-determination to the Palestinian People, and the establishment of an independent Palestinian state; the PLO was the real and only representative of the Palestinian People; and the Arabs in Israel are an inseparable part of the Palestinian People.[178]

An analysis of this "Charter" displays that it mainly focused upon the nationalist aspect of the relationship between the Arab minority and the government. There were no special demands made in the charter for the Arab population in Israel as far as economic and civil issues were concerned – apparently because those who composed it were interested in emphasizing that the Arab minority in Israel was an integral part of the Palestinian and Arab nation. This document reflected the dominant mood that existed at this time among the Arab citizens of Israel, and surveys carried out during this period indicate that most of them defined themselves as "Palestinian Arabs" or as "Palestinians."[179] As such they were demanding that the government recognize the leadership of the Palestinian People and open negotiations to solve the Palestinian question.

The Umm el-Fahem document led to the establishment of the "National Coordinating Committee," which was a kind of roof organization established by power factions in the Arab minority that acted as a framework for the activities of nine political bodies that did not include the Communist Party.[180] The National Coordinating Committee intended to work in a similar way to the Committee for National Guidance which was operating in the West Bank and even to cooperate with it.

The Palestinian national consciousness did not express itself only in protest activity but also in attempts to establish institutions to be alternatives to those offered by the state, and in this context a prominent attempt took place in 1979. A year earlier, in Nazareth, an Ottoman association was registered under the name of "*ha-Qol*" (the voice),[181] whose members wanted to establish an independent university in the Galilee. George Kanazi, one of the core members of the foundation group believed that there was a need for a university that would fight for the neutralization of nationalism. Najwa Makhul, another of those who promulgated the idea, explained that a Palestinian national university was needed and Sami Mi⁽ari, a lecturer at Haifa University, noted that education was needed for Arab students "who would fulfill their essential beings and no longer study in Israeli institutions that impose a Zionist ideology upon them".[182]

The government's policy towards this initiative was unequivocal; it disallowed any possibility of establishing an independent Arab educational institute.[183] In spite of this policy, the idea did not die and various circles tried to revive it from time to time.

The activities of the new movements in the Arab villages and their participation in the election campaigns of professional organizations almost always took place without interference from the government. The chosen patterns of protest that exploited the political opportunities made possible by a democratic regime included holding conferences, demonstrations, and assemblies; and forms of expression that emphasized nationalist (Palestinian) motifs, denial of the Jewish state, and demands for equal rights between the Jewish majority and the non-Jewish minority in the country. None of the activities at these events broke the law or led to violence, although some cases of localized and minimal confrontations with security forces were recorded – but these ended very quickly and did not turn into any form of violent protest. When the authorities did identify any intention to undermine the state's character, as happened in the case of the mass congress in December 1980, it used its power and neutralized the activity. The importance of the events during this period was the fact that they produced new ways for the Arab minority to contend with the authorities over issues from both a nationalistic and civilian point of view; these methods included protest activities, both from the standpoint of the form of the participation and the forging of content that was of a nationalistic, demanding, and oppositional character vis-à-vis the government.

During these years another central political phenomenon was identified, when at the end of the 1970s, the Islamic Movement took its first steps and began working along two parallel tracks. One track turned towards the Arab population; its main goal was to convince people to come back to religion through preaching (*"da⁽wah"*), accompanied by demanding that businessmen close their businesses on festivals and stop selling alcohol. The other track turned against the State of Israel. Under the influence of Islamic organizations in Arab countries, a group of young people, approximately 200 in number in their widest circle, established an underground cell that was called the "Jihad Family" (In Arabic: *Usrat al-Jihad*). Its members believed that Palestine was once an Arab and Islamic country and should remain so. The motto they adopted was based upon the Muslim Brothers' platform and consisted of Palestinian nationalism. At the beginning, they acted violently, even murdering a man from Umm el-Fahem who was suspected of assisting the authorities. The members of the cell were arrested – some were tried and sent to jail for a period – but this development only stimulated the movement's activities. Sheikh ʿAbdallah Nimr Darwish from Kafr Qasem, the leader of the group, after his release from jail, adopted a non-violent approach toward the government and chose a strategy of recruiting as many believers as possible. The call he made to *daʿwah* (Call) turned out to be successful, because the Islamic Movement turned out to be a central political force from the middle of the 1980s by virtue of widespread educational, religious, welfare, health, and transport arrangements it managed to introduce into the Arab sector in Israel. The political changes were mainly recorded on the municipal level, when the movement succeeded in placing its candidates into the councils of the cities and smaller settlements and by its gaining control of the municipality of Umm el-Fahem in 1989.

12
Signs of Growing Activism on the Background of the First Lebanese War

The year that preceded the War for the Peace of Galilee in 1982 was continuously marked by the political activity of all the power factors in the Arab minority that reflected the nationalist mood of this public. One of the prominent expressions of this was the call made together by the "Sons of the Village" and the Progressive National Movement (PNM) to Arab voters to boycott the general elections that had been set for June 30, 1981, in which they argued that the Arabs had no real chance of changing their situation by taking part in the parliamentary game. This call was responded to, if only partially, and the Arab voter turnout was 68% as opposed to 74% in the 1977 general elections. The heads of the Communist party, which took part in the elections, were disappointed at the number of votes they received from the Arab voters, and explained that as a result of the party not adopting a more militant approach against the government as was expected of them by the "Sons of the Village," the PNM, and other parts of the Arab sector.[184] One of the lessons the heads of the Communist party learned was that they had to make way for a more activist, although not necessarily violent, approach in order to make progress towards achieving the goals of the Palestinian population on both sides of the Green Line. In this spirit the heads of the Communist stream decided that the "Land Day" events which were planned for March 30, 1982 would be devoted to the housing discrimination suffered by the Arab population. The shortage of housing in the cities of Jaffa and Lod had long since become a subject that was being used by the Arab minority to agitate against the authorities, and in order to provide a response in the form of a protest, local committees were formed under the aegis of the National Committee for the Protection of Lands – the same committee that had organized "Land Day" in 1976.

The decision made by the Communist faction to steer the struggle in the direction of purely civil affairs as a result of feelings of having suffered long-lasting and continued discrimination fit the wave of national feelings at this time. At the beginning of 1982 a rise in the intensity of force used by the Israeli authorities against the Palestinians was recorded in the West Bank and the Gaza Strip, and this activity was condemned by the leaders of the Arab public in Israel. Practical effects of this new line of action could be seen about a month before March 30, 1982, which was the "Land Day" anniversary commemoration. At the end of an assembly of support for those lacking housing in Acre it was decided that "Land Day" would be marked with processions to villages in which Arabs had been killed. "The National Committee for the Protection of Lands" adopted this course of action suggested by the Communist Party based on the assumption that it would be difficult to mobilize the public to take part in a more violent demonstration. During the month of March 1982, however, the confrontation between the Israeli security forces and the Palestinian population in the West Bank and the Gaza Strip escalated to the point that Israeli authorities issued administrative orders placing political bodies outside of the law; this led to violent clashes in which two IDF soldiers and six Palestinians in different places in the West Bank were killed.

This reality created agitation in the Arab street in the State of Israel, and against this background, the Communist stream chose to mark "Land Day" with a more militant display of activity than originally planned. "The Committee for the Protection of the Lands" decided to hold a general strike on "Land Day." This decision aroused opposition from members of the leadership, mainly from the heads of local councils, who wanted to prevent an escalation of the situation in the field and preferred a memorial day that would be characterized by memorial ceremonies. These heads of council believed that the situation should not be exacerbated by holding a strike that would provide free time to the public, and that might lead to an inflammation of the atmosphere in the field. They supported continual dialogue with the government representatives. Muhammad Watad, one of the leading spokesmen of this faction, explained, "Every person needs to raise his voice because of what is going on in the territories but the Arab citizens of Israel should make a distinction between our strategy here and the strategy of the Arabs in the (West) Bank and the (Gaza) Strip".[185]

The 1982 "Land Day" was characterized by local incidents, including setting up stone barriers in the main traffic arteries, burning tires, and throwing stones at the security forces and vehicles in a small number of villages. One possible explanation for the low number of events and their rapid passing was the decision made by the police not to enter the Arab centers of population and to allow a limited amount of protest. Another explanation is that in March 1982, unlike in March 1976, the Arab leadership did not call on the public to confront the security forces, and preferred to call for a strike through which the Arab minority could express identification with the Palestinian struggle in the West Bank and the Gaza Strip.

The first reactions of the Arab citizens of Israel to reports of the IDF having hit the PLO command headquarters in Lebanon in June 1982 were a mélange of helplessness, confusion, shock, and anger; many Arabs experienced fears for the fates of their families living in Lebanon.[186] Among the Christians, signs of identification with Israel could be seen, as was the case with the Six Day War, and in a number of the villages in the Galilee Christians collected contributions for IDF soldiers. The Israeli Public Committee to Aid Lebanon published a public statement supporting the campaign, expressing sorrow at the deaths of IDF soldiers, which was signed by some Christians who were Arab Israeli citizens. This public sympathy, however, very quickly disappeared, and was replaced by expressions of condemnation of Israeli policy and of the force Israel was using in Lebanon. The protest activities included, for example, the publication of a public statement that called upon the Israeli government to stop the war immediately and enter into negotiations with representatives of the Palestinian People. This statement was signed by the heads of the Arab local councils as well as by people who had traditionally supported dialogue with the authorities and distanced themselves from violent activities – such as Member of the Knesset Muhammad Watad (Mapam), Yussuf Khamis, a member of the Central Committee of the Histadrut, Muhammad Khabaishi, the Qaḍi of Acre, and others.[187] The heads of the local councils who called upon the government to immediately stop the war also decided to begin collecting contributions for those hurt in Lebanon and to transfer them through the offices of the Red Cross in Lebanon.[188]

The Communist party led the non-violent protest activities in the way they traditionally did and, on June 6, 1982, the Political Bureau of Rakah condemned the war and Israel's aggression, and accused it of an attempt to eliminate the Palestinian People and to begin a military confrontation with Syria. Along with this, the party's members of the Knesset presented a motion of no-confidence in the government. It was only a month after the beginning of the war, in July, that the Arab protest was expressed in the field in the form of a demonstration in Nazareth, which was organized by the Communists and in which the participants called for the arrest and sentencing of those responsible for the war and for a retreat from Lebanon.[189]

The more time passed, the greater the feelings of anger were among the Arab minority – following the call that Rakah made to the public to take part in the planned protest activities. Parallel to this, the leaders of the Communist organization passed on a message to the public which said: "The Israeli government is about to expel you from the country".[190] These calls found a response in the Arab public, and at the next demonstration, which took place in Nazareth on July 31, about 10,000 demonstrators turned up, according to police estimates. The demonstration was organized by the National Committee against the War in Lebanon, a body set up by Rakah according to the same formula used to establish the National Committee for the Protection of the Lands – which was established in 1975 within the framework of the struggle against the appropriation of land. The assembly itself was stormy, and the speakers used volatile and threatening language against the government, such as the words of Jamal Tarabiyyah, the mayor of Sakhnin, who declared, "They will not succeed in killing Arafat; we are all Arafat."[191] This demonstration was also marked by waving placards, whose contents expressed complete identification with the Palestinian struggle and the resistance of the Palestinian fighters in Lebanon against the IDF. On the placards was written, for instance, "Whoever goes into Lebanon will come out in a coffin".[192] The solidarity of the Arab citizens of Israel with the suffering of the Palestinians in Lebanon expressed itself in various ways, including the organization of protest meetings, hunger strikes, symbolic commemorations for those killed, and demonstrations in which Palestinian flags were flown.

The change in the patterns of protest took place following the events of Ṣabra and Shatila refugee camps in September 1982. When the proportions of the massacre became known, the leaders of Rakah convened a meeting of the Heads of the Local Councils on September 20, at which they decided to hold a general strike two days later as a mark of protest and identification with the suffering of the Palestinians. They also decided to cancel all the events and festivities marking ʿId al-Adḥa (Sacrifice Feast), to fly black flags, to hold symbolic mourning processions, and to hold mourning prayers in the mosques in memory of those killed in the massacre. The organization shown by Rakah, as it had when they organized "Land Day" in 1976, proved their skill at mobilizing the masses. Smaller political bodies, such as "The Sons of the Village," "The Muslim Youth," and others all supported the decision to hold a general strike.

On September 21, 1982, a day before the strike was to take place, a notice was issued calling for the Arab public to join the strike in order to express disgust at the massacre, which the Arab population believed was carried out by Israeli forces and perceived as a frontal attack upon the Palestinian People everywhere.[193] Tawfik Zayyad chose to use caustic language publicly and compared the Ṣabra and Shatila incident to the horrors carried out by the Nazis at Auschwitz and other extermination camps, called the heads of the Israeli government by shameful names, and warned that anybody who did not lend a hand in protesting would be considered to be provoking the will of the Palestinian People. Zayyad even suggested the possibility of violence when he said that "Our brothers have made sacrifices and so have we made sacrifices when we were defending our land and homeland . . . we are ready to contribute to the caravan of victims . . . we are a nation of fighters. I look at your faces, youths that can destroy walls."[194]

September 22, the day of the strike, turned into a day on which many incidents of public disorder were registered, in addition to violent clashes that were more widespread than on "Land Day" in 1976. During the strike in the northern region of the Israeli Police Force, no less than 146 events involving clashes and confrontations between demonstrators and the various security forces took place – including cases of throwing stones (47), arson (18), blocking roads and junctions (19), burning tires (17) and more. All in all, 59 Arabs and 43 policemen were injured, and the police arrested 25 people that day. The widespread political violence included atypical phenomena such as: erecting barriers at the entrance of Bakah al-Gharbiyyah and beating up Jewish drivers; blocking main traffic arteries such as the highway through Wadi ʿAra and the main street in Nazareth; loading trucks with stones which were thrown at passing vehicles; attacking vehicles belonging to the police and the IDF; and beating up policemen (most of whom, incidentally, were Arabs). For the first time, Bedouin also took part in the violent events.[195]

13
Accelerated Processes of Politicization, 1982–1990

The violent protest events carried out by the Arab Israeli citizens following the Ṣabra and Shatila massacre were a concrete expression of ethnic and national identification with the Palestinians living outside the borders of Israel and the conversion of their group identity to Palestinian. After these events, the process of politicization continued among the Arab citizens of Israel; its immediate expression was the establishment of a new political entity in the form of The Higher Monitoring Committee. In October 1982 the Arab members of the Knesset, Watad and Hamad Khalailah, met with the Rakah members of the Knesset, Zayyad and Tubi, and together they reached an agreement to establish the new political body. The goal they set for themselves was to improve the situation of the municipalities in the Arab sector by demanding higher budgets and a master plan, and by opposing enlargement of the regional jurisdiction of the Jewish settlements.[196] Seven heads of local councils, the most prominent being Nimr Murkus from Kafr Yassif, Muhammad Zaydan from Kafr Manda, and Ibrahim Nimr Hussein – who at the same time was the chairman of the Committee of Heads of Local Councils to which he had been elected in June 1981 – from Shfarᶜam, joined the four members of the Knesset who had come up with the idea.

From this point onwards, The Higher Monitoring Committee was to play a central role in setting the agenda and patterns of activity of the Arab population regarding both national and civil issues. During the 1980s it became the central leadership body of the Arab minority in the State of Israel, which is the status it still enjoys today, mainly because it consists of representation from all the political power factions: the Communists, the groups with a nationalist orientation such as the Progressive Nationalist Movement, "The Sons of the Village," The Progressive List for Peace (PLP), as well as political bodies with links to Zionist parties and Islamic groups. The committee adopted a policy that is an attempt to carry on a dialogue with the central Israeli authorities while leading the struggles and protest against steps taken by the regime in the local-civil arena and the Palestinian arena.

Along with membership in the institutions of the committee, the political groups continued to be independently active during the 1980s, which were marked by accelerated political processes and things other than the establishment of the Higher Coordination Committee. For the first time an attempt was made to put together a political framework that had a Palestinian nationalist orientation but whose aim was to play a role in the parliamentary arena and not be separate from the Jewish state. One such body was the PLP led by Muhammad Mi‘ari, one of the founders of *"al-Arḍ"* in the 1960s, whose political platform was based upon Palestinian nationalist foundations with a call to demonstrate greater commitment to the Palestinian issue, which appealed to the Arab public. In this context, the appearance of the PLP just before the general elections for the Eleventh Knesset (1984) was appropriately timed from the Palestinian point of view, since it was benefiting from the nationalistic public mood that was dominating the Arab streets during these years. The results of the elections proved that the PLP had successfully identified the mood, since 51 percent of the Arab vote went to the PLP and Rakah, while only 49 percent went to the Labor Party or other Zionist parties.[197]

The tense relations between Rakah and the PLP at this time were fed by the opposing positions the two bodies adopted towards the organizational crisis taking place in the ranks of the PLO. Rakah, in line with the stance adopted by Moscow, supported the leftist organizations in the PLO, which included the Popular Front for the Liberation of Palestine, the Democratic Front, and the Palestinian Communist Party, while the PLP clearly supported the central stream led by al-Fath and its leader Arafat.[198] The immediate significance of this tension was difficulty in agreeing on ways of acting together in the struggle against the government in matters of both nationalist and civil importance. The PLP was not the only power group that was active in the political arena, since a member of the Knesset from the Labor Party, ‘Abd al-Wahhab Darawsha, at the invitation of the PLO, took it upon himself to appear before the Palestinian National Council at the end of 1984 "in order to bring about a breakthrough in the relations between Israel and the PLO." Darawsha's attempts to develop his status as an agent who could negotiate between the Israeli government and the PLO leadership in Tunis continued on and off until 1992.

While Rakah and the PLP were leaders in political activity that dealt with nationalist aspects, it was the Higher Monitoring Committee that led in matters dealing with civil issues. At times, however, as the committee contained all the political power groups – including those with a clearly Palestinian nationalist platform – it found itself dealing with activities that were a mixture of nationalist and civil issues. One example of this kind of activity was the meeting of the heads of local councils that took place in February 1984, which Nimr Hussein convened, to discuss matters on the agenda. The announcement that summed up the meeting first focused upon the national issues and stressed that the Arab public in Israel was an inseparable part of the Palestinian People and that it aspired to quickly realize its legitimate national rights. In civil matters and the (traditional) demand for an improvement in the situation of the Arab minority in the State of Israel, the announcement made clear that the Committee of the Heads of Local Councils, supported by the Higher Monitoring Committee, would act in cooperation with the Center for Local Government and the members of the Knesset and its various committees in order to achieve equality between the populations of Jews and Arabs.[199] This announcement contents indicate the direction of activities that Nimr Hussein was taking, which was essentially an ongoing dialogue with the authorities and not a pattern of violent activity at events in the field.

A small number of participants, mostly activists from Rakah and the PLP, took part in the demonstrations and symbolic mourning processions that made up the events marking the second anniversary of the Ṣabra and Shatila massacre and no disturbances of the peace were registered. The population showed little interest in the events and the public mood was characterized by disinterest on the part of the power factions.[200] A similar pattern of activity was registered in September 1985 on the third anniversary of the massacre and in September 1986 when the PLP coordinated the quiet memorial events in Nazareth and Tira.[201] In February 1985 a delegation from the Higher Monitoring Committee visited the Temple Mount following the publication of reports that said that the Israeli government was planning to do damage to the mosques – by permitting Jewish religious circles to enter the Temple mount area. Nimr Hussein announced that the Higher Monitoring Committee had decided to join in the effort to protect the holy places, and his fellow delegation members, Tawfik Zayyad from Nazareth, Tarek ᶜAbd al-Hayy from Tira, and Miᶜari, the head of PLP, warned that this was a case of political and religious discrimination; but they did not threaten to act violently since the various reports were not supported by any events in reality.

A year later, in February 1986, after a wave of additional such reports on the subject, the Higher Monitoring Committee held a special discussion about the issue of protecting the mosques which was attended, apparently for the first time, by a representative from the Islamic Movement, Kamal Rayan, the head of the Kafr Bara council.

Nimr Hussein warned that any damage to the *al-Aqṣa* Mosque would be a dangerous and detestable thing, so the Arabs and the Muslims had to begin an ongoing campaign to prevent this.[202] The announcement that summarized the meeting called for protection of the mosques and did not call for any violent action to be taken to achieve this goal. Hashem Mahamid, a member of Hadash and mayor of Umm el-Fahem, sent a letter to Prime Minister Shimon Peres, Minister of the Interior Yosef Burg, and Minister of Religion Yitzhak Peretz, as well as to Speaker of the Knesset Shlomo Hillel, in which he condemned the Israeli provocation against the Mosque. He was satisfied with expressing condemnation and demanding that this provocation never be repeated, but did not threaten to take any violent steps to stop what he and his friends in the Arab sector were calling attempts to do damage to the mosques on the Temple Mount.

In October 1985 the Israeli air force bombed the PLO headquarters in Tunis, and in response to this, the Committee of the Heads of Local Councils held a meeting at the end of which the participants expressed sorrow at the bloodshed, and called for the establishment of a Palestinian state alongside the State of Israel. They also decided to hold a one-day strike of solidarity with the PLO, but their call to the public did not include a call to take any violent action, to disturb public order, or to confront the security services.[203]

A month later, in November 1985, the mood in the Arab sector became stormy following the appropriation of a small amount of land in the area of the villages of Majd al-Kurum, Sakhnin, and ʿIlut, where a number of villagers were arrested during the activities.[204] The decision the government made to appropriate this small amount of land came at a time in which there was a heavy shortfall of funds in the Arab local councils. On December 16, 1985, a demonstration was held opposite the Knesset building in Jerusalem at which thousands of Arabs called on the government to take action to halt the policy of discrimination, appropriation of lands, and the demolition of buildings in the Arab sector, and to adopt a policy whose goal would be to create equality between the two populations. The demonstration ended with a call made by Member of the Knesset Zayyad to the Arab public to come in masses to another demonstration that would take place in Nazareth five days later on December 21. He added the threat, "We learned the lesson of 'Land Day' in 1976, and if the situation does not change, we will turn each Arab city and village into a hell that will scorch the land beneath the policy of discrimination and racism."[205]

Despite his threat and his call to act violently in response to the massacre in Ṣabra and Shatila, Zayyad this time was an "isolated voice" making such a threat. In contrast to this line, Nimr Hussein continued to adhere to the line of dialogue with the government and sent letters to the Prime Minister and Minister Ezer Weitzman, who was in charge of matters concerning the minority populations, in which he demanded that they immediately make arrangements to settle the budgetary problems of the Arab local councils. In the proceeding demonstration in Nazareth, a decision was made to intensify the protest, without defining what concrete steps would be taken if the government did not solve the crisis. In practical terms, the line of moderation proved itself, and negotiations between representatives of the government and representatives of the Committee of the Heads of Arab Local Councils began in which an agreement was reached to urgently transfer assistance (about six million dollars as opposed to the ten million dollars demanded by the Arab councils) to cover the deficits of the Arab local councils.

In June 1986 the heads of the Arab local councils convened an emergency meeting in Sakhnin to discuss the accumulation of a number of specific problems – the budgetary distress of some of the councils, the intention to carry out fencing work in the area next to Sakhnin,[206] and the continuation of the government's uncompromising policy of demolishing illegal buildings in Arab villages. At the end of the discussion a number of decisions were made: to demand that the government recognize the illegal buildings; to request a meeting with the relevant government factors (The Ministry of the Interior) in order to immediately arrange to solve the problems of planning and building in the Arab villages; to open a media campaign whose goal was to present the details about the buildings marked for demolition in the Arab villages; to demand that the government budget fifteen million dollars to cover the deficits of the Arab local councils (instead of providing half this sum); and to mobilize Jewish members of the Knesset to help in the struggle against the planned appropriation of lands. In this instance as well, the leadership parties who took part in the discussion did not call for any form of violent activity in order to achieve the goals they had set themselves. This struggle was only partly successful since, while the Prime Minister's Office issued instructions to halt the appropriation activity next to Sakhnin, the orders issued to demolish illegal buildings were carried out in Arab villages. These demolitions led to a decision being made by the Committee of the Heads of Local Councils to continue with their struggle against carrying out planned demolitions.

What characterized the behavior of the Arab leadership during 1987, the year in which the Intifada broke out in December,[207] included activities that ranged from negotiations with the authorities to staging demonstrations within the limits of the law – while the strike weapon became the main instrument used by the Arab leadership to threaten the public agenda. The most troubling issue from the point of view of the Arab leadership was the ongoing budgetary deficit of the Arab local councils, which led to the committee organizing "Equality Day" in June 1987 around this issue. The goal the organizers set for themselves was a reduction in the gaps that existed between the Jewish majority and the Arab minority, and the leaders made sure not to break any laws and satisfied themselves with expressions of protest that were acceptable in a democratic regime.[208] During this period the Higher Monitoring Committee was enjoying unequivocal support from all the political power players in the Arab sector – including the Knesset members, the heads of local councils, and the political movements and parties – which made it easier for it to persuade all the factions to abide by their decisions and not to disregard them.

Throughout 1987 the Higher Monitoring Committee and the other leadership bodies in the Arab sector continued to follow what was going on in the West Bank and the Gaza Strip; regarding national issues – dominated by the struggle of the Palestinian People, the Arab leadership bodies consistently expressed their verbal identification with the struggle in the territories and avoided using violent types of activity which sometimes characterized what was taking place there.

The outbreak of the Intifada in the West Bank and the Gaza Strip surprised the Arab citizens of Israel. In the days preceding its beginning, the only daily Arab newspaper, *al-Ittihad*, printed a wide-ranging survey of the preparations being made for the summit meeting between President Reagan of the United States of America and Gorbachev, the USSR leader. On December 9, 1987, the newspaper printed a report about a road accident that had taken place a day earlier in which four people from the Gaza Strip had been killed and which was considered an excuse for riots breaking out. The next day, on December 10, the newspaper continued to focus its attention on the American-Soviet summit, and on the front page they printed a political commentary by Zayyad, while the monthly issued by the PLP reported on the "fervor that held the territories" in its December 12 issue.[209]

On December 12, *al-Ittihad* began to publish the lists of those killed in the territories; in that day's issue there was an article dealing with the protest events in the Israeli Arab sector. The newspaper reported that Rakah had organized protest demonstrations on December 11 in Nazareth and Tel Aviv against what they called "the crimes of the occupation in the occupied Palestinian territories".[210] During the demonstration in his city, Emil Jarjura, one of the senior members of the Nazareth branch of Rakah, said, "From every home in Nazareth and in every respectable place in it to the refugees in Balata and in the refugee camp of Jibaliyah we send our blessings to the Palestinian People who are courageously facing the bullets of repression and destruction."[211] On the same day, December 11, demonstrations took place in Tur⁽an, Kafr Kana, and Tamra during which banners were waved with slogans saying: "The blood of the fallen will not be for nothing," "Long live the courageous struggle of the Palestinian People," "Yes to the establishment of an independent Palestinian state," and "The iron hand of Rabin the conqueror must be taken down."[212] Two days later, on December 13, demonstrations were held opposite the Prime Minister's office in Jerusalem and the Defense Minister's Office in Tel Aviv. The Arab and Jewish students at the Haifa University also demonstrated against the deterioration of the situation in the territories, and at the end of their demonstration issued a public statement that condemned the steps taken by Israel in the territories. The National Committee of the Arab High School Students held a similar demonstration in Nazareth.

On December 15, *al-Ittihad,* along with a news report on the events of the previous day and statistics about the people killed, published an article that called upon Israel to cease the repressive acts and to embark on a course that would lead to a just Israeli-Palestinian peace. The public institutions in the Arab sector in Israel, including the institutions that dealt with education and religion, as well as the local councils and professional organizations, were called upon to deliver an urgent outcry against what was taking place in the West Bank and the Gaza Strip – but there was no call in the publication to take violent steps against the governmental authorities.[213] The government reacted to these publications and protest activities by taking steps to prevent any escalation in the Arab sector in Israel on the basis of the Intifada (the name that had already appeared in the newspaper) that was taking place in the West Bank and the Gaza Strip. The police arrested Rakah activists in Jerusalem and Nazareth, and made it clear to the heads of the party that it would intercede in any illegal demonstration or procession that might take place in Arab villages in Israel.

On December 16, the Nazareth Municipality presented the Committee of the Heads of the Arab Local Councils with a proposal to hold a non-violent general strike in the Arab sector as a sign of protest against what was taking place in the territories. On the same day, the Hadash faction in the Knesset proposed a motion of no-confidence in the government on the basis of the events in the territories. The next day, on December 17, in a meeting held by the Committee of the Heads of Local Councils, the participants formulated a statement that included: a condemnation of Israeli crimes; a call for the withdrawal of Israel from the territories; a call for the holding of a national demonstration because "we are part of the nation and will not remain silent about what is taking place."[214] At the end of the discussion the members of the committee decided to pass on the decision about holding a general strike to the forum of the Higher Monitoring Committee. *al-Waṭan,* the PLP organ, also devoted the main headline of its December 18 issue to the PLP's call to declare a general strike and this was printed next to a statement made by the priest Riyakh Abu ʿAsal, one of the leaders of the party, which called upon world leaders to intervene and put a stop to what he called "the slaughter in the territories." Miʿari chose to express his identification with struggle in the territories through a speech he gave in Arabic to the Knesset in which he declared his demand for "Freedom for the Palestinian People and independence for the Palestinian state."[215] Similar motifs appeared in January 1988 in *al-Ṣirat,* the monthly organ of the Islamic Movement. Alongside articles that mainly called upon the public to return to religion, the Islamic Movement chose to express a position that had been coordinated with other leadership bodies. Articles in the monthly publication, like that of Khaled Mahaneh, one of the movement's leaders, reflected the dominant mood on the Arab street while emphasizing the unrest among the Palestinian prisoners in Israeli jails on the basis of the situation in the West Bank and the Gaza Strip.[216]

The developments in the field created an additional focus of tension between the Arab minority and the government, and during a discussion in the Knesset, Roni Milo, a deputy minister in the Prime Minister's Office, called on the Arab citizens of Israel "to not get involved in what is going on in the territories and to deal with civil matters." He also told them to act responsibly and prevent harm being done to the state of which they were citizens.[217] His comments aroused a storm of criticism among all the political power factions in the Arab sector – who hastened to condemn what he said and to express their solidarity with the Palestinians in the territories.

On the basis of a meeting called by the Committee of the Heads of Local Councils on December 17 and the tense atmosphere following the protest demonstrations and the comments made by Deputy Minister Roni Milo, the Higher Monitoring Committee met (December 19) to discuss how they should react to the events in the territories. At this meeting the participants made the following decisions: to declare a general strike in the Arab sector in Israel on December 21, which would include the educational institutions, the local councils, the welfare services and commercial bodies; to mark their solidarity with the struggle in the territories by making calls from the Mosques and ringing bells in the churches; to hold a minute's silence in memory of the victims at 12 noon; and to call upon Jews of conscience to join the strike.

Among those who participated in making the decisions were the representatives of Rakah (Tubi and Zayyad), Arab Democratic Party (Darawsha), PLP (Micari), representatives of the Islamic Movement, representatives of the students and teachers' organizations, women's representatives, and members of the Committee for the Protection of Lands.[218] Nimr Hussein made a call to solve the problems in diplomatic ways and explained that "nobody can prevent the Arab citizens of Israel from expressing their solidarity with their brothers living in the territories".[219]

An analysis of the decisions and the accompanying declarations made by some of the participants, among whom were some who had in the past called for violent actions, shows that this time, there were no calls to act violently. Zayyad suggested calling the strike day "Peace Day" and Watad explained that a general strike was the minimum the Arab Israelis could do for those living in the territories. Darawsha explained that the world was looking at the Arabs in Israel and was waiting to see what they would do, and a general strike was the best reaction to what Deputy Minister Milo had said about the Arab population. Not a single Arab leadership group that took part in the meeting questioned the decisions made at its end or called for violent forms of activity against the authorities because of the situation in the territories.

"Peace Day" took place in the spirit of the decisions made by the Higher Monitoring Committee, and in most of the Arab villages the day was marked by an absence of disturbances of the peace or confrontations between the Arab population and the security services. In a small number of villages there were some instances of public disorder recorded; the Wadi ʿAra highway was blocked with stones for a short period of time, and in Jaffa there were some clashes between Young Arabs and Jews. Hashem Mahamid, the then mayor of Umm el-Fahem, was observed "running after excited young people in an attempt to prevent them blocking Wadi ʿAra."[220] In Shfarcam a local incident was recorded – supporters of Rabbi Kahana who wanted to visit the ancient synagogue there and in Nazareth arrived in the city; leadership figures such as Tubi hastened to calm down tempers in localized confrontations between demonstrators and the border police. After a few days it became clear that this incident was atypical as a reaction to the decision to make sure the day would be marked by restraint. According to a report made by Deputy Minister Milo, the incident began with young people throwing stones at the Nazareth police station, following instructions given by Tawfik Zayyad.[221] During the same discussion Milo explained that the government's policy was to encourage the moderate factions among the Arab citizens of Israel and to aspire to co-existence and cooperation.[222] About a week later the Minister of Police presented a report on the events of "Peace Day" and noted that public disturbances were recorded in only six Arab villages; the Arab press also reported that the incidents were minor and took place in no more than a few Arab villages.

On the evening of that day, the Committee of the Heads of Local Councils condemned the violent expressions, and even the nationalist political forces such as "The Sons of the Village", Rakah, and the PLP came out against throwing stones and Molotov cocktails at a vehicle. In the days following "Peace Day," the Arab leadership in Israel dealt with the lessons learned from the events of the day. After expressing satisfaction with the public's readiness to strike in an orderly fashion, the leadership called for the release of those arrested in the small number of incidents that had taken place, and declared that it would continue to support the struggle of the Palestinian People.

14

Central Government Decisions and Politics in the Aftermath of Two Waves of Violence

Earlier studies that have tried to analyze the mutual relations between the Arab minority and the Israeli government have done so up till the 1990s, and some of the studies have divided the relationship into six periods:

(a) The first period continued from the establishment of the state until 1956, and was characterized by the Arabs' search for a way of adjusting to things and the expectation of a miracle that would prevent the need to identify with the new-born Jewish state. During this period what stood out was the fear the Arab citizens of Israel had of the possibility that they would be expelled from their homes, which resulted in their adopting a pattern of activity aimed at surviving the new reality. This situation prevented them from acting violently, as did the fact that Israel's War of Independence had proved that it was strong and that no Arab country was able to destroy it. During this period the Arab citizens of Israel chose the option of waiting, while they examined whether the Arab countries would be capable of ending the State of Israel's episode and to revenge the defeat they had experienced with the establishment of the State of Israel.[223]

(b) The second period was from 1956 until June 1967. In the eyes of the Arabs Israel's victory in the 1956 Egypt–Israel war was the final confirmation that Israel had become an established fact. This period was marked by economic growth which, together with easements given by the military government, made the rapid integration of the Arab minority into the developing labor economy possible. Even though this was the case, it was during this period that the first incidents of political violence, albeit in small numbers, were recorded. The most noteworthy of these was on May Day 1958, when a violent demonstration broke out in Nazareth during the events of "Workers Day."

(c) The third period began after the 1967 War and ended after the War in October 1973. Many researchers believe that during this period the process of the Palestinization of the Arab citizens of Israel was accelerated and that the removal of barriers between them and their relatives in the West Bank made it possible for them to absorb some of the deeply nationalistic atmosphere and consciousness of the people living in the territories. During this period the Arab population in Israel became more extreme in its relations with the State of Israel and this was expressed in political activism.

(d) The fourth period began in 1973 and ended with the Intifada in December 1987, and was characterized by the maturation of the process of the Palestinization of the Arab citizens of Israel and the strengthening of nationalist feelings. One of the practical expressions of this, but not the only one, was the establishment of national and local political organizations. The patterns of activity adopted by these organizations during this period included demonstrations and strikes but not terrorist activities.

(e) The fifth period began with the outbreak of the Intifada in 1987 and ended with the October events of 2000. During this period, a significant rise in the number of violent activities within a nationalistic framework took place, along with a large number of protests in the form of demonstrations and strikes about social and political issues – these also became larger and more demanding.

(f) The sixth and last period has continued from 2001 until today, and has been characterized by the internalization of lessons learned from the bloody events of October 2000, growing endeavors to integrate into the public space in Israel, and a growing sense of alienation by the establishment from the minority population despite the change in policies of the executive authorities.

An analysis of the network of relations over a historical time axis shows a number of trends. The first is that the Arab minority, both the leadership and the public, moved from a passivity that aimed at minimizing damage from the government in the 1950s and 1960s to an activism that began to blossom at the beginning of the 1970s and reached its peak at the end of the 1980s. Secondly, The Arab minority moved from having a traditional leadership, some of whom were members of the satellite parties of Zionist political frameworks, to the development of a leadership that had Palestinian nationalist characteristics and which also became more insistent in the demands it made of the Israeli government. Third, there was a significant growth in the number of political branches that took on the form of new movements from the 1970s onwards; this was made possible not only because of direct contact with residents of Judea and Samaria and the Gaza Strip, but also because of the growing integration of young Arabs into the education system in Israel and their exposure to conventional political ideas and values of democratic regimes. Fourth, patterns of dealing with the situation during the first decades with such behaviors as obedience and subservience, together with attempts at dialogue and mild protest – except for the events in Nazareth in 1958 – took on a more activist character colored by bold protest that spilled over into violence, in events that were viewed by the Arab minority to have caused severe damage to its status. This is true for both the nationalist component (Ṣabra and Shatila, for example) and for the civil component, in the case of the appropriation of land and the events of Land Day in 1976 – which, in the eyes of the Arab public, also had a nationalist aspect.

These developments in the ranks of the Arab citizens of Israel exacerbated the dilemma faced by the Israeli government concerning the policies that needed to be formed towards this population. On the declaratory level, expression was given to the need to reduce the gaps in civil matters and pointing out the security risks that might arise from the Arab collective, but in practice, two contrasting trends stood out. In matters of security, the central government did not hesitate to use its forces to frustrate any threats of terror or any other dangers that might come from the Arab minority – but, in contrast to this, the area of civil life did not receive sufficient attention from the government and this was attested to by some of the policy makers during the first decades of the establishment of the state. The result was the constant and continuous growth in the gaps that existed between the statuses of the Arab and Jewish citizens. This complex reality was something recognizable at the political level at the beginning of the 1990s as well – when things began to change in relations towards the Arab minority. This will be described and analyzed in the coming sections.

PART TWO

The Government's Policy, 1987–2010

There are methodological and conceptual differences between this analysis of the Israeli government's policy towards the Arab population from 1990 onwards and our analysis up until that year. This is the result of changes in the political, social and public agendas in Israel. If up until the beginning of the 1990s, the analytical emphasis had been on the steps taken by the executive arm of the government, mainly through security stance, during the next two decades, the analysis emphasized the system and included components of mutuality between the regime and the minority group. The activity of the government thus not only included decisions made by the executive arm but also legislative steps taken both in favor of and against Arabs and a growing, sometimes activist, involvement of the judicial branch in Jewish–Arab relations. The public mood and media discourse, mainly the informal discourse, which became a prominent cultural phenomenon in Israeli society and provided a forum for every citizen to express his or her opinion in the social media, constituted a variable that influenced the sensitive relationship between the majority and minority groups. This makes comparing the policy and operations of the executive arm with the character of relations and dialogue taking place in the shared public arena, including the parliament, possible. In contrast, there were a number of arenas of activity that obliged the Arab minority to react or initiate its own activity within the framework of the mutual relations that existed with the government.

This period, which has continued for more than two decades, can be divided into sub-periods according to the political key of changes in government in the State of Israel. This key makes it possible to observe the policy adopted by each government towards the Arab minority from both the points of view of security and of civil matters. The first sub-period ended in the middle of 1992, when the Likud government made way for the Labor government headed by Yitzhak Rabin under whose government real changes took place for the first time in the Arab centers of population as a result of the adoption of a new policy. The second sub-period began in May 1996 and continued until the beginning of 1999 with the Likud government headed by Benjamin Netanyahu, which adopted the previous government's policy towards the Arab minority. The third sub-period, with the Ehud Barak government in office, only lasted two years and ended in 2001. During this period serious clashes, which came to be called the October 2000 events, took place between the state and the Arab minority. The fourth sub-period, in which the government was led by Ariel Sharon and Ehud Olmert, continued from 2001 to 2009; this can be called the golden age of the Arab minority in Israel because of, among other reasons, significant steps that were taken by the political establishment towards this minority group. The fifth and last sub-period took place after 2009 when the second, third and fourth Netanyahu governments were in power. A gap between the official policy of the executive arm of the government – which continued to improve the status of the Arab minority – and both the public climate and political dialogue (including that within the parliament) developed and expanded. The more Jewish influences, both political and social, supported the Arab minority's exclusion from the public space in the State of Israel.

From the end of 1987 until the second half of the 1990s, a number of significant developments took place in both the Israeli and Palestinian internal arenas. All of them directly or indirectly influenced the network of relations between the Israeli establishment and the Arab minority, as well as the formation of the government's policy towards this population. In the Israeli arena the state, from 1990 onwards, found itself having to deal with the challenge of absorbing more than a million new immigrants; this not only necessitated the attention of the authorities in the governmental ministries but also the allocation of enormous resources for the new immigrants. This situation naturally siphoned off significant sums from the budgets of the ministries of welfare, housing, health, education and others. Despite this, an analysis of the data that was collected reveals that programs for the Arab minority which had received large budgets were carried out in municipal and many other areas.

In the Palestinian arena two important developments were recorded. In December 1987, there was a serious escalation in security issues in the occupied territories, which came to be called the Intifada by the Palestinians, and within a year the U.S administration, under President Reagan government, just before it ended its term in office, made preparations for negotiations with the PLO. This led to political discussions between the Israeli government and representatives of the Palestinians in October 1991.

On the basis of the Intifada in the territories and because of the traditional concern about the possible negative influence of Palestinians on Israeli Arabs, the state tried to create effective deterrence in the Arab minority and prevent its joining in with the violent protests of the Palestinians, which also included acts of terror. The deterrent included severe steps involving enforcement in the political arena. In its preparations for the Eleventh Knesset elections in 1988, the Central Elections Committee, after consultations with the legal advisor of the security authorities, decided to prohibit the participation of the Progressive List for Peace (from now on PLP) in the elections. It was only the intervention of the Supreme Court of Justice that led to the cancellation of this decision and made it possible for the PLP to participate in the elections. Even earlier, as part of the policy of separating the Israeli Arabs from the PLO, the authorities prevented Kamal Daher and the priest Riakh Abu ᶜAsal, who were senior members of the PLP, from traveling abroad, because of their links with the PLO. Following this, in August 1990, the Minister of the Interior signed an order preventing Ahmad Tibi, who at that time was a prominent public figure but who later became a member of the Knesset, from leaving the country. The security argument was to forestall Tibi's intention of meeting with elements of the PLO.[1]

During the same month procedures were begun to remove the parliamentary immunity of Member of the Knesset Muhammad Miᶜari, who was suspected of providing support for the PLO during 1988 when the organization wanted to send "the ship of the return" towards the coast of Israel as a symbolic statement of identification with the issue of Palestinian refugees.

These years were also characterized by growing protests in the Arab minority about the Israeli establishment. Demonstrations were held about various issues such as the destruction of illegal buildings in the Arab sector, the financial deficits of the local Arab authorities, and the security situation in the territories. The protests grew stronger during the first year after the outbreak of the Intifada, and in 1988 a sharp increase in the number of acts of public disorder and security incidents was recorded in areas of the State of Israel – with 226 terror attacks as opposed to only 69 in 1987, and 507 incidents of a nationalistic nature such as stone throwing, holding demonstrations and flying the PLO flag, as opposed to 101 in 1987. Arab citizens of Israel were involved in some of these events but not in terror attacks, and their participation, given the generally prevalent public climate, increased the security threat to the Arab minority.

The situation in the territories had its effect on the Arab population in Israel and, parallel to Arafat's declaration of an independent Palestinian state in December 1988, the Higher Monitoring Committee declared "Home Day".[2] The goal was to protest the demolition of about 500 buildings over the past year.[3] The police met with heads of the villages in Wadi ʾAra and the Galilee district, as well as the mayor of Nazareth, Tawfik Zayyad, and informed them that they expected a peaceful day.[4] The advance preparations worked, and the events signifying solidarity with the Palestinians and protest against the demolition of buildings proceeded without any significant public disorder. The events, which were accompanied by local incidents in Jaffa and along the Wadi ʾAra Highway, along with multiple public disturbances over the whole year, attested to the widespread nationalist identification of the Arab minority with the struggle in the territories. This reality had the potential to influence various civil aspects of Israeli policy towards the Arab sector in the long run.

1

The Civil Dimension of the Policy towards the Arabs: The First Signs of a Change in the Direction of Narrowing the Gap

Despite the escalation of the security situation that strengthened the policy of separation between the population of the territories and the Arab minority in Israel, signs of a change in the Israeli government's policy could already be seen in 1987. The then Prime Minister Yitzhak Shamir met with Knesset Member ᶜAbd al-Wahab Darawsha – a clear indication of Israeli readiness to see him as a bridge between the Israeli leadership and the PLO leadership in Tunis, but the political aspect was not the only one being pursued. During those years, the Israeli leadership's recognition of the need to separate the tough approach, taken to dealing with security threats, from a change in the policy in civil areas of life, strengthened. At the height of the Palestinian insurrection, the Israeli government introduced a policy approach based upon differential lines: side by side with the consistent avoidance of recognizing the leadership of the Arab minority, meaning the Higher Monitoring Committee, and the prevention of their involvement in general Palestinian processes, the government acted to broaden economic aid to Israeli Arabs and to encourage their recruitment into the IDF, while embarking on a comprehensive examination of the question of national service for the Arab minority instead of military service. For the first time since the establishment of the state, a statist conception was established based upon the idea that Jews and Arabs in the State of Israel had a shared interest in a peaceful life together. Accordingly, the state had an obligation to provide for the needs of the Arab minority without making any demands of it.

During these years, under the leadership of Prime Minister Shamir, a permanent mechanism that involved consultation with Arab members of the Knesset in matters of internal policy, such as the question of national service, was introduced. It was Minister Mosheh Arens, who was responsible for Arab minority affairs, who initiated the increased integration of minority citizens into the IDF and who set out a path towards integrating them not only into security branches but also into state institutions in general. This policy bore fruit at the beginning of the 1990s when the number of minority members (Christians and Bedouins) who signed up stood at several hundred.[5]

Along with this, the government during these years (1988–1990) made a series of decisions that were aimed at advancing special sectors within the Arab population – such as allocating half a billion shekels to settle the problem of Bedouin lands, determining the first criteria for settling the issue of illegal concentrations of populations of Bedouin in the South, and establishing the foundations for the integration of educated Arabs into the civil service. In response to strengthening the identification with general Palestinian values, the recruitment of Bedouin and Christians into the IDF was broadened. This was a profound and fundamental change, at least from a conceptual point of view, which arose out of the growing recognition at the political level of the need to change the situation of the Arab citizens, and from the fear that perpetuating the gaps between the groups – which resulted from a policy that moved between complete denial and extinguishing fires – would not lead to any remedy for the basic affliction.

One of the central issues during these years was the phenomenon of illegal building in the Arab sector which could be looked at two ways. The first claimed that because of procrastination by the authorities, which did not allow for authorization of master plans for Arab villages, many minority citizens had to break the law and build unauthorized dwellings for themselves due to population growth. This phenomenon, according to the other viewpoint, should be seen as something illegal irrespective of the reasons for its existence. One way or the other the issue attracted the attention of the authorities beginning in the middle of the 1980s, resulting in the appointment of the Markowitz Committee, which presented its recommendations to the Minister of the Interior in August 1986. The main recommendations were to grant retroactive licenses to illegal buildings that had been built in areas that were included in master plans for Arab villages, to impose restrictions on other buildings, and to be satisfied with a reduced number of demolitions of unauthorized buildings.[6] The members of the committee did not stop at presenting their report, but instituted an orderly and methodical follow-up study of the way the execution of the recommendations was progressing, which clearly expressed how the political level viewed this issue.

A study of the protocols of the committee's discussions reveals that the government's recognition of the need to pay attention and allocate resources to solve the problems of illegal building was authentic. Following the presentation of the report to the Minister of the Interior, the government decided, on February 15, 1987, to adopt the principles set out in the report.[7] The stages of implementation of the decision also included publishing a booklet in Arabic containing the committee's recommendations, which was sent to the heads of the Arab local authorities. Parallel to this, government officials held meetings with the heads of the municipalities in order to present the material and to explain that their goal was to regulate the issue of building – which had been an ongoing source of bitterness for the Arab minority. The Markowitz Committee's report was the first sign of a change in the government's approach to the Arab minority. It not only expressed recognition of the need to regulate the issue in a way that would satisfy the aspirations of the Arab minority, but also constituted a process that included an ongoing dialogue with the leaders of the Arab minority, and that applied a strict follow-up to ensure that the solutions proposed by the government would actually be realized in practice.

From a historical point of view, the Markowitz Report was the formal basis for the master plans of all the Arab villages, and between 1990 and 1999 the Ministry of the Interior authorized master plans for twenty-five Arab villages.[8] During 2000–2002, the Ministry of the Interior continued the process and authorized master plans for other Arab villages as part of the real progress that was being made on this issue.[9] From 2000 onwards, master plans for 47 Arab villages were authorized,[10] and in 21 of them implementation of the plans began in 2002. By the beginning of 2010 the master plans for 125 Arab villages were completed, out of the 128 master plans that had been authorized.[11] As a result of this policy the percentage of lands that the Israel Lands Authority allocated for the purposes of housing to the Arab population between 2006 and 2008 grew from 5 percent to 13 percent.

Another important issue that was constantly part of the dialogue between the government and the Arab minority was the situation of the Arab local municipalities which were traditionally funded by the Ministry of the Interior through two different channels: one, the regular budget which was for the current running of the local municipality, and the other a development budget for various enterprises in different areas such as education, health, sport, and culture. The budgetary deficits the local authorities were suffering from have, over the years, become a chronic sickness for a number of reasons, including poor management by the heads of the local authorities, the lack of government funding, and low levels of municipal tax collection. Some researchers believe that the situation is so serious that the basket of services provided by the Arab authorities is already a critical situation.[12]

This budgetary deficit, which became a permanent feature, and other municipal issues have been a perpetual subject of discussion between the government and the Arab minority; over time, the understanding of the government ministries about the need to provide aid for the management of the Arab villages has grown. This, for example, can be seen in the letter the Director-General of the Ministry of the Interior Aryeh Deri wrote in response to Ibrahim Nimr Hussein, the mayor of Shfar‛am and head of the Higher Monitoring Committee. From data appearing in the letter one can see that the Ministry of the Interior had transferred the sum of 22.5 million shekels to the Arab authorities from the original budget allocation and that Deri was making it clear to Hussein that his ministry expected the heads of the authorities to increase the collection of municipal taxes in order to allow the municipality to function and progress.[13] The growth of the budget for the Arab local authorities also continued during the following years – in 1989 the Ministry of the Interior allocated a sum of 60 million shekels to the Arab villages, and in 1991 an additional 106 million shekels were transferred, as an expression of the growing recognition of the need of the Arab population.[14]

The subjects of illegal building and the budgets for the local authorities did not reflect the whole picture regarding the policy. At the end of 1987, then Prime Minister, Yitzhak Shamir, Minister of Finance, Mosheh Nissim, and Minister in Charge of the Minorities, Mosheh Arens, agreed upon a development program for the Arab minority in which special budgets would be provided for development, and they all agreed to increase the original budget for the program by 11 million shekels. This was, in fact, the first time that the political level acted with an initiative intended to respond to the needs of the Arab minority. The continual increase in allocations took place despite the low levels of tax collection in the villages. Several days after the violent "Peace Day" events in December 1987, the Deputy Minister Milo, sent a letter to the Minister of Finance containing data on the non-Jewish population in anticipation of a government decision to allocate budgets to the Bedouin population and to moderate factors in the State of Israel. The letter included an analysis of the way the Arab minority was managing its affairs and, among other things, said that the strike that took place on "Peace Day" had made the process of Palestinization taking place among the Arab citizens of Israel more concrete and had strengthened the loyalty of the Bedouin (and the Druze) populations, which had not taken part in the strike, to the state. The letter went on to state that there was a great national need to aid and strengthen the moderate elements among the Israeli Arab citizens through a significant allocation of financial resources. The letter defined the Bedouin and Arab villages headed by people who belonged to Zionist parties as moderate elements. The sums required for immediate allocation were 15.4 million shekels for the Bedouin and 22 million shekels for the Arab local authorities that were defined as "loyal"; the funds were meant for the purposes of initiatives in the areas of education and housing. This letter reflected the prevalent mood at the political level and, in fact, contained indications of a policy of double separation – first, between the Arab minority in Israel and the Palestinians in the territories and second, between the radical elements in the Arab minority and elements that can at least be called normative that were operating within the framework of the law.[15]

In the Office of the Advisor to the Prime Minister on Arab Affairs, a new policy paper relating to the Arab minority was prepared, and its character was influenced by both the rise in the number of events in the field and the decision made by the Higher Monitoring Committee to declare a general strike on November 15, 1988 – as a sign of identification, albeit symbolic and declarative, with Arafat's declaration of the establishment of an independent Palestinian state. Among other things, the document reported that there was a noticeable trend towards radicalization in the Arab street, and it recommended examining the legal possibility of declaring the Higher Monitoring Committee an illegal organization in accordance with the emergency defense regulations.[16] This climate in the relevant government circles also found expression in the press. Amos Gilboa, who had acted as the Advisor on Arab Affairs during the period in office of Arens as the Minister in Charge of Arab Affairs, pointed out the link between the Israeli Arabs and the Palestinians in the West Bank and the Gaza Strip, which was based upon a shared national identity. He also pointed out the difficulty for the government of enforcing the law in the Arab villages, and called upon the government to deal with the challenges being raised in the Arab sector.[17]

An analysis of the above chain of events raises the question of whether recognition of the government's need to pay attention arose out of the deterioration of the security situation in Judea, Samaria and the Gaza Strip and its potential ramifications for the Arab minority in Israel, or whether it signified a change in policy as a result of long term thinking. The impression one receives is that recognition of the need to improve the situation of the Arab minority already existed in the minds of the policy makers even before the outbreak of the Intifada in December 1987. Evidence for this can be found in Prime Minister Shamir's agreement to authorize the development program for the Arab villages before the deterioration of the security situation in the field took place. In practice, this program suffered from long delays because of bureaucratic obstructions, and only in December 1988, which was the month in which Ehud Olmert took over minority affairs, did the governmental apparatus go back to dealing with the civil issues of the Arab minority. Olmert believed that it wasn't enough to provide budgets to improve the conditions of the minority population but that a lot of attention had to be paid to the problems of this society and that solutions to these problems had to be found. He succeeded in raising the question of the Arab minority for discussion in the security cabinet, and although it took three meetings to have a thorough, searching and meaningful discussion, the conclusion reached was that the issue was of little interest to the ministers. He himself described this by saying: "There is awareness of specific problems but no interest in any more comprehensive thinking".[18]

At the end of the discussions in the cabinet, Prime Minister Shamir appointed Olmert to set up a committee to make recommendations for how the Arab sector should be dealt with. This committee consisted only of Minister Dan Meridor, the police commissioner and the head of the general security services. There were no representatives of the government ministries who dealt with civil issues that were vital for the daily lives of the minority population, and there were no representatives of the Arab minority. This was an expression of the fact that there was still no consciousness or readiness among the decision makers to allow the Arabs to take part in that decision making, which dealt directly with their quality of life. The committee presented its recommendations to the Prime Minister – these included allocating financial resources and establishing a mechanism that would be attached to the Minister in Charge of Minority Affairs. According to Olmert the then Minister of Finance, Shimon Peres, objected to the recommendations, and because of political differences they were not put into practice.

Throughout his period Olmert refused to cooperate with the Higher Monitoring Committee, and thus adopted the policy that had become permanent after the events of "Land Day" in 1976. According to this policy, all discussions were only to be carried out with the heads of the local authorities separately and not with any umbrella organization that represented them based on different nationalism identity.[19] In June 1990, when he completed his term in office as the Minister in Charge of Minority Affairs, Olmert presented the government with a long term program for dealing with the Arab population entitled "The Advancement of the Minorities in Israel". Among other things, it included a recommendation to allocate a sum of 850 million shekels over a period of ten years in order to solve the main problems that were interfering with the daily lives of the Arab minority. The importance of the program was not only the unprecedentedly large sum of money that he had proposed to grant the Arab minority, but that his explanations for this included recognition of the fact that the Arab population had not been given equal status with the rest of the country's citizens because of historical and political circumstances.[20]

In the Office of the Advisor, the staff was aware of the gap that existed between the circumstances of the Arab minority and those of the Jewish majority and the need to reduce this. The main approach that was taken up till the time of the dismantling of the Office of the Advisor in the summer of 1992 was that the government's policy, from a national point of view, should be to strengthen the civil components of the Arab minority because of the profound gaps. This view was also expressed publicly by one of the advisors who believed that "in everything that affects the relations between the Arab minority and the Jewish majority there is a state of tense co-existence in the country. If the government manages to find answers for the civil components of the issue there is a chance that the two sides can live in a reasonable state of co-existence".[21]

The Advisors on Arab Affairs, and like them, the ministers responsible for dealing with the minority population, made sure that they regularly visited the Arab villages. Minister David Magen, who was the Minister in Charge of the Minorities from 1990 to 1992, adopted a policy of ongoing dialogue with the heads of the local authorities, and in a meeting with 16 heads of authorities in 1991, he told them about his intention to carry on an ongoing discussion with them, and informed them of the immediate transfer of budgets to the municipalities[22] – which was an expression of his policy of accelerating the processing of help for the various civil issues.

From a historical point of view, all of these steps taken from 1987 to the middle of 1992 were the first significant steps taken to reduce the gaps between the Jewish majority group and the Arab minority. The totality of influential factors – both external, such as the situation in the territories, and internal, such as the municipal issues – led to a growing recognition among the decision makers that something had to be done to for the Arab population. The government that was elected in June 1992 adopted the policy in principle and expanded it.

2
After the 1992 Elections: From Intentions to Deeds

After the general elections to the Knesset in June 1992 there was a change in government and the Labor Party headed by Yitzhak Rabin formed Israel's 25th government, which was based upon a coalition that was supported by five Arab members of the Knesset who remained outside the coalition. In exchange for this, the newly elected Prime Minister promised a change in policy towards the Arab minority. The Rabin government inherited a document which provided a picture of the situation in the Arab sector and a series of recommendations. From a historical point of view the document was the touchstone for the policy that was pursued from 1992 onwards. It contained a series of operative policy recommendations relating to the Arab minority, which were divided into sections according to a key that referred to the government ministries. Section One of the document included, the following proposals: the integration of suitably educated Arabs into the civil service,[23] the appointment of a Muslim Arab Deputy to the Prime Minister's Advisor on Arab Affairs, the appointment of an inter-ministerial committee that would act to solve the problems of the Arab sector's unrecognized centers of population, and the establishment of a fund for the advancement of the Arab citizens of Israel.[24]

Other sections of the document recommended the following in areas controlled by the Ministry of the Interior and Ministry of Religious affairs: additional funding over and above the regular budgets, in order to achieve full equality between all Israeli citizens as decided upon by the government; the provision of a sum of half a billion shekels from 1993 to 1997 (a five-year plan) for development budgets for the Arab sector; an examination of the possibility of giving Rahat and Sakhnin the status of cities (a step that was realized in 1993 and 1994); and the provision of budgets for the repair and rehabilitation of Muslim and Christian holy sites.

Other proposals that were included in the document were: planning an additional seven industrial zones throughout the country in which special encouragement would be given to initiatives of minority group members; allocating seven million shekels for the encouragement of enterprises in the Arab sector to be led and handled by the Ministry of Industry; constructing a maternity hospital in Rahat and examining the need to establish additional baby care centers under the supervision of the Ministry of Health; allocating a sum of about a million shekels for agricultural development (the Ministry of Agriculture); providing street lighting in the Arab villages (the Ministry of Energy and the Infrastructure); allocating a hundred million shekels for settling the problem of the Negev land issues (the Ministry of Housing and Construction); the application of a five-year program by the Ministry of Education and Culture to reduce the crowding in classrooms; and building new schools according to need and the integration of suitably educated Arabs into the Ministry of Education. In regard to government ministries that dealt with security matters, the document recommended increasing recruitment of minority members into the IDF and police organizations.[25] As far as could be ascertained, this was the most comprehensive document written at the beginning of the 1990s regarding the Israeli establishment's treatment of the Arab minority.

The situation of the Arab minority was discussed in one of the first meetings held by the new government, which was a concrete expression of the seriousness of its intentions towards this population. Resolution 31 of the government on July 26, 1992 appointed a committee made up of directors general to ensure that the government's policy of integrating the Israeli Arab citizens into areas of the daily life of the state would be carried out. This decision was quickly translated into deeds in the field by the governmental ministries. In November 1992, the Ministry of Transport announced that it was investing the sum of 15 million shekels in the rehabilitation of the transport infrastructure in fourteen Arab villages in the Galilee. Yisrael Keisar, the then Minister of Transport, explained that the government was acting with the intention of closing the gaps that earlier governments had created.[26] In January 1993, the leaders of the Arab public welcomed the government's decision to classify most of the Arab villages as "A class areas of priority" and "B class areas of priority" since the significance of the decision was increased funding for budgets in industrial zones, benefits for education and tax relief.[27] About half a year later Shimon Shitrit, the then Minister of Economics who was also in charge of minority affairs, announced that the government would allocate a sum of 300 million shekels for the development of physical, economic and social infrastructures for initiatives in industry, tourism, and agriculture in the Arab sector. He also announced that the government had decided to employ 100 Arab academics in the civil service and subsequently 70 Arab academics were integrated during 1994.[28]

In the middle of 1993, Binyamin Ben Eliezer, the Minister for Housing and Construction, announced that his ministry would allocate a sum of 105 million shekels to settle the problems of the Bedouin in the Negev. A third of the sum would be dedicated to developing infrastructures for the new settlements and the rest would be paid as compensation to the Bedouin who were moved from where they had been living. [29] During that same summer Haim Ramon, the Minister of Health, authorized the establishment of twenty new family health centers in Arab villages.[30] At a ceremony for the dedication of a new road in Sulm village, Prime Minister Rabin announced that his government had taken upon itself to close the gaps that had been created over 45 years since the establishment of the state between the different groups that made up the population. Ibrahim Nimr Hussein, the chairman of the Higher Monitoring Committee, expressed himself by saying: "We feel that something is moving," and Mustafa Abu Raya, the mayor of Sakhnin, admitted that "there is movement with the budgets".[31]

During 1994, the first results of the new policies began to be seen in the field, and the gaps, for instance in the field of education, began to close relatively quickly as indicated by elements that supported full equality in the provision of allocations to the sectors. These budgets made the provision of additional hours of study possible (for example 11,000 hours in 1994) to strengthen the learning of Arab students, to increase their numbers in technological education and teacher training, and for the provision of psychological services to Arab minority students.[32]

In June 1995, the Law of Equal Opportunity in Work was amended and prohibited discrimination based upon nationality or religion. It also proscribed employers in the private sector from making army service a condition for getting a job unless service in the army was essential for functioning in the position. The improvement in the area of employment continued until 2000, when the number of people employed from the Arab minority in the civil service was 2.5 times higher than it had been in 1992, and stood at 5 percent of all those employed.[33] All in all, during this period about 2000 Arab employees were added to the work force in the civil service.

Table 2 shows the continual growth that took place in numbers and percentages for the number of Israeli Arab citizens who were employed in the civil service. From the point of view of the Arab minority these figures were not enough to close the long existing gaps but the positive and ongoing trend in this area reflected the government policy adopted towards the Arab citizens during these years.

The budgetary deficits of the Arab local authorities also received special relief during these years. By the middle of 1995 the regular budget of the Arab authorities had risen in real terms by 13 percent

Table 2 Employment of Arabs as civil servants, 1992–1996[1]

The percentage of Arabs employed as civil servants of the total number of employees	Number of Arabs employed	Year
2.1	1,117	1992
2.5	1,369	1993
3	1,679	1994
3.5	1,997	1995
4	2,231	1996

[1] Sikkuy Voluntary Association, *Annual Report 2000–2001* (Jerusalem, 2002), p. 4.

compared to the budget that was provided in 1992, while the development budgets of the authorities grew by 160 percent during the same period. According to the data that was collected and presented to the Orr Committee the grants to the Arab local authorities grew 5.5 times during the 1990s compared to previous years. As a follow-up to the growth in budgets, a development program for the Arab villages was prepared; a sum of 4 billion shekels was budgeted, half of which was allocated for investment in physical infrastructures in order to complete the connection of the Arab villages to the national infrastructure of roads, electricity and water; and a considerable amount of money was also allocated for laying out a sewage network for the local authorities in the Arab sector. What was special about the program was not only that this was the first time in the history of the state that a comprehensive program was being provided for the Arab minority, but also that it was presented to the heads of the Arab local authorities for their comments and ideas. Despite the criticism leveled at the program by public and other bodies that had political interests, there were also those among them who described the program as "historic" and saw its realization as having potential for changing the situation of the Arab minority in the country. This observation was not the only one that attested to the change in its relations with the government.[34]

An analysis of the activities of the different government ministries shows that from 1992 onwards the Israeli government moved from the stages of discussion, talk and the planning of programs to the stage of their execution in the field. This was a policy that drew a line between national and civil factors and that reflected a desire to reduce the gaps between the majority and minority groups. Interestingly, this process took place during the decade when the State was, in parallel, struggling with the complex challenge of absorbing large numbers of immigrants from the former Soviet Union and other countries. In spite of the enormous resources that were being invested in the absorption program, the government ministries did not neglect the execution of the various projects for the Arab population; this process was carried out during these years in an almost one-sided way, while discussions on specific issues were held from time to time between the government ministries and representatives of the Arab minority. This dialogue would become a regular feature after 2000.

3
The Civil Policy from 1996 to 2000:
One-sided Striving to Reduce the Gaps

The basic guidelines of the government elected in May 1996 did not include the goal of achieving equality between the Jewish majority and the Arab minority.[35] The efforts here to clarify and to analyze the government's subsequent policy, beginning in the middle of 1996, are based on the responses given by ministers to parliamentarian queries asked by members of the Knesset. The ways in which they addressed these queries makes clear the necessity to close the gaps between the different groups in the population, and from the ministers' answers, as they were recorded in the protocols of the Knesset discussions, one gets a wide and comprehensive picture of the policy which, in many ways, was a direct continuation of that of the outgoing government. The different ministers also adopted most of the civil components of the policy because of this need to close the gaps and improve the status of the Arab minority.

On the 2, 9 and 22 of July 1996, about a month after the Netanyahu government was sworn in, three discussions were held in the Knesset on the government's policy towards the Arab population in Israel. None of the government ministers attended the first discussion. Tzahi Hanegbi, the minister responsible for the liaison between the government and the Knesset, turned up at the second discussion. Mosheh Katzav, the then minister of tourism who was also responsible for Arab affairs, attended the third discussion. During this discussion, Arab members of the Knesset raised a number of areas which they claimed suffered from government discrimination, although some of them also admitted that during the five preceding years there had been a clear improvement in the situation of the Arab minority in Israel. Minister Katzav requested not to respond but postponed his answer to a later occasion.[36] In October 1996, the government issued an announcement to the Knesset about its policies during the first months of its activity, but the announcement did not contain any mention of a policy relating to the Arab citizens of Israel.

About a half a year later, on December 18, 1996, a discussion took place in the Knesset on issues that were affecting the minority population. Salah Salim, a Balad–Hadash member of the Knesset, demanded full equality between the Jews and the Arabs in order to achieve a situation in which Israel would be a state of all of its citizens. Minister Katzav rejected this demand and explained that Israel would preserve its Jewish character as set out in its Declaration of Independence.[37] A month after the discussion the Prime Minister, Netanyahu, met with representatives of the Committee of the Heads of Local Councils and at the end of the meeting the Arab representatives expressed satisfaction at what Netanyahu had said about his obligation to close the gaps and to bring about equality between all the sectors. Satisfaction was also expressed about Netanyahu's readiness to meet with them again.[38]

On July 8, 1996, Member of the Knesset Azmi Bishara raised from the podium an issue regarding the demolition of the house of an Arab family in the city of Lod. Eli Suissa, the then Minister of the Interior, answered that the house had been demolished because it had been built outside the boundaries of the neighborhood in Lod, and explained that if the Lod municipality was interested in expanding its building plans it would have to do this within the framework of the law. Suissa used his appearance in the Knesset to clarify that his ministry's policy was to remedy the discrimination that had been imposed in the past and that the process of reducing gaps, as had already begun in the outgoing government in 1992, should continue. He supported his words with the following figures: an increase of 15 percent in the development budget of the Arab sector since 1993 as opposed to a drop of 2 percent during the same period in the Jewish sector's development budget. He promised to continue in the same direction, but at the same time he demanded that the heads of the local Arab councils enforce the collection of municipal rates and taxes.[39]

A similar policy approach was suggested by Hanegbi, the Minister of Health, who believed that the solution for the reduction of the gaps was the allocation of more resources to the Arab sector. Hanegbi announced to the Knesset that the policy in practice in his ministry was to prevent gaps between the populations and to ensure an equal distribution of resources to all the citizens. He also announced that he intended to appoint a doctor from the minorities to be part of the staff in his bureau partly because, he admitted, this was an initiative taken by the Minister of Health and not "on the level of a national under-taking in face of a national problem".[40]

At the beginning of 1997, a comprehensive discussion took place in the Knesset about the budgetary crises of the Arab local munici-palities which, despite the considerable increase in their current budgets, were continuing to suffer from deficits as a result of the irreg-ular management by the heads of the villages that were not collecting all the municipal rates. The Minister of the Interior rejected the claims of the Arab members of the Knesset that there was prejudice towards the Arab local councils and demonstrated that there had been a steady and continuous rise in the sums allocated by the Ministry of the Interior to the Arab sector since 1991. The overall sum provided for 1996 was 516 million shekels and an additional special allotment of 70 million shekels from other government ministries. At the same time, Suissa was not sparing in his criticism of the management practices of the heads of the Arab authorities, and he claimed that there had been what he called an "unworthy" decrease in the collection of municipal taxes. He summed up by saying that the policy of his ministry was to support the Arab sector and to act towards reducing the gaps.[41]

In March 1997 Limor Livnat, the then Minister of Communic-ations, was asked to reply to a query about the integration of the Arab minority group members into the civil service. She noted that, in line with the decisions taken by the ministerial committee for coordination and administration during 1994–1995, government action was initi-ated to integrate Arabs into the civil service. Following this, in accordance with the Prime Minister's decision of January 20, 1997 and directions issued by the commissioner for the civil service on January 31, 1997, the work of the command post whose aim was to unfreeze additional positions for the absorption of Arabs into the civil service had begun. She went on to note that altogether, up to the time of the discussion, there were already more than 2,200 members of the minorities employed.[42]

In another discussion that took place in the full plenum of the Knesset, Minister Katzav said that the government was not ignoring the basic problems of the Arab citizens of Israel and was interested in solving them. He promised that the government would "devote itself with all its strength to solve these basic problems in all areas". Katzav reviewed a series of actions that had been taken in aid of the Arab minority during the recent years and noted that the present govern-ment was already running special development programs in a number of Arab villages such as Jisr al-Zarka, Nazareth, and Bir al-Maksur. In Nazareth the government had invested 250 million shekels in the area of development, had provided benefits in property taxes, and had transferred 4,750 computers to schools in the Arab sector.[43] Mosheh Peled, the Deputy Minister of Education, told the Knesset that his ministry was working towards closing the gaps between Jews and Arabs and announced that his ministry had transferred an additional 600 weekly hours for special education students in the northern region. Concerning equality in aspects of employment, Peled, in response to a query raised by Azmi Bishara, noted that both Jewish and Arab teachers had to swear an oath of allegiance to the state as a condition of employment.[44] Ali Asadi, the person responsible for Arab education in the Ministry of Education, ratified the figures stated by Peled and declared that in 1996 Arab education had received the total development budget allocated it while only 75 percent of the sum budgeted for Jewish education had, in practice, been transferred to Jewish educational institutions.[45]

The then Minister of Welfare, Eli Yishai, always made sure to present a policy aimed at achieving equality for the Arab minority. In response to a query raised by Member of the Knesset Taleb al-Sana, he stated that in the budget allocations for his ministry there were no separate sections for Arabs, and that the treatment given by all the units in his ministry was provided equally to all parts of the population. He also added that his ministry had completed work which had increased the number of social workers for the Arab sector by 120 positions.[46]

In 1997, Minister Katzav announced to the Knesset plenum that the government had decided to recognize seven as yet unrecognized Arab villages.[47] At the end of the discussion he presented the government's policy and pointed out a series of subjects that needed to be dealt with in order to improve the situation of the Arab minority, such as: adding six Bedouin villages to the national priority A zone, building 161 classrooms in Arab schools – which were 75 more than originally planned for in the budget, adding 160 million shekels to the regular budget of the Arab local councils and 40 million shekels more to the development budgets – despite the cuts made in the government ministry budgets of 7 billion shekels. Katzav also updated the Knesset about the fact that the government had adopted the policy of the previous government in matters concerning increased employment of academics in the civil service as well as the intention to establish industrial zones in the Arab villages, among which were Kabul, Sakhnin, and Tamra, and to encourage the initiation of industrial zones for Arab–Jewish cooperation in the triangle area and Bakah el-Gharbiyyah.[48]

This trend of striving for a reduction in the gaps between the population groups and for equality was also reflected in the policies of the

Ministry of Housing. Deputy Minister of Housing Meir Porush announced to the Knesset that in 1997 there had been a steady rise in the number of young couples from the Arab minority that were asking for mortgages and that he himself had given the workers in the Ministry instructions to make the procedures easier for those from the Arab minority to receive assistance from the Ministry.[49] Government officials also presented a similar policy in 1998 when, in March, the Minister of the Interior announced that budgets had been allocated for completing the master plans for seven Arab villages in the Galilee – in this way he was in fact confirming that the government had adopted the policy of the previous government, since the decision to recognize these villages had been made in December 1995. Hussein al-Heib, the head of the Tuba Zangariyyah council, expressed satisfaction at the decision to recognize the villages and noted that he felt that in his decision the Prime Minister had recognized his previously mistaken attitude towards the Bedouin villages in the north.[50]

In March 1988, Minister of Justice Hanegbi responded to a query raised by Darawsha about the policy involving the employment of minority group members in the Ministry of Justice. He presented a figure according to which 81 Arabs (58 Muslims and 23 Christians) were being employed in the court system. He made it clear that the policy was in favor of employing any Muslim or Christian Arab worker on the condition that he satisfied one criterion – which was that he lived in Jerusalem.[51] Two months later, the activities of the Civil Guard in Arab villages were discussed, following a query raised by Arab Member of the Knesset Walid Ṣadek. Minister of Internal Security, Avigdor Kahalani, replied that 351 Arabs were being employed in the Civil Guard in eight Arab villages.[52]

In July 1998 a comprehensive, wide-ranging discussion was held in the Knesset about the situation of the Arab minority, and Minister Katzav respond that the government's policy did not see the Israeli Arab citizens as either a security risk or as an existential threat to the State of Israel. "In regard to those few who were committing security crimes, they will be taken care of by the security forces," he emphasized.[53] He made it clear that the government's policy recognized the need to carry out affirmative action for the Arab minority, and pointed out that despite a cut of ten billion shekels in the government budget, the Arab local councils had not suffered any consequences. Katzav went on to say that in another area the development budget for the Arab villages would reach 570 million shekels in 1998, which was a rise of 8 percent compared to 1997. In relation to the employment of minority members in the government ministries he reported that, as of mid-1998, their number stood at 2,500 in addition to the 15,000 teachers – and that in the area of education the government intended to build 1,600 new classrooms.

The change in the government's policy and its execution could not only be seen in the steps it took. In the judicial system there were also signs of change towards the beginning of the 1990s in everything connected with pleas made by Israel's Arab citizens.[54] Israeli Arabs, whether as individuals or as associations that were widely established, identified the judicial system as a channel that could provide them with assistance, and remedy what they saw as longstanding injustices. The more time elapsed, the more pleas were presented by Arab Israelis to the courts – in such areas as equalizing budgets, preservation of the Arab language and culture, education, and street signs.[55] At the end of 1998 and the beginning of 1999, Netanyahu's government continued its policy of closing the gaps between the sectors, along with use of governmental power in security matters and a growing use of demolition orders against illegal buildings in Arab villages. In November the government decided to invest the sum of 615 million shekels in Bedouin villages in the north of the country over a period of five years. This was after it had budgeted 185 million shekels for taking care of the problems of the Bedouin in the Negev in 1998, in a program that included establishing public institutions, developing new neighborhoods for demobilized Bedouin soldiers, developing road infrastructures, and advancing master plans. The villages that were included in this program were Tuba Zangariyya, Buᶜeineh-Nujaidat, Zarzir, and Bir al-Maksur.[56] The Katz Report, which developed recommendations to improve the state of education for the Bedouin in the Negev, was presented to the government as part of the program, and recommended building 146 new classrooms in existent schools in Bedouin villages and constructing additional education centers. Other recommendations included budgeting positions for social workers and kindergarten assistants, as well as for learning hours, which would raise the number of students gaining the matriculation certificate. The cost of the budget for this program was 24 million shekels and ᶜAwad ᶜAbd el-Fraih, an educator and one of the senior members of the northern branch of the Islamic Movement in the Negev welcomed the government's decision to adopt the recommendations.[57]

At the beginning of 1999, Ariel Sharon, the then Minister for the Infrastructures, reported to the Knesset that the Israel Lands Authority was marketing lands for building 154 residential units in the Buᶜeineh-Nujaidat village, which had been included in the framework of the program, and for the sake of the program, 84 dunams of land had been taken from the nearby forest reserve and attached to the jurisdiction of the village.[58] During the same month, Prime Minister Netanyahu announced that the government had decided to recognize the unrecognized Bedouin village Arab al-Naᶜim, which was a step greeted with satisfaction by the Committee of Forty.[59]

As part of the integration policy during this period, the Prime Minister's Office prepared a program for the mobilization of minority members into national or civilian service; this idea was greeted with protests by Arab public figures. Ahmad Saᶜad, a member of the Knesset from the Balad-Hadash faction, called for cancellation of the program; ᶜAbd Anabtawi, the spokesman of the Higher Monitoring Committee, announced that, as long as the conflict between Israel and the Palestinian People continued, it opposed the initiative, and Ramez Jiraisi, the mayor of Nazareth, told the Minister of Defense who was visiting the city that the program was a mistake.[60] This issue of national or civilian service was not expressed with violence in the field, but it did feed feelings of discrimination and frustration, as well as different nationalism identity and affiliation among the Arab leadership who always came out against it.

The policy that strived for equality between the sectors continued in the field of education as well, and Eliezer Zandberg, the Deputy Minister of Education, announced in a discussion in the Knesset that, according to the five-year plan, 130 new classrooms would be built in the Arab sector in 1999 which was 100 more than had originally been planned.[61] In a follow-up discussion he announced that the approach of his ministry was positive and that the goal was to adopt the five-year plan for advancing the situation of Bedouin education. This would be done in cooperation with the Ministry of Finance so that financial resources could be found for continuing the necessary activities as recommended by the Education Committee. On December 23, 1998, Zandberg responded to a query raised by Member of the Knesset al-Sana, explaining that according to the ministry's policy, every classroom in the area of special education in the Arab and Bedouin sectors was budgeted exactly the same as in the Jewish sector. In addition, in the budgets for special education, 30 percent of hours allocated were for the Arab minority, which was 10 percent higher than their number in the population.[62]

On January 18, 1999, Eli Yishai, the Minister for Welfare, responded to a query about preventing Arab citizens from taking part in the training courses of his ministry. He announced that his ministry's policy was to give everybody eligible for it in all sectors of the population an equal opportunity for training. He presented data about the training of minority members in 1997 and 1998, which showed that 20 percent of all the training in the youth and apprentice tracks, 28 percent in the technician and practical engineering track, and 16 percent in adult training courses were taken up by the Arab sector. He concluded with the announcement that he even intended to strengthen the policy of equalization in all sectors of the population.[63]

The responses of the ministers responsible for the various areas indicate that they intended to integrate the minority population, and were striving to reduce the gaps between the sectors in all civil affairs. This policy covering the main areas relative to the Arab population was also presented in publications issued by public bodies and associations striving to achieve equality between the sectors. These areas mainly concerned the Ministries of Welfare and Education, the budgets of which rose for the Arab minority during these years above the percentage of the minority in the overall population. Thirty percent of the development budgets of the Ministry of Education were devoted to the Arabs, and 25 percent of the development budget of the Ministry of the Interior was planned for the Arabs.[64]

In May 1999, elections for the 15th Knesset took place, after which the Labor Party formed a coalition government, partly because of the Arab minority's massive support for the candidate for Prime Minister, Ehud Barak. On June 23, 1999 the outgoing Minister of Finance, Meir Shitrit, informed the Knesset that his ministry had allocated the sum of 700 million shekels for development in the Arab sector for 1999, which was 18 percent higher than the 1998 development budget. He summed up the period in office of the outgoing government, saying that it could claim for itself a series of achievements in everything connected with the advancement of the Arab minority.[65] Three months after the elections, in August 1999, as a follow-up to Shitrit's announcement, a ministerial committee headed by Matan Vilnai, the Minister for Culture and Sport, was set up and given the task of dealing with the needs of the minority population.

In the summer of 1999, a general policy paper about the Arab sector was prepared in the Prime Minister's Office, and the program proposed was titled "A Long Term Program for the Social-Economic Development of the Arab Villages". Many professional people from the Arab minority were involved in its preparation, including city planners and businessmen, in addition to research bodies and associations that dealt with strengthening ties and producing inter-sectorial shared projects. The guideline for the program was "the obligation of the Israeli government to act in order to provide equal and fair conditions for Arab citizens of Israel in social and economic areas".[66] The program set the goal of producing suitable solutions for problems in areas such as transport, infrastructures, building and housing, industry, commerce, education, employment, as well as health and agriculture; the sum allocated to actualize these was 4 billion shekels over a period of four years. The disadvantage of the program was the red tape involved in the process of getting authorizations. It took from September 1999 to October 22, 2000, three weeks after the outbreak of the violent events in the Arab sector, for Minister Vilnai to get the necessary authorizations.

Parallel to the preparation of the program, the government ministers continued to vote for policies whose goals were equality between the sectors, Minister for Science, Culture and Sport, Matan Vilnai, in response to a query asked by Member of the Knesset Taleb al-Sana, emphasized that the demand for equality seemed right to him and he reported to the Knesset that the Prime Minister had appointed a ministerial committee to deal with Arab minority matters, which he would head. The committee asked the Minister of Justice to present a proposal for a law governing the integration of Arab minority members into the boards of directors of government companies. The committee also decided to deal with master plans for the Arab villages and education. Regarding the latter, Vilnai announced the intention to immediately build 473 new classrooms out of the 2000 planned for the Arab sector.[67]

The Ministry of Education also presented programs in the spirit of the policy expressed by Vilnai, and in October 1999 Yossi Sarid, the Minister of Education, responded to a query by Member of the Knesset Ahmad Tibi about positions for psychologists in Arab education, by saying that over and above the five-year plan, which had already begun to be implemented, a special budget to pay for positions for psychologists would be provided.[68] At the beginning of 2000, Sarid announced that he had decided to establish an Arab college in Nazareth which would serve in the future as the basis for the establishment of an Arab university in the city. He noted that the college would begin to function in 2003, and thus repeated the promise he had made to Member of the Knesset Bishara about this matter. In this same month he authorized the construction of four schools in unrecognized Bedouin villages in the Negev, which was a decision welcomed by al-Sana,[69] and reported to the Knesset about his intention to use affirmative action to increase the number of Arabs employed in senior positions in his ministry.[70] What Sarid said expressed the trend towards improvement that was taking place in the field, and by 1999 the number of classes and positions made available for special education increased so that it reached 5000 yearly hours. In addition, science subjects were strengthened, thousands of computer units were installed and upgraded, and equipment was acquired for laboratories in dozens of schools in the Arab sector.[71]

During 1999–2000, a five-year plan was prepared whose declared goal was the achievement of full equality between the Arab minority and the Jewish majority. Among those who prepared the program were three education experts who influenced its formation; despite criticism leveled at it by people with interests that were not included in it, there were members of the Arab minority who welcomed it, including the Ministry of Education's regional supervisor Mahmud Diab, who understood the needs of the system and said: "The program is a step in the right direction, if the resources are used properly".

The Minister of Finance, Avraham Shohat, was also asked about the government's policy towards the Arab minority; he responded to a query raised by Member of the Knesset al-Sana about sales tax and the absorption of Arab academics into state organizations by saying that a policy of cancelling fines, linkage to the cost of living index, and deferred payments had been put into practice for minority members. Concerning the absorption of Arab academics, the Minister of Finance announced to the Knesset that on January 31, 2000, a long-term program for integrating non-Jewish candidates into the civil service that was prepared by the state employment commission was presented to the ministerial committee for minority affairs, which stressed that the aim of the program was to achieve a rate of 20 percent non-Jewish employees in the civil service by the end of 2004. Shohat pointed out that this was a policy that they were obliged to carry out from both a public and ideological point of view, and also noted that the first phase of the program to absorb 300 Arabs into the civil service into positions defined as "intermediary" and "high" had been completed.[72]

The last decade of the 20th century was characterized by a change in the policy of the government towards the Arab minority. If for the first four decades of the state the approach was mainly security driven, and Israeli governments, as an outcome of the democratic regime, satisfied themselves with granting basic rights to the Arab minority, the last decade of the 20th century was marked by a change towards a policy of integration. This included continuing to thwart security threats that might come from the Arab minority, which was influenced by, among other things, the situation in the occupied territories and the adoption of an approach aimed at reducing the gaps between the populations in civil areas. All of this was taking place during a decade that was complicated and challenging – mainly because of the efforts being made to absorb a million new Jewish immigrants who had taken advantage of the breaking up of the Soviet Union and wanted to see Israel as their new home. The new citizen-based policy expressed itself in increased attention being paid to the needs of the Arab population by allocating resources, by (occasionally) recognizing villages that up until then had been illegal and unrecognized, and by paving ways towards dialogue that would remain open not only during times of crisis, but that would also enable representatives of the Arab sector to be partners in decision making – at least in decisions that directly affected the Arab minority.

Although, which became clear after 2000, it would have been possible to do more to reduce the gaps – compared to the first four decades of statehood, as our analysis will soon show, this was a turning point. All of this also took place in a decade in which political entities emerged in the Arab sector who established themselves as ideological leaders calling for a change in the character of Israel, and who refused to accept it as a Jewish and democratic state. Two groups stood out within this framework: the Islamic Movement – mainly its northern branch that vowed to protect the *al-Aqṣa* Mosque (and all the other mosques in the country) and whose vision was to see a Muslim entity ruling Palestine – and the Balad Party, whose platform supported the conversion of Israel into a state of all its citizens.[73] Different spokesmen for both of these parties constantly leveled criticism against Israeli policy and repeatedly pointed out what they called the injustices committed by the government in the areas of religion (harm to the mosques) and citizenship (inequality between the groups).

Along with the significant changes in the lives of the citizens, the Israeli establishment continued to deal with security threats. Member of the Knesset al-Sana was investigated by the police because he was suspected of incitement following a statement he made about the Israeli police after an event in which a young Bedouin man was shot dead by an inspector from the Nature Reserve Authority.[74] Member of the Knesset Darawsha was also investigated on suspicion of a similar crime, as was Nimr Hussein for something he stated during a visit to Jordan.[75] Sheikh Raᶜid Salah and Nimr Hussein were summoned by the police for investigation into trespassing during a clean-up campaign of Muslim cemeteries in the City of Nesher. In the area of security, the terrorist attack that failed in September 1999 when two car bombs exploded, one in Haifa and the other in Tiberias, stood out. The subsequent investigation showed that activists from a number of villages in the Galilee, who were members of the northern branch of the Islamic Movement and who had been recruited into the ranks of Hamas, were behind the attack. Despite the declarations made by the Sheikh Salah that his movement only operates within the limits of the law the government decided to tighten the supervision and surveillance over the activities of the northern branch.[76] This decision, which was moderate considering the calls made by members of the Knesset to outlaw the northern branch, aroused much bitter criticism in the Arab sector as a whole and especially by the heads of the northern branch.[77]

Ultimately the first Netanyahu government, without determining for itself what its aims and basic guidelines were, continued the policy approaches of the previous government headed by Rabin, because of a similar way of viewing the need to separate the Arab citizens from the Palestinians and the understanding that closing the gaps and increasing civil integration might reduce security threats and add content to the democratic make-up of the country.

4

After the Events of October 2000: Strengthening the Effort to Compensate the Arab Minority

The serious violent events of October 2000 took place during the Barak government's period in office, from May 1999 to March 2001. In contrast to its predecessor, this government's basic guidelines did include the need to deal with the Arab minority in the area of civil life. In accordance with this it took additional steps in a number of areas that influenced the lives of the Arab citizens. These steps directly affected the extent and qualities of the way things were handled by the different government ministries to improve the quality of life of the Arab citizens in Israel.

The first change was structural. Prime Minister Barak appointed a ministerial committee headed by Matan Vilnai to deal with the affairs of the Arab citizens. This committee encouraged a built-in ongoing dialogue with representatives of the Arab sector in its work setting up a program to provide this population with comprehensive care. Its role was to find solutions for the problems of unemployment, poverty, the housing shortage, and the appropriation of lands. Another committee headed by Minister Haim Oron, which coordinated the treatment of the Bedouin in the Negev, recommended the allocation of the sum of 1.2 billion shekels over a period of four years in order to create physical, social and economic infrastructures in the recognized villages of the Bedouin in the south of the country.[78] In December 2000, a division was established in the Prime Minister's Office to deal with the civil affairs of the Arabs in Israel. In 2003, in the government of Ariel Sharon (after the Barak's period), a government authority for the advancement of the minority sectors was set up in the National Security Council – which was a permanent advisory council on the subject in which representatives of the Arab minority were members as determined by governmental decision. In June 2004, again as the result of a governmental decision, the government Authority for the Advancement of the Minority Sector was set up.

The second change was subject and area based, and arose out of the understanding that a comprehensive program that would affect every area of civil life that directly influenced the population needed to be put into action. The practical expression of this was a development program for the Arab villages which would include infrastructures for sewage, roads, education, completing public buildings, developing employment, forming policies involving lands, and legally enforcing planning and construction.

The third change was the allocation of increased resources to put these different plans into action. This was a continuation of the understanding that was already put in place in the 1990s, according to which substantial budgets were needed in order to produce and improve things from a development point of view in the Arab villages. The government had already made a decision in 1998 (Resolution 4464) about the development of Bedouin villages in the north. Eighty-eight percent of this decision was put into effect in 2000 when 540 million shekels were invested in the advancement of the villages included in the program.

The fourth change was the appointment of members of the minorities to public positions, one of whom was Oscar Abu Rizk to the post of Director-General of the Ministry of the Interior in 2005 – which was a position that traditionally had a dramatic influence over the quality of life of Arab citizens. Another prominent appointment was that of Member of the Knesset Ghaleb Majadllah to Minister of Science in 2007.

An analysis of the way the government ministries managed things during this period shows that the events of 2000 had accelerated the improvement in the treatment of the Arab population by the executive authorities. This was, in fact, carried out under the shadow of the bleeding wounds of the violent events and against the background of the severe crisis of credibility that had developed between the Arab minority and the state and; despite these, the government decided to continue applying the policy of affirmative action towards the Arab population. This policy arose out of recognition and understanding of the effects of the gaps between the majority and minority groups and the need to close them. It was clear that the government was seeking channels of dialogue with the leaders of the Arab sector in order to soften the harsh atmosphere that was enveloping the relations between the parties after the violent events. In this respect, from the beginning of 2001 onwards, an additional change took place in policy – not only would efforts be made to reduce the gaps, but initiatives would be taken to develop dialogue with different representatives of the minority. Up until then the government had focused upon initiatives for dialogue on security issues, while discussions on civil matters were usually initiated by the Arab sector in its efforts to improve its status.

The events of October 2000 led to the presentation of a comprehensive program for the development of the Arab sector at an overall cost of four billion shekels.[79] This was the most comprehensive program for the Arab minority since the establishment of the state; the sum was budgeted for four years and the development was planned for seventy-three Arab villages. Ultimately the sum was reduced by 20 percent because of an across-the-board cut in the budgets of all government ministries. Out of the 3.15 billion shekels that was allocated, close to 90 percent was actually provided.[80] Most of the sum was funneled through the ministries whose activities had a crucial influence upon the daily lives of the citizens, such as the Ministry of Industry and Commerce, the Ministry of the Interior, the Ministry of Housing and Construction, the Ministry of Education, the Ministry of Transport, and the Ministry of National Infrastructures.[81]

After October 2000, various government programs were prepared for the advancement and treatment of the Arab population, three of which stood out and are worth mentioning: the development of Arab villages, the integration of Arab citizens into the civil service, and the advancement of education in the Arab sector.[82] The program for the development of the Arab villages was prepared during 2000 by the Coordination and Control Wing of the Prime Minister's Office. It was aimed at all the Arab villages in Israel, except for mixed towns and cities. People from all the relevant government ministries were involved in the planning of the program for the treatment of the Arab minority, as were the heads of the Arab authorities along with businessmen and planners from the Arab sector – all contributed their experience in order to map out the needs of this minority. People from the Prime Minister's Office and Minister Vilnai visited the Arab villages in order to examine the problems that needed rapid, close-up solutions. These actions indicate how important it was for the then Prime Minister Barak to place the management of this project into the hands of people from his office so that they could coordinate the activities of all the ministries involved in this matter. The participation of representatives from the Arab minority was also a clear expression of the realization of the policy of encouraging dialogue about civil matters towards expanding of integration of the Arab minority.

The goals of the program were reducing the gaps between the Arab and Jewish sectors; providing suitable solutions for the problems and main needs of the Arab sector villages in areas such as transport, infrastructures, housing and construction, industry and commerce, education, employment, health, and religion; and establishing the foundations for the continuation of economic investment. Those who prepared the program recognized the low level of the infrastructures in the Arab villages despite the financial investments during the 1990s. Therefore, half of the sum was allocated for physical infrastructure such as paving roads, laying down sewage pipes, street lighting, connection to the national water pipelines, completing the master plans for the villages, constructing high density housing neighborhoods, accelerating the building of public institutions, and developing internal infrastructures in the villages. The program became a working one for all the government ministries and exact sums were allocated for every enterprise.

Another main area that the five-year program was designed to develop was the economic sphere; the planners characterized the Arab sector as a market segment that had high unemployment, a low level of participation of women in the workforce, and that lacked developed industrial zones. The goals that were set were development of industrial zones that could be shared by several groups of settlements, including industrial zones for Jews and Arabs, directing Arab employment into the areas of technological research and development, and developing human capital through investing in education. A sum of 700 million shekels was designated for building new classrooms within the framework of economic development for building classrooms, and 280 million shekels were designated for pedagogical programs aimed at gifted students, special education, and science and technology education.[83]

Yet another main program that the government developed after 2000 was one designed to increase the integration of Arab citizens into the civil service. Behind the preparation of this program was amendment 11 to the Civil Service Law that the Knesset had passed, which stipulated that suitable expression would be given to the representation of members of the Arab population in the civil service workforce at all levels and in all professions.[84] This amendment reflected, in the legislation, a reality that had already begun to exist in the 1990s when the integration of more members of the Arab minority came into effect in the various government ministries.[85] The following table presents the ongoing growth in the number of Arabs employed in government service during the decade between the entry of the Rabin government into office and the end of 2015.[86]

An analysis of the data of Table 3 leads to a number of conclusions. First, from 1992 on there was a continuous annual growth in the

Table 3 Arabs employed in government service, 1992–2015

Year	Percentage of number of Arab workers	Total number of Arab workers	Total number of government workers
1992	2.1%	1,117	53,549
1993	2.5%	1,369	53,914
1994	3%	1,679	55,278
1995	3.5%	1,997	56,183
1996	4%	2,231	56,809
1997	4.1%	2,340	57,286
1998	4.4%	2,537	57,580
1999	4.8%	2,818	58,115
2001	5.7%	3,128	54,337
2007	5.7%	3,429	60,549
2008	6%	3,737	61,938
2009	6.4%	4,092	63,852
2010	7%	4,543	65,366
2011	7.4%	4,852	65,749
2012	8%	5,433	68,520
2013	8.4%	5,937	70,586
2014	8.8%	6,266	71,469
2015	9%	6,440	71,797

number of Arab minority members employed by government service. The very fact of this growth expresses the, at least partial, actualization of the policy adopted by the government of integrating minority group citizens. Over the two decades presented in the table, the percentage of minority group citizens employed in the civil service grew four and a half times (and these figures do not include the ever-growing number of young men and women who want to do national/community service), while their relative percentage in the population has remained similar to the end of 2015, which was the beginning of the period (by 19 percent Israel's population).

The last program that stands out is the five-year program for the advancement of education in the Arab sector, which was prepared by a steering committee of nine members, including three minority group people. The program was put into action in the 2001–2002 school year and was funded with 250 million shekels. One of the members, Ṣalaḥ Taha, believed that the sum was insufficient but that "something could be done with it".[87] The goal of the program was to increase learning achievement by Arab students by placing special emphasis on mathematics and languages. [88] During the first year, the program was put into action in 240 schools out of the 570 in the Arab sector – in other words in close to 50 percent of the schools.

5

The Sharon Government: Continuation of the Government's Treatment of the Arab Minority

The change in government that took place after the elections in February 2001 did not lead to a change in policy, and the following was written in the basic guidelines for the new government headed by Ariel Sharon: "The government will ensure full equality for all Israeli citizens . . . in education, employment, housing and infrastructures as well as correcting the distortions that existed in the allocation of resources and the provision of public services. The government has likewise taken upon itself to create places of work for the Arab sector".[89]

In practice, changes in municipal practices were evident, and The Ministry of the Interior authorized master plans for Arab villages during 2000–2008.[90] From 2000 on, master plans were authorized for 47 Arab villages[91] and in 21 of them the plans were already operative in 2002. By the beginning of 2010, master plans for 125 Arab villages (out of 128) were authorized by The Ministry of the Interior.

Between 2006 and 2008, the percentage of lands allocated by the Israel Lands Authority for the purposes of housing for the Arab population grew from 5 percent to 13 percent. A study of the different plans shows that they included procedures for rehabilitating the authorities, providing development budgets (at the rate of 60 percent of the original budgeted sum), constructing and renovating religious institutions, developing new and old neighborhoods, and establishing public institutions. Another area in which real improvement was evident was the installation of sewage systems in the Arab villages, and by the end of 2004, more than 80 percent of the Arab households had been connected to the sewage systems.[92] The Ministry of Transport along with the Ministry of the Interior, which was responsible for the local authorities, chose to provide funds for improving the road infrastructure at a cost of more than 270 million shekels, which was 30 million shekels higher than the sum determined by the government decision.

Efforts were also made to improve the situation in the Arab sector in other civil areas as well, such as developing industrial zones, encouraging initiatives and employment, and closing infrastructure and pedagogical gaps in education. Quite a few of these programs came up against barriers or only enjoyed partial success. In one of these areas, agriculture, which was traditionally thought to be central and important for the Arab minority, the development budget grew to four times greater between 1999 and 2002. The activity here more than once came up against difficulties, and in some of the cases there was a slowdown in the work because of bureaucratic barriers; but problems also appeared because of lack of readiness by the Arab minority to accept modern developments, power struggles between clans, a lack of faith in the government's intentions, frequent changes of the heads of the local authorities, and the continuation of the phenomenon of illegal building.

6
The Olmert and Netanyahu Governments: Acceleration of Improvements in Treatment of the Arab Population

Improvements in the treatment of the Arab population were further accelerated in Olmert's period in office from 2006 to 2009 – his government made a point of advancing the status of the Arab population. Olmert put a policy into practice which focused upon a number of new levels of activity that were over and above those of previous governments. First he singled out the problem of the low independent incomes for improvements in the educational system and later the need to make a change in the curricula. Finally he prepared programs for shared Jewish–Arab enterprises for businessmen in order to develop the Arab villages.

During the first decade of the twenty first century, the Israeli governments made a series of decisions whose future realization meant even greater reduction in the gaps that had begun to close during the previous decade. Olmert's period in office was characterized by putting some of these decisions into action, and in August 2003, the ministerial committee for non-Jewish affairs decided to instruct the government ministries to give priority, for a period of two years, to minority members in obtaining employment and promotions at work.[93] In January 2004, the government decided to advance the integration of equality and of the Arab citizens of Israel into the civil service as a continuation of the procedures that had been introduced by previous governments in the 1990s.[94] In March 2006, the government adopted the recommendations made by an inter-ministerial team, which included representatives of the Ministry of Justice, the Ministry of Finance, and the Civil Service Commission, to decide on additional ways to advance the suitable representation of Arab minority members in the civil service. The goal set by the government was to have 8 percent, by the end of 2008, of all those employed in the civil service be Arab minority members.[95] In the area of housing the government decided to subsidize the costs of developing building infrastructures for dwellings for demobilized soldiers in the villages of minorities in the north. The goal was to market 600 housing units per year for demobilized soldiers, including the Druze and Circassian soldiers, and the annual sum budgeted for this was ten million shekels.[96]

Olmert, as Prime Minister, was not satisfied with just navigating a policy whose main purpose was the preparation of comprehensive programs to reduce the gaps. He also encouraged direct dialogue with the leaders of the Arab minority and their participation in making decisions that directly affected the quality of their lives in the country. As a direct result of this policy Olmert initiated the Prime Minister's Conference on the Arab Minority which took place in May 2007, and in his speech to the participants he chose to emphasize the point that the Arab citizens of Israel did not represent a strategic threat and enjoyed equal rights in the country. The conference was the high point of the process of dialogue that had become more regular and organized after 2000. In his summing up of the conference Olmert gave instructions to prepare wide-ranging programs for the Arab population in the areas of education, economics, and for municipal affairs. Three programs were presented to the second Prime Minister's Conference that took place in July 2008, and representatives of the Arab minority took part in the preparation of all of them.[97]

The government made another series of decisions that were aimed at advancing the Arab minority – one in February 2007, to establish an authority for the economic development of the Arab sector, which prepared an economic program. The program defined the vision of turning a segment of the Arab population into an advanced economic and social group, in an effort to utilize its economic potential as an integral part of the national economy. Among the goals of the program were raising the standard of living of the Arab citizens, the encouragement of productive economic activity, and raising the personal incomes of the Arab population.[98] Appointed as the head of the authority for economic development of the Arabs was Aiman Saif, a member of the Arab minority, which was a clear expression of the intention to actualize the policy of integrating the sector into the state institutions. The contents of the program represented another step forward by the government. From almost complete neglect of the minority – apart from a limited number of specific discussions, most of which involved security matters – until the beginning of the 1990s, through a process of passive and limited dialogue and recognition of the gaps that existed between the groups which included the initiation of dialogue in the 1990s, the government now constantly made efforts to reduce the gaps and strengthen the integration to the point that the Arab minority was seen as part of the national economy.

Rapid steps were taken in the field and in February 2007, the government decided to establish an authority for the economic development of the minority sector, and it was agreed that "the authority would act as a body whose aim was to fully exploit the economic potential of the minority population by encouraging productive economic and commercial activity in the minority sector and its integration into the wider national economy".[99] At the Prime Minister's Conference, Olmert explained the importance of their integration to the heads of the Arab minority using the expression "one country, one economy" and agreed that there was discrimination against the Arabs in Israel.[100] He also declared that "the Israeli Arabs are not a strategic threat and I do not see them as a threat. The Israeli citizens have to be educated to understand that the Arabs in Israel are citizens with equal rights".[101]

These years were marked by a surge in development in the Arab villages. The Prime Minister's conscious perception that there was no threat contributed to the application and actualization of programs in the field. The authority for the development of the Arab, Druze and Circassian sectors worked vigorously to put the different programs into action, and published this in annual reports such as that of 2009–2010 when the authority presented the principles governing its activities, which included: providing assistance for integrating Arab workers into the workforce with emphasis on women and academics, encouraging initiatives in Arab villages, integrating Arab businesses into the national economy, and improving assistance and government services to Arab owned businesses and business activities shared by Jews and Arabs.[102] The latter activity included the provision of incentives to employers in the private sector who were hiring Arabs, raising awareness among Jewish businessmen of the potential of the work market in the Arab sector, developing professional courses for Arab women to encourage them to seek employment, and preparing candidates for positions in demand. The efforts made to integrate Arab women into the workforce during these years not only included directly approaching them, but also establishing a supportive logistic foundation in the form of child care centers that supervised the children until late in the afternoon. The goal of this activity was two-fold: the removal of logistically problematic and cultural barriers together with raising the gross national product as a result of the Arab woman workforce.

Parallel to this, the economic authority worked to remove barriers that existed in the government bureaus in a way that would allow an accelerated rate of employment of Arabs in the civil service. This activity was the actualization of the decision by the government in November 2007 when they defined the goal of having, by 2012, ten percent of those employed in government service be Arabs.[103] The activities of the authority were carried out closely accompanied at the political level, and in March 2010 the government made another resolution (Number 1539) to set up a five-year plan for the development of the Arab sector (2010–2014) at the cost of 800 million shekels. The guiding principles of the program were the development of the economy, employment, housing, accessibility of transport, and increasing personal safety along with enforcement related to the latter. The program emphasized cooperation and involvement of the Arab local authorities in order to put its components into action. Among the villages and towns that were included in this program were Shfarᶜam, Sakhnin, Nazareth, Tira, Kafr Qasem, Rahat, Umm el-Fahem, and Tamra. This was a clear signal by the executive level that it intended to invest in the leading areas of the Arab sector and that the goal was to bring the sector closer to the national public space. About 140 million shekels were budgeted for the building of 4,200 housing units in the Arab sector in order to provide quick solutions to the distress of young couples.

The government also allocated government owned lands for building initiatives in different municipalities, and provided 100 million shekels for another area important for the security of the citizens – for improving connections with the community police and constructing police stations that would bring about a reduction of the level of criminality in the Arab villages. In the area of employment, guidance centers were opened in Tira, Sakhnin, and Umm el-Fahem in order to help those seeking employment to integrate. Business guidance was also given, and business programs prepared by entrepreneurs were budgeted to the tune of 10 million shekels till the end of the year 2000[104] – even though claims were made that more could have been done in this area to mobilize employers (mainly Jews) in order to change the pattern of employment in Israel and get to the point where Arabs would become an integral part of the workforce.[105] This initiative, with the motto, "Welcoming the Arab Citizen," continued in 2011. The annual report of the Authority for Economic Development showed that the government's resolution to be more active in the field had become a reality. Eighty percent of the program's budget (about 640 million shekels) was applied during 2010–2011, half of which was for the planning of housing.[106] Terminals for public transport were built in Sakhnin, Tamra, and Umm el-Fahem; internal transportation lines were introduced in the village for the first time since the establishment of the state. In ʿArabeh and Nazareth children's day care centers were built in order to make it possible for women to go out to work; in Shfarʿam and Umm el-Fahem a regional industrial zone was set up and opened. In other Arab villages there was a noticeable improvement in the areas of housing, community policing, and employment.[107] Netanyahu, the then Prime Minister, followed the lead of his predecessors and also established a conference for the Arab sector, and among the things he said to those who came was the clarification that "there is still a gap . . . the conditions have to be provided to help all parts of the population . . . the integration of the minority population into the Israeli economy is possible and the Arab sector should become integrated into the national economy".[108]

The government was not satisfied with just making declarations and requested updates from the Authority for Economic Development about the progress of the comprehensive program's various components. In a meeting that took place in March 2012, the government decided to broaden the program to include all the villages in the minority sector, and 10 million shekels were added to the original budget for the planning of housing on both private and state land; for the subsidization of the infrastructure development of land reserves for housing; and for marketing and public relations that would present to the Arab population.[109]

The results of the policy of closer ties could be seen not only in the field but also in the government ministries themselves; between 2002 and 2015 the trend towards the absorption of minority people into government service, as described above, grew. The process of absorbing them into the civil service came up against various barriers, and the government, which recognized this, appointed an inter-ministerial team headed by the Director-General of the Ministry of Justice whose task was to accompany the efforts of the government ministries to remove the bureaucratic barriers. Among the recommendations made by the team was one that became a government resolution

(4436) – it ordered that new employees of minority origin being absorbed into the civil service would be eligible for benefits, such as rent assistance up to 2000 shekels per month for each employee who was forced to move his residence.[110] Additional governmental and bureaucratic barriers were the slow process of issuing master plan authorizations, poor economic foundations, low quality municipal management, and the lack of strategic planning. Included in the area of cultural barriers were factors such as the effort required to make inroads in a society that had a traditional character, the lack of experience in employment, the lack of social networks, and the low level of education of the potential workforce. The multiplication of programs and the application of at least some of them indicate the government's permanent occupation with issues involving the Arab minority and efforts made to advance it.

Since 2008, an ongoing effort has been made to integrate Arab academics into the workforce, and in 2012, the Prime Minister's Office initiated a public relations campaign to encourage this. The research done before this campaign revealed that 81 percent of Arab academics were employed in the economy but fewer than two percent were working in the profession they had studied. It appears that the main barrier to absorbing Arabs was discrimination and prejudice, but at the same time, it was shown that 94 percent of the Jewish employers who had already employed Arabs answered that they would be interested in employing additional Arabs.[111]

The trend towards integration and the allocation of resources have also continued during recent years, and Prime Minister Netanyahu has continued with the annual conference devoted to the needs of the Arab minority. At the beginning of 2012, he announced that: "it is incumbent upon my government to integrate the minority population into the national economy and to grant them equal civil, economic and social opportunity".[112] Like his predecessors he differentiated between these components and the nationalist component; the practical expression of this announcement was the implementation of a long-term program for the development of the Arab villages with a comprehensive budget of five billion shekels. Since its establishment in the Prime Minister's Office in 2007, the Development Authority has created a series of initiatives that has encouraged entrepreneurship and investment in the Arab sector. During these years the Development Authority focused upon four areas of activity: the economic empowerment of the Arab local authorities, the upgrading and development of the business sector, the upgrading of the human capital and its integration into the workforce, and the strategic planning and development of the Arab local authorities.

Various programs began to be implemented as a result of the government's activity, among which was the housing program whose goal was construction for the housing of young Arabs. This program became part of the wider steps taken to authorize the master plans for Arab villages. In Sakhnin the construction of a modern residential neighborhood was begun along with a growth in the reserves of government-owned land to be used for dwellings for Arabs. In the areas of economics and commerce there was considerable growth in the number of Arab exporters, while in the social and employment areas three centers for employment counseling were opened in Sakhnin, Tamra, and Umm el-Fahem.[113] In addition to these the government decided to increase the rate of employment among the Arabs; the significance of this in practice was the allocation of 150 million shekels to increase the areas for businesses in the Arab villages.[114]

This activity, in all its areas, led by the Prime Minister's Office, was not the only channel that linked the establishment to the Arab minority. In October 2005, the government adopted the recommendation made in the report of the "Ivri Committee" to allow national service for all the citizens and residents of Israel who had not been called up to serve in the defense forces or who had been exempted.[115] The National Service Administration had been established in 2007 in the Ministry of Welfare and was later moved to the Prime Minister's Office and then to the Ministry of Science. The National-Citizen Service offered the minority population the option of volunteering to work for the public's benefit in a long list of areas such as education, welfare, legal aid, health, transport, the elderly and pensioners, internal security – which included bodies such as the police, prison services and the border police, and social security services. According to data from the National Service Administration, in 2010 there were 14,000 volunteers, including 1,500 Arabs.[116] The number of young Arabs who volunteered reached 4,500 by the end of 2015. A more exact analysis shows that from 2005 on there was a constant rise in the number of Arab volunteers, most of whom chose to volunteer in the area of education (about 60 percent) and health (24 percent). Thus, in 2011, there were 2,400 Arab volunteers which were 200 more than the designated goal, and among the volunteers were Muslims (76 percent) and Christians (13 percent), while the rest were Druze.

Another area in which the government was more and more involved because of its desire to solve ongoing problems was the arrangements made for the Bedouin lands in the Negev. From a historical point of view the government had dealt with the Bedouin issues in three phases since the establishment of the state. First, after the commencement of the military government over the Arab minority in September 1948, the government concentrated the Bedouin in the Negev into the restricted area which was called "the Restriction" (*Hasyag*) area south and east of Beer Sheba in 1952, and the settlement there was limited to a million and a half dunams. The transfer of the Bedouin to the area was completed in 1954, which was the year the state granted the Bedouin citizenship.[117] The second step was taken in the 1960s when the government decided to establish seven permanent settlements for the Bedouin in the Negev; and the third step was the attempt to solve the issue of the Bedouin ownership of lands in the Negev. In 1976, an inter-ministerial committee determined that the lands in the Negev were a kind of dead land (land that is not suitable for cultivation – *arḍ mawat*) but authorized partial compensation of 20 percent of the lands to those who made a claim, for over 400 dunams. Along with this compromise proposal, the government's policy towards the Bedouin hardened; this was expressed in the enforcement of the law in the areas of building and pasturing and in the establishment of the Green Police (1977) – which was given the task of enforcing the law in an uncompromising fashion.[118]

At the end of 2007 the government gave the Minister of Housing the responsibility of appointing a committee to make recommendations about establishing order in the Bedouin settlement in the Negev. In the spirit of the government policy of encouraging dialogue with the Arab minority, the committee included two Bedouin representatives from the south. The committee heard more than 120 people involved in the subject including Bedouin who lived in the Negev and it recommended that the government recognize most of the unrecognized villages and declare that the existing illegal buildings "in the territory of the master plan and doing no damage to the implementation of the program" should be seen as "gray" area buildings – a definition that would pave the way to their approval. Together with this the program recommended the empowerment of the Bedouin population by introducing social and economic initiatives at an overall cost of more than a billion shekels. The government adopted the recommendations in a meeting that took place in January 2013 and since then the dialogue has continued with the Bedouin in order to implement the recommendations in the field.[119]

The law that was finally proposed was put on the table of the knesset on May 2013, after years of discussions between the representatives of the establishment and the heads of the Bedouin tribes, and in this case as well the step was taken after continuous discussions had taken place. The goal of the law proposed by the government was to make arrangements for ownership of the lands in the Negev that were related to the claims made by the Bedouin population in this region. The organizing principle of the proposal touched upon a number of levels of activity. From the point of view of infrastructures, the aim was to regulate the status of the unrecognized Bedouin settlements and their inclusion into recognized settlements, and from the social-economic point of view the program's intention was to invest the sum of 1.2 billion shekels in the creation of places of employment and in providing solutions in the area of education.[120]

The complete picture that one gets from an analysis of the activity of the different government ministries, under the encouragement, guidance and permanent supervision of the Prime Minister's Office, is of a policy whose main idea is the reduction of gaps between the Jewish majority and the Arab minority. This can be seen both in the progress made in the physical infrastructures in the field, in regulation of the status of the Arab villages and in the integration of the minorities into the public and citizen based domain of the state.

The government's policy during these years came up against not a few barriers, and it is important to mention them in the framework of the discussion, because they can teach something about the gap between the policy that was adopted by the government and the negative public and parliamentary discourse that has taken place during recent years regarding the Arab minority.

To begin with we have the political barrier which is, in fact, an unwritten principle in the Israeli political system according to which the Arab representatives are regularly excluded from the decision-making centers. This barrier arises out of the definition of the country as "Jewish" but also contains the component of hostility between the Jews and the Arabs that rests upon prejudiced and stereotypical ideas.[121] Despite continual efforts made to discuss things with the Arab representatives, the important decisions of the government have been made in the cabinet in which there is no representation of Israeli Arabs.

A second barrier is in the area of institutions – this arises out of the multiplicity of double roles that exist in the governmental structures as well as over-centralization in cases such as that of the Ministry of the Interior vis-à-vis the local authorities and that of the Israel Lands Authority and the Ministry of Housing regarding the question of who is responsible for state lands.[122] The direct result of these disagreements between the different state institutions have, more than once, held up the implementation of decisions. In the same context, there is the third barrier of the complicated bureaucracy as attested to by official documents that have significantly delayed the implementation of programs in the field, because the clerks responsible for their implementation did not believe that the political level had really given instructions to implement certain programs for the Arab minority. In other cases, we have found that the bureaucratic professional level has blocked the implementation of programs when it has lacked the interest, readiness, or ability to carry out the policy of equality and to correct the long existing injustices. The bureaucratic barriers do not end with the behavior at the civil service level – since, when the implementation of the different initiatives commenced, it became clear that in a number of the authorities there were also bureaucratic-planning barriers that were characterized by a lack of effective planning, limited availability of lands for building, the high rate of privately-owned land, weak infrastructures, and difficulties in mobilizing sources of funding the initiatives and tenants.[123] Another barrier that became a significant problem was the economic-budgetary one. The incompetent management of the local authorities in the Arab sector over many years legally prevented the establishment from transferring the resources and budgets that were to be provided for the development of a number of authorities because of the foreclosures of their bank accounts. This situation demanded the rehabilitation of these authorities before it was possible to implement the various programs in the field.[124]

Finally there is the cultural barrier that comes from the Arab and Muslim tradition. There are Arab custom which deal with family structure, the characteristics of employment, the status of women and their role – which focuses on housekeeping and raising children – who have made it difficult for the various government ministries to implement certain projects that were prepared for the Arab population and were part of the efforts to reduce the gaps.

Despite these barriers and the inherent difficulties, the totality of the widespread activity of all the government ministries during these years was expressed in concrete ways and was visible in the field. The provision of enlarged budgets and the increase in initiatives fostered by the authority for economic development gradually came together in the form of industrial regions, improved infrastructures, growth in the number of employed people and availability of government services for the Arab population.

All of these were not lost on the leaders of the Arab public who understood there was a disparity between the policy of the executive authority and the hostile discourse that was growing among the Jewish majority and members of the Knesset in reference to the Arab minority.[125] The work done contributed positively to the dialogue between the establishment and the leaders of the Arab minority, among whom were the heads of the authorities, educators and businessmen – this softened the tension that had developed with the worsening tone of the public discourse regarding this charged issue.

Moreover, this policy for improvement in conditions for the Arab minority, despite the various difficulties that existed in its implementation, was put into practice in a period in which Israel was busy dealing with the second Intifada in the territories and with the frustration from and prevention of the terror incidents being carried out by a small number of Arab Israeli citizens. One of these that stood out was the suicide bombing carried out by an Israeli Arab in the Nahariyah in northern Israel train station in September 2001, in which three Israelis were killed. During these years dozens of other Arab Israeli citizens provided assistance to terrorist actions as drivers and as providers of shelter and work for residents of the territories; some of these were arrested by Israel's security forces. This involvement in terror was naturally perceived negatively by the Israeli public and contributed to damage being done to the image of the Arab public as a whole after October 2000 events. From the beginning of the Intifada, which broke out in September 2000 and included violent events that took place in the Arab sector in Israel, there was a clear change for the worse in the way the Jewish majority related to the Arab minority. This issue in itself deserves discussion, since it not only reflects profound social processes among the Jewish majority group but has also found institutional expression in anti-Arab legislative steps that were taken. Despite these changes, which will be presented anon, the executive authority is still adhering to the favorable policy towards the Arab population.

7
The Attitude of the Jewish Majority to the Arab Minority: Increasing Radicalization, Hatred and Alienation

A series of processes in the internal Israeli arena and in the regional Palestinian arena has gradually and continuously eroded the social steadiness and sense of security of the Jewish majority group in the State of Israel since 2000. All of the events that will be analyzed further on had a direct or indirect influence on Jewish–Arab relations in Israel. Unsurprisingly, the cumulative result of the erosion of steadiness and the sense of security led to an increase in negative feelings towards the Arab minority. Despite the more radical public tendencies that were also expressed in legislative steps taken, the executive authority continued with a policy whose main idea was the reduction of the gaps between the majority group and the minority group – and an analysis of the various subjects involved in the external and internal areas will henceforth be made.

The first subject is the process of Iran's nuclearization, which has led to a continuing discussion in the regional area on Iran's nuclear program at least up until the signing of the nuclear agreement between Iran and the major powers in July 2015. From the Israeli point of view, this issue was featured prominently in the media because of the degree of interest, more than once public personalities and the IDF had to emphasize the threat. The powerful media preoccupation with this issue influenced the level of national anxiety of the Israeli public, if only because the discussion included potential ramifications for Israel's continued existence as a country in the era of a nuclear Iran. Among the many expressions of this that stood out was an opinion poll published in the summer of 2012 in which 37 percent of Israelis believed that nuclear weapons in the hands of Iran might lead to a second holocaust. Only 25 percent believed that such a holocaust was impossible and the rest answered that they didn't know. The data not only indicated an authentic fear of the reality of a nuclear armed Iran but also the difficulty that close to 40 percent of those polled had in forming an opinion. This confusion, naturally, arouses security fears because of the uncertainty of some of the public.[126]

Another significant event in the regional arena was the Second Lebanese War in the summer of 2006 during which 4,000 missiles fell on Israeli territory which made the vulnerability of the Israeli home front real. The Vinograd Committee which investigated the readiness of the army for war found that the IDF was not properly prepared for a long military campaign or, in the language of the committee, "We are talking about serious and profound failings whose full significance and the dangers inherent in them must not be muddled by current events, specific one-time successes and initial corrective measures".[127]

The Palestinian arena was also experiencing changes, some because of Israeli initiatives that awakened national resolve, followed by a rise in the extremity of expressions used against the Arab minority. First of all there were the Oslo Accords that were signed in September 1993 and that laid down the foundations for the establishment of an independent Palestinian entity. The agreement aroused public discussion centered on a dispute between Israel's political blocs over the future of the country. There was no argument about one thing and that was that the accords, which were implemented in May 1994, reduced the territory that was under complete Israeli control since 1967, certainly in Judea and Samaria, and these areas were divided into three categories. One of them there was under complete Palestinian control (area "A");

the second was under Palestinian civil control and Israeli security control (area "B"); and the third was completely under Israeli control (area "C"). During the 1990s, the geo-political and security reality was characterized by waves of violence including harsh terrorist activities in the heart of Israel. These fed growing feelings of hostility, alienation, and hatred in the Jewish majority towards the Arabs, which did not distinguish between Palestinian and Israeli Arabs.

From 2000 on, serious escalation of protest and violence took place in Israel, after the failure of the "Camp David 2" talks, the aim of which was to arrive at a political arrangement between Israel and the Palestinians. The attacks carried out by the Palestinians in different ways significantly eroded the feelings of personal security of the Jewish population which paid the heavy price in hundreds killed and thousands wounded. The difficult scenes broadcast by the media also contributed to undermining personal feelings of security, and for years a high level of fear of terror remained – this fear had direct ramifications for the way Jews related to the Arab minority in Israel.[128]

The Palestinian Intifada was not the only change in the reality of Judea and Samaria and the Gaza Strip. In the summer of 2005, the process of unilateral disengagement from the Gaza Strip was completed; but from the very beginning, the process of leaving was seen as something illegitimate by many within the Jewish majority group – this sense was augmented by the fact that the geographic space over which Israel had control was reduced so that the country which was already small became even smaller. In June 2007, following the disengagement, Hamas forcibly and violently took control of the Gaza Strip and compelled the Palestinian Authority supporters to flee for their lives. A new geo-political reality was created by the fact that the physical territory of Israel became smaller, and in the south a strong Islamic Palestinian entity that threatened and attacked the Israeli home front had established itself. The Israeli public felt that it was trapped in pincers since in the southern border they were being threatened by Hamas and in the northern one by Hizbullah.

Two steps initiated by Israel in Judea and Samaria as well had ramifications for relations with the Arab minority since it was part of the overall Arab threat. At the beginning of 2006, an outpost called Amona, in the central of the West Bank was evacuated by force by the state as an act against the settlers who refused to obey the rule of law. Against this background, a public debate took place about the possibility that the then Prime Minister, Olmert, might embark on a program of retrenchment in Judea and Samaria that would lead to the evacuation of settlements and their concentration into three settlement blocs, within the framework of an arrangement with the Palestinians.

In 2008 the security forces evacuated "Beit ha-Shalom" (house of peace) in Hebron, parallel to the government making a decision to freeze building in the Jewish settlements for a period of nine months.

All of the above changes fed the feeling of hostility towards the Arabs that already existed in the Jewish public, without their distinguishing between Israeli and Palestinian Arabs. It seems that the events of October 2000 and the wave of Palestinian terror had had a crucial influence upon the change in attitude of the Jewish majority towards the minority group. This influence was not only expressed in public opinion polls but was also reflected in discussions that took place in the parliamentary arena. In a series of sessions in the Knesset in 2000, some of the members expressed the public's feelings as they understood them from their visits in the field and from remarks made by public figures and professors. In this way, for example, Arab members of the Knesset pointed out trends towards incitement and the phenomenon of racism that was developing among the Jewish majority and aimed at the Arab minority.[129]

Member of the Knesset Hashem Mahamid cited Minister Danny Naveh (2001–2006) who had made the statement, "The Muslims are rapists" and Uzi Landau, the Minister for Internal Security from 2001 to 2003 who had asserted, "Whoever demands equal rights will end up as a hater of Israel". These public statements, like the attacks that had been carried out by the Palestinians, had a cumulative effect on the behavior patterns of the Jewish majority. During the same debate in the Knesset, Mahamid, a resident of Umm el-Fahem, said that the Umm el-Fahem youth football team does not host teams from the Jewish sector because the players' parents have forbidden their children to enter the city".[130] Benny Eilon, the then Minister of Tourism (2001–2004), presented his data that supported the trend towards hostility and the severance of ties between the Jewish public and the Arab minority. He informed the Knesset that all the attempts of his ministry to invest in tourist enterprises in Arab villages had been a failure during 2001, while in Jewish villages there had been a record full occupancy of Jewish internal tourism. He blamed the Arab leadership in Israel for the situation that had been created, because it had chosen to join the Palestinian Intifada and copy the violent performances that had happened in the October 2000 events in the territory of the State of Israel.[131]

A report prepared by the Center for the Struggle against Racism at the beginning of 2007 found that half of the Jewish public was afraid when they heard people speaking Arabic in the streets, and 31 percent of the Jewish respondents answered that they hated Arabs – which was almost twice the number compared to a similar survey that was taken in 2005. Seventy-five percent of the respondents in a survey of 1,600 high school students in 2004 replied that the Arabs were violent.[132] The democracy index that was published in June 2007, about a year after the Second Lebanese War and two years after the disengagement from the Gaza Strip, showed that 87 percent of the public believed that the relations between Jews and Arabs were not good. Fifty-five percent of the Jewish respondents supported the idea of the government encouraging the emigration of Arabs from Israel, and almost 80 percent opposed the idea of an Arab party or minister joining the government. The findings showed that this was the highest rate of opposition since the beginning of the 1990s.[133]

Some of these findings found their way into the media. No less relevant were the reactions of the Jewish public to the findings, which included statements such as, "I hate them!"; "This is not about racism but about self-defense and a national struggle"; "This is the only Jewish country"; "The Arabs are loyal to enemy countries"; and the call "to boycott Arab businesses and exclude them from the public domain".[134] These figures and assertions, like the opinion pieces in the newspapers and the continuous media discussions, made the extremes that Jewish–Arab relations had come to since 2000 more concrete.

The hostility towards the Arabs among the Jewish public was also reflected in public opinion polls; a survey taken by the Israeli Institute of Democracy that was published at the end of 2010 showed that more than half of the Israelis (54 percent) supported making the right to vote conditional on swearing an oath of allegiance to the state of Israel. Among the Jewish respondents, about one third (32 percent) replied that the definition of Israel as a Jewish state was more important than its definition as a democratic state, and only 17 percent thought the opposite. About a third of the respondents even believed that in a state of war or serious security crisis Israel should behave towards the Arab minority the way the United States acted towards its Japanese citizens during World War II, meaning that they should be incarcerated. 70 percent opposed the appointment of Arabs to senior positions in the state.[135]

A survey carried out by the institute a year later, and published in 2011, presented findings that supported the above claims. Twelve hundred people took part in this survey, which was a representative sample of Israeli society made up of 879 Jews, 141 Russians, and 180 Arabs.[136] Fewer than 70 percent of the Jewish public supported equal rights for Arabs, as undertaken by the state in its Declaration of Independence. In everything connected with the need to improve the relations between Jews and Arabs in the country only 74 percent of the respondents believed that this should be aimed at. Other issues such as reduction of the economic gaps, aiding young people with housing, strengthening Israel's military power, and other issues were found to be higher priority items for the Jewish public than its relations with the minority group.

These and other surveys are not the only measures that reflect the trend towards more extremity towards the Arab minority in the Jewish majority. From 2000 onwards a real increase began in the number of publications distributed in the names of rabbis and Jewish public figures that preached hatred towards the Arab citizens of Israel, immigrant workers, and refugees, and that called upon the establishment to remove such groups from the country.[137] At the end of 2009, the book *The King's Torah*, which contained things that incited towards rebellion and violence against Arabs and other minorities in the State of Israel, was published, and the contents of the book appeared to make the use of violence against non-Jews legitimate and permissible.[138] Added to this were the comments made by Rabbi Dudu Batzri, who declared that the "Arabs are a donkey nation, an evil affliction, an evil Satan . . . the Arabs are beasts".[139]

Some of these publications came out as reactions to the terror attacks carried out by Palestinians against Jewish targets in the streets of Israel and almost always contained encouragement of reprisals. One of them written after an attack on a yeshiva in Jerusalem (March 2008) in which eight Jews were killed contained the statement: "Every one of you has to imagine what the enemy is planning to do to us and respond with measure for measure. Have no mercy for them because they will have no mercy for you".[140] Following another attack, also in Jerusalem (August 2008), in which an Arab tractor driver ran down and injured 24 Jews, rabbis published a declaration entitled "A Response to the Bloodshed". This declaration did not satisfy itself with calling for a reaction to the attack but widened the discussion about Jewish–Arab relations to additional issues. The attack was exploited by those who signed the declaration to point out the dangers existing in employing Arabs in the Israeli economy, the attempts being made by Arabs to acquire real estate in Jewish neighborhoods, and the deliberate and systematic attacks by Arabs on Jewish daughters. The public was called upon not to employ Arabs any more, not to buy goods from the enemies, and not to invite the enemies, meaning Arabs, into Jewish homes.

In recent years the calls made by rabbis to not rent apartments to Arabs and foreign workers have increased; such calls by public figures and rabbis have found receptive audiences, and have created a public climate that encourages the use of violence by Jews against Arabs – either initiated or as a reaction to some violent action by Arabs. Such attacks have become common in different places throughout Israel where there is constant friction between Arabs and Jews living close to each other, such as in Jerusalem, Upper Nazareth, Safed, and other places.

The public mood which can be characterized as focusing upon Jewish elements has also changed the parliamentary dialogue. If in the 1990s, the Knesset legislated a series of laws that were aimed at improving the situation of the Arab minority. Despite government's policy which can be named affirmative actions, during recent years the characters of the laws, or at least the legislative processes that are relevant to the Arab population, have taken on the tone of exclusion and alienation. It is important to discuss the legislative proposals because they act as an institutional expression of the prevailing mood of the Jewish public towards the Arab minority, which is the mood that fashions the image of the parliament. Moreover, such a discussion makes it possible to examine the significant differences that exist between the nature of the activism of the legislative branch and that which characterizes the government's policy and its implementation by the different ministries.

In May 2009, the government supported the proposed legislation banning the marking of the "*Nakba*" which is the name given by the Palestinians and the Arab minority in Israel to the celebration of the establishment of the Jewish state. The reason is simple: if it is a celebration for Jews, for the Arab-Palestinian it is a disaster. The proposed legislation also included imprisonment for anyone who celebrated this occasion.[141] The public storm caused by this formulation of the law ultimately led to an amended formulation that did not include the punishment of imprisonment. During this same period, the then Minister of Education, Gideon Saᶜar, decided to ban teaching about the *Nakba* in schools, using the argument that learning about a subject that encouraged extremism and strengthened the processes of de-legitimization of the State of Israel was unacceptable.

Parallel to this, in the summer of 2009 the then Minister of Transport, Yisrael Katz, decided to remove the Arab names from the road signs throughout the country. The Minister's decision – whether to support or oppose it – was contrary to the judgment made by the Supreme Court of Justice, which states that the Arab language in Israel has the status of an official language. In March 2011, the legislation was passed into law in the Knesset.[142]

Another legislation proposal whose purpose was to discriminate between Jews and Arabs involved the civil service, and aimed to give preference to those who had served in the army or who had done national service for employment in the civil service. The proposal discriminates against members of the minority population who did not do such service and is contrary to the law of equal opportunity in the workplace. The government supported the proposal which passed the preliminary reading but the processing of the issue was frozen as a result of the intervention of the Government Legal Advisor.[143]

In January 2012, Member of the Knesset Danny Danon proposed a law that required an oath of allegiance to the state and its citizens as a condition for any one requesting documents from the state such as a driver's license or passport. The proposal has not yet been brought to the ministerial committee that deals with legislation, but its contents attest to the climate that is antagonistic to the Arab minority. Eventually, left wing parties within the Israeli Parliament did manage to cancel this law, but obviously did not succeed to change hostile feeling against Arabs in the public sphere. Another law in the same vein entitled "Israel is the national home of the Jewish People" is also worth analyzing since the proposal aims to redefine the identity of the state and establish arrangements which will subordinate the democratic character of Israel to its definition as a Jewish state.

8
Two Decades of Change: Not Only Security But Civil Integration Issues as Well

Two decades that began in 1990 and ended in 2010 have been marked by real changes in the relations between the Israeli establishment and the Arab minority group. This change has been expressed in the continual dialogue that has been carried on between the establishment and public figures in the Arab population, in the large allocation of resources compared to the past whose purpose was to reduce the gaps with the majority group, and in the series of legislative steps in the parliament which were aimed at finding a balance between the Jewish character of the state and its democratic character and to bring about increased integration of the minority group members into public life through utilizing the workforce, employment in government offices, and advancing the status of the Arab villages.

This change took place during two decades in which Israel had to deal with complex national challenges which included the absorption of more than a million immigrants, harsh rounds of violence with the Palestinians in Judea and Samaria and the Gaza Strip, regional threats (both direct and indirect), and an acute self-examination following the assassination of its Prime Minister. All of these also affected the Arab minority that, during these two decades, became more educated, prouder, more daring, and more prepared to ask for its share in the public domain (see more in Part Three).

This share moved between different ideas such as total integration and the solution of two states for two peoples (an idea supported by the Communist stream and other Arab political parties); separation and the establishment of an Islamic political framework (the Islamic Movement); or the conversion of the character of Israel into a state of all its citizens (Balad). This last idea succeeded in situating itself at the heart of the consensus of the political elite which adopted the vision as documented from the spirit of the ideas of Azmi Bishara.

Despite all this, and perhaps because of it, the Israeli government decided to change its policy, and side by side with its "security vision," it added a civilian vision intended to reduce the friction and tension between the Arab minority, whose nationality is different, and the majority group.

The Israeli leadership at the beginning of the 1990s internalized the need to reduce the gaps between the majority group and the minority group. The Palestinian Intifada in the territories, which were characterized by high levels of violence, accelerated this understanding that the Israeli interest was to prevent the copying of the violence from the territories into the Arab community in Israel. The adoption of a policy of equality and affirmative action was perceived by the Israeli establishment to be a means by which they could reduce the expressions of foment, protest, and violence in the Arab minority. Another reason for the change in policy, at least until the end of 1995, was rooted in the field of politics and can be divided into two. First, there was the political level, headed by the late Prime Minister Rabin who honored the IOU he had given on the eve of the general elections in June 1992 when he promised to work for a change in the status of the Arab citizens. Second, the political constellation that developed when the Rabin government had to rely upon a narrow coalition supported by Arab members of the Knesset outside the formal coalition, also contributed its part to payment of the price of the promises that had been made. In later years the first Netanyahu government, the Barak government, the Sharon government, and the Olmert government, also as the result of external developments such as the October 2000 events, continued to improve the situation of the Arab minority. The trouble was that it was the last decade of the 20th century, during which there was a clearly positive change in the Israeli policy towards the Arab minority, that contained the most violence by this minority – as will be analyzed in the next chapter.

PART THREE

Political and Social Changes within the Arab Minority

Part Three deals with the way the Arabs related to the state and its institutions and the patterns of their actions as reactions or as initiatives taken relative to the steps taken by the government.

As a general rule, any distinguishable group that is examined within the context of its society (immigrant group, national group, religious group and so on) will adopt a policy that moves between four alternatives: separatism, dialogue, protest, or violence. In practice, it appears that in the case of the Arab minority in Israel, there are situations in which this minority chooses to adopt more than one alternative at a time at particular points, its position depending on the given issues and whether those are national, civil or religious ones.

Thus, in the group of Arab citizens of Israel – which is made up of various sub-groups that are different in aspects of religion and ethnicity (Muslim, Christian, Druze and Circassian) and political ideologies (Islamists, Communists, Pan-Arabists) one can identify different attitudes ranging from separatism to dialogue since 2000. When it comes to perceptions, some of the above groups, like some citizens' social organizations, support alienation and disengagement while others call for commingling and more integration. The practical level examines patterns of actions vis-à-vis the establishment, and both levels will be analyzed in relation to attitudes of the minority and its patterns of activities in civil, national, and religious matters, with the emphasis placed upon critical events.

This chapter also will analyze the demographic aspects of the Arab minority during the last two decades and their influence upon the direction of the actions this population has taken vis-à-vis the regime. Following this, we will present the growth of the political frameworks in the Arab sector and the ideological platforms during these two decades, as well as the sociological, economic and cultural changes that the Arab population has undergone.

1
The Political Reality in Israel at the Beginning of the 1990s

At the beginning of the 1990s, the Arab public in Israel had to face a complex and problematic reality. It was seen as a security threat by the Jewish majority even though only a marginal few were involved in terrorist activities. The 1987 Intifada in Judea and Samaria and the Gaza Strip which led to expressions of identification with the

Palestinian people and to humanitarian aid campaigns by elements in the Arab sector only strengthened the sense of threat for the Jews and the government in Israel. In many civil areas significant gaps were visible between the standard of living of the Arab citizens and that of the Jews; added to this was the significant development of the diversion of large amounts of the resources available for national budgets to the absorption of the new immigrants, most of whom came from the former states of the Soviet Union.

The reality which has sharpened the ongoing dilemma of the Arab minority since 1948 has primarily surrounded the question of personal and group identity, which has led to disagreement between the two different approaches. One side has argued that the Arab minority was in the process of Israelization, whose main effect was integration into Israeli society and the striving for a country in which there would be co-existence and full equality for all its citizens. The other school has believed that the dominant trend is in fact towards Palestinization of the Arab minority which, in its way, means identifying with the struggle of the Palestinians in Judea and Samaria for independence.[1] There are researchers who believe that during the last decade of the 20th century the Arab minority, the public, and the leadership gave up on the struggle for equality and actually chose the idea of political separatism. This process accelerated after the events of October 2000, which deepened the crisis of trust and identification of the Arab citizens of the country.[2]

We would like to argue that the Arab population of Israel has developed a unique identity for itself which can be called Palestinian nationalism and Israeli citizenship and that this identity is directly influenced by the way the Israeli establishment relates to it. The change that took place in the government's policy from the beginning of the 1990s became a real factor during these years and made a contribution to this unique identity. For example, in 1994, a year in which the first buds of change began to be seen in the field, a survey was carried out in the Arab minority, which involved 768 interviewees. 94 percent of who answered that it was very important, or important, that full equality be achieved in the country in order to advance the status of Israeli Arabs.[3] At the same time most of the interviewees supported the idea of striving for administrative autonomy for the minority that would enable them, for example, to manage their own Arab education system and establish an Arab workers system that would be separate from the state institutions. The responses of the interviewees and the public statements made by public figures reflected the national-citizenship duality at the height of the process of forming a unique identity.

The definition of a personal and collective identity naturally influences the way the Arab minority acts towards the establishment. A thorough examination of history shows that it is difficult, if not impossible, to make generalizations and deterministically claim that the Arab minority was either moving towards separatism, integration, protest, or even violence. In fact, all of these options of activity were taken place by the Arab population during the last two decades, sometimes simultaneously as a result of several reasons.

First of all, the Arab minority is not a homogeneous group from a religious, class, and political point of view, and since this is the case, the sub-groups that make up this community in Israel have different agendas, interests, and ideologies as well as separate ways of behaving that might combine in certain scenarios.

Even the political maneuver of running as a joint list for the Knesset in March 2015 did not merge the different ideological political parties. Thus, for example, the Islamic Movement, which became a significant social and political force as early as the 1980s, has constantly striven to establish Islamic alternatives in Palestine.[4] Balad has been trying to instill the slogan "a state of all its citizens" into the heart of the Arab public and to implement this in practice,[5] and the communist branch has traditionally adhered to a solution to the Palestinian problem based upon the platform "two states for two nations". Despite the three different ideologies, the three groups have managed to come together from time to time around some common interest to decide upon a united action against the establishment, while in parallel, each of them has been working to realize other interests, even at the cost of doing damage to the other groups.

Secondly, during the 1990s, the political consciousness of the educated class matured and spread and developed into new political clusters, the most prominent of which was Balad. The multiplication of political groups, each of which had a different ideology, more than once caused damage to the effort to reach agreement about the steps that needed to be taken against the Israeli establishment. The Northern Branch of the Islamic Movement is mainly interested in separation from the state, but it finds itself against its will maintaining contacts with the government, sometimes in the context of municipal affairs and sometimes as a partner in a national leadership framework that is making demands of the various government ministries. In contrast, the Southern Branch of the Islamic Movement sees itself as part of the parliamentary system and public life in Israel. Balad has chosen a dual approach of integration into Israeli society and involvement in parliamentary life, together with separatist demands involving autonomy in education, communications, and culture.

The phenomenon of Balad and its media activity contributed to the dialogue which centered upon raising the bar for demands made of the state, including the widening of both individual and collective rights and the granting of national rights to the Arab minority.[6] These were not necessarily the same demands and the same directions taken in action as those of the Islamic Movement, but the growing public, academic, and media involvement with the subject ultimately led to the production of documents that described the vision of the Arab population in 2006. These documents, which to a great degree are the embodiment of the basic views of Balad, were accepted, albeit with a lack of enthusiasm, by all of the political factions, if only because being a member of the Arab minority did not allow anybody to come out vigorously against them. In essence the documents aim at the conversion of Israel into a state for all its citizens and a definition of it as an ethnocratic state that endows minority groups with partial equality.[7]

Thirdly, during the two previous decades there had been a sharp rise in the number of civil associations that were active in the Arab sector. Some of them, mainly those operating in the name of, and on behalf of, the Northern Branch of the Islamic Movement, wanted to establish alternative institutions to those of the state, while others in fact chose to go in the opposite direction and work towards integration. Prominent in this framework were the activities of law-centered associations such as *Adalah* (Justice in Arabic) and *Musawa* (Equality in Arabic). Other associations, in contrast, aimed at advancing the trend towards integration of the Arab minority into the Israeli public domain, and when they encountered different barriers, turned to the judicial authorities for assistance.

The activities of the Arab associations have also been a subject of research controversy. Some researchers believe that the activity is aimed at gaining civil equality; this is supported by the fact that many associations involved in justice, economics, land and development, education, and the media are trying to create relationships with groups from the Jewish majority based on cooperation in decision making.[8] Others claim that the goal should be to establish an ethnic citizenship society and to empower a community that has its own ethnic characteristics. The methods adopted by these associations have been taken from similar associations throughout the world, but the ultimate goal is not striving for equality but separatism based on ethnicity.[9] One way or another the establishment of the associations reflected the process of empowerment of the Arab society in Israel, including strengthening political consciousness about the status of the minority compared to the majority group, and aspiring to improve its status through the activity of the associations.

2
The Political Power Frameworks

The complex relationships of the political power factors in the Arab sector with the Israeli government led to patterns of action that, from time to time, included cooperation between these factors and sometimes operating separately in parallel channels. It is important to deal briefly with the centers of political power, their ideological platforms, and which centers acted as bases for decision making and activities that were directly aimed at the Israeli government.

(a) **The communists.** This faction in its various forms and under different names in history is the oldest political body in the Arab sector in Israel, and its roots go back to 1919 when a group of Jewish leftist activists established the Socialist Workers Party. Four years later, after they had overcome differences of opinion and divisions, the activists united the ranks and established the Palestinian Communist Party – in short the PCP.[10] Beginning in the middle of the 1920s, Arab members also joined the party and, in this way, it became a political body in which there were members belonging to different national and ethnic groups. This was in itself important throughout history, since it created ongoing tension between the unifying communist idea and the national-ethnic differences that divided the members. The communist body under its various names was the strongest and most significant power in the Arab sector at least until the mid-1970s, a decade in which new political bodies appeared. The success of the communists can be attributed to four factors: 1. a political-ideological platform that adjusted itself to the prevalent mood of the time but which basically propounded the idea of solving the Palestinian question through "two states for two peoples"; 2. efficient political organization; 3. socio-political changes that developed in the Arab sector; 4. a strategy that provided an answer to the changing needs of the population. From the 1980s on, the communist faction, in order to preserve its political power among the population, has found itself in an ongoing battle with the new political factors that arose in the Arab sector, and this battle has been fought on several levels. On the national level it is being fought with other political groups over the Arab vote in the national elections. In the internal sectorial arena there is a struggle going on over the character of the Higher Monitoring Committee.[11] On the local level there is the traditional rivalry over the elections for the municipalities and for the character of the Committee of the Heads of the Arab Local Authorities and the ways in which it fights the government in national and civil issues.

(b) **The Sons of the Village.** This movement was founded in 1972 by a group of young educated men from the free professions.[12] Their leader was the lawyer Muhammad Kaywan, a resident of Umm el-Fahem where the first nucleus of The Sons of the Village was established. The movement did not publish a well-formed platform and relied upon the power of local groups in Arab villages. In Tira (the "Sons of Tira"), Taibeh (*al-Nahda*-Resurrection), and Nazareth (*al-Ṣawt* – the Voice) was founded.[13] The ideological approach of The Sons of the Village was based upon the ideas of denial of the sovereignty of the State of Israel over the whole territory of Palestine, including inside the "Green Line," unequivocal identification with the PLO, and the acceptance of the platform of the Popular Front for the Liberation of Palestine. In the platform of the movement they state that the Jewish People have no rights to self-determination and that they should strive for the establishment of a secular democratic state in the whole territory of Palestine within the pre-1948 borders. The way to realizing this goal was defined as "an armed Palestinian revolution," and all parts of the Palestinian People would take part – in the territories and in the State of Israel. The leaders of the movement inscribed the slogan *"al-khalil mithl al-Jalil"* (Hebron equals to the Galilee) on their banner in order to emphasize the shared national identity of the populations on both sides of the Green Line. Raja Aghbariyyah, who was also one of the senior members of the movement, declared that The Sons of the Village identified itself with the ideological line of the Popular Front for the Liberation of Palestine and does not recognize either the existence of the State of Israel or the Knesset as the state's legislature".[14]

A clear expression of the rejectionist and separatist line of the movement was its non-participation in the elections to the Knesset. The separatist policy expressed itself in its efforts to establish independent institutions for the Arab minority, one of the prominent ones being the effort to establish an Arab university in Nazareth. The attempt failed because the movement failed to raise enough funds, but The Sons of the Village continued their activities anyway. They began with deepening Palestinian consciousness in the Arab sector, and from the beginning of 1988, they began to publish a weekly entitled *"al-Raya"* (The Banner), which they used to spread their view of the world. From this year onwards The Sons of the Village's political power began to diminish on the municipal level because of, among other things, the appearance of the Islamic Movement and the growing moderation of the PLO, which was signaling its desire for political negotiations with

Israel. From the 1990s until today, The Sons of the Village is usually seen as one of the power factors in the politics of the Arab sector in Israel, but its influence upon the agenda of the Arab minority is minimal and it has not succeeded in enlarging the circle of its supporters which is smaller, in any case, than other political frameworks in the sector.

(c) **Balad.** The National Democratic Alliance (Hereinafter: Balad) was founded in 1995 by a group of young Arab Christian and Muslim activists, the most prominent of whom were activists from the Alliance for Equality[15] which was led by Dr. Azmi Bishara, members of The Sons of the Village, ex-members of Hadash (the communists), ex-members of The Progressive List for Peace, activists from The Committee of Forty and other activists from other marginal groups from the Arab minority in Israel.[16]

The movement participated for the first time in the elections for the 14th Knesset in 1996 in a single list with the communist branch despite their basic ideological differences. Bishara was elected to the Knesset after he was placed fourth on the list. After the elections there was a rift between Hadash and Balad because of conflicts over finances as well, and Bishara decided to end the partnership with Hadash. Since then Balad has taken part in all the elections for the Knesset and has succeeded in gaining between two and three mandates.

Balad's platform defines the party as a "National Patriotic Palestinian" party that aspires to a just solution to the Palestinian question. The basic premise of Balad is that the Arabs in Israel are discriminated against by the government both as individuals and as a collective that is part of the Arab nation. The solution that the party suggests is to give prominence to the Arab nationalist component (and not, in fact, to the Palestinian component) and to present this as the basis for the unity and organization of the Arab public in Israel. It aspires to convert Israel into a "state for all its citizens," in contrast to what it defines as a state with a Jewish character. Balad demands recognition for the Arab population as a national minority and the granting of collective national rights and full equality in line with international law and the relevant UN resolutions and declarations, with emphasis upon the 1992 declarations about the rights of minorities. The party gives prominent place to the need to struggle for the fostering of Arab nationality, the organization of the Arab public as a collective that has equal rights to the Jewish public, the granting of cultural and institutional autonomy to the Arab citizens of Israel and the expression of solidarity with the Palestinian struggle. This identification has more than once, in the past, led to the expression of open support for terrorist organizations and, to put it mildly, condemnation

of the government's policies.[17] From Balad's point of view the definition of the Arab public as a national minority would, according to UN
resolutions, grant it the right to autonomy in all areas of life that differ-
entiate it from the rest of the citizens in the country in which it lives.
In the area of education, the party wants to establish an Arab university, to independently manage Arab schools, to decide upon curricula,
and to appoint teachers. In the area of religion the party demands the
right to appoint Qaḍi's and administer the sacred sites. In the area of
communications Balad demands the right to open, independent radio
and television stations and to do similar things in other civil areas such
as health and welfare. This was also expressed in the political platform
that the party composed in preparation for the elections to the
Seventeenth Knesset which contained the following: "The Arab
minority has the right to actively participate in the decision-making
process about things that affect it; the government will not make any
decisions that have far-reaching consequences for the lives of the Arabs
without the active participation (in the decision-making process) of the
Arabs as a nation. The Arab minority has the right to reject any decision that might be made without its active participation or that is
contrary to its interests and legitimate rights".[18]

During the first years of its existence Balad focused its ongoing
activities around a series of subjects that directly touched upon the
Arab minority in general and especially upon the effort to cancel the
Jewish character of the State of Israel. In a brochure published by the
party in November 1999 they wrote: "All the while that Israel
continues to be a state for the Jews, instead of being a state for its residents, and the national Palestinian minority in it is not receiving its
rights as individuals and as a collective, then Israelization will be no
more than a fictive option"[19]. In a proposed law that Balad presented
to the Knesset in October 1999, it demanded the cancellation of all
the easements and privileges given to Zionist institutions, such as the
Jewish Agency and the Jewish National Fund. At the same time the
leaders of the party expressed public opposition to any attempt to integrate Arab minority members into the various state institutions.[20]
Together with the calls to change the character of the state, the heads
of Balad acted to put a series of separatist initiatives into practice. The
party began to publish a weekly called *Faṣl al-Maqal* (The Determined
Words) which, during the second half of the 1990s, had a circulation
of 20,000 copies and provided an ideological forum for the party like
its internet site. Balad established an association called "The Arab
Culture Association" which ran summer camps and excursions to
abandoned villages for youths. In all these events, emphasis was placed
upon the fostering and strengthening of Palestinian and Arab nation-

alism. Another of Balad's associations, "*Baladna*," (Our Country) had a membership made up of young Arabs, youths and students; its task was to strengthen Arab and Palestinian nationalism in the younger generation through, among other things, the publication of a monthly magazine, the organization of exhibitions connected with the Palestinian struggle, and holding processions to collect donations for Palestinians in the territories.

Parallel to deepening the connection to the land, the leaders of Balad radicalized their public message against the state and the government by advocating "support for security prisoners, calls for a physical struggle against the appropriation of land and the active participation of party members in this struggle, support for terrorist organizations in the arena of the Middle East (for example, Hizbullah) and the condemnation of Judaism and Zionism".[21] Based upon this, the Israeli establishment tried to have the candidacy of Balad for the elections to the Sixteenth Knesset in 2003 cancelled, but the Supreme Court of Justice, by a vote of seven to four, rejected the request. In March 2007, the defense forces published material which showed that during the Second Lebanese War (summer 2006) the leader of the party, Member of the Knesset Bishara, had passed on information to Hizbullah.[22] In response to the publication, Bishara fled the country; since then Balad has continued to act to advance its ideological platform while staying legitimately within the limits of the law.

(d) **The Islamic Movement.** The growth of the Islamic Movement among the Arab citizens of Israel is connected to the Islamic wave that gained force in the Middle East during the 1970s and which was reflected in the revolution that took place in Iran in 1979. During these years, the phenomenon of a return to religion and the adoption of the motto "Islam is the Solution" became widespread among the Arab citizens of Israel, especially among the young people. The driving spirit behind this activity was Sheikh ʿAbdallah Nimr Darwish (1948–2017) from Kafr Qasem; he and others – the most prominent among them being Sheikh Raʿid Salah from Umm el-Fahem and Sheikh Kamal Khatib from Kafr Kana – absorbed their Islamic values during their period of study at the Islamic College in Hebron. In 1979, Darwish gathered together dozens of born-again Muslims in underground groupings which were called "*Usrat al-Jihad*" (the Jihad family).[23] Its members collected weapons, burned fields, and in Umm el-Fahem, murdered an Arab that they suspected was a collaborator with the authorities.

The heads of this group were captured in 1981 and imprisoned for various lengths of time. This was the first concrete expression of their involvement in violent activities against the state. After their release from prison in 1983 and 1984, the members of the group changed their modus operandi that was aimed at implementing their ideology. Sheikh Darwish came to the conclusion that the way of Jihad would not lead to the hoped for results, and declared that the movement would now operate within the law and express itself in a number of areas.[24] The first of these was the strengthening of the *"da'wah"* system, which meant educational preaching of the values of Islam. This activity was carried out during these years especially among the younger generation, within the framework of a campaign to capture and train hearts, by establishing a system of country-wide institutions that provided health and welfare services, educational institutions, and charity in the form of meal provision and campaigns to collect donations for the needy.

Starting at the beginning of 1983, the leaders of the Islamic Movement gave themselves an additional goal to achieve – control of the local municipal authorities. In the elections that took place that year, the movement for the first time ran its own list and achieved gains in two municipalities. In the next round of elections in 1989, the movement gained control of six authorities, the most prominent being Umm el-Fahem, where it is in control almost three decades. Entering the municipal election campaign had two advantages – creating direct contacts for the movement's senior members with the different government ministers, and allocating government budgets for the public through the local authorities, which were controlled by the movement. This served as a boost to the establishment of the movement's political power among the Arab citizens of Israel during these years, without having to recognize the central Jewish sovereignty. During this period, and even more so since the outbreak of the Intifada in 1987, the connection between the Islamic Movement and the Islamic branch in the West Bank and the Gaza Strip strengthened.

In 1992, the leaders of the movement issued instructions to its supporters to vote in the elections to the Knesset, but avoided recommending any particular list to vote for. Four years later, close to the general elections of 1996, an internal dispute appeared in the movement over principles related to whether or not to compose a list that would run in the elections. This dispute was a turning point in the history of the development of the movement. Sheikh Darwish decided to support forming a list of candidates; this paved the way to a split in the ranks of the movement and the creation of two branches – one led by himself, known as the southern branch because of its location in his domain in Kafr Qasem, and the second, headed by Sheikh Salah, known as the northern branch because of its location in Umm el-Fahem.

The ideology of the Islamic Movement is identical to the central one of the "Muslim Brotherhood" movement, and its ultimate and strategic goal is to establish a theocratic Islamic state in Palestine even if "its leaders avoid disclosing this as their goal in public and in the territory of the State of Israel".[25] There are a number of basic principles that make up the ideology of the Islamic Movement. The movement sees Islam as a world embracing entity whose rulings govern all areas of life. It is interested in basing its society upon the model of the ancient Islamic community (*Salafiyyah*) and to establish state institutions based upon Islamic law (Sharia). The ideology also supports the unification of all the Islamic peoples into one camp which will create the Islamic nation. Because of this point of view, it opposes the rule or hegemony of western powers which is called *Ṣalibiyya*, taken from the word "*Ṣalib*" (cross) which is considered to be a Christian symbol. In the concrete context of life in Israel the movement's ideology negates Zionism and the State of Israel and sees the state as a temporary phenomenon. In order to implement these principles, the movement aims to uproot western cultural influences and to extinguish secular phenomena. Because of this, it aspires to spread the ideas of Islam using the system of sermonizing and propaganda. In some of the cases where its values have clashed with those of the policies of the authorities, legitimization has been given by the leaders of the movement to the use of violence in order to achieve the movement's goals.[26] Issam Abu Raya, a member of the Arab minority in Israel, has claimed: "This movement aspires to creating a state that operates according to the laws of Sharia, instead of the existing regimes. The Muslim Brotherhood sees the State of Israel as a foreign body that has been "implanted" in the region by the West in order to fight the Muslims and the Arabs. Thus, according to the movement, the State of Israel has no right to exist and, moreover, the liberation of Palestinian lands and the elimination of the State of Israel are, in its eyes, necessary conditions for the struggle against the social, economic and political illnesses the Arab and Muslim world are suffering from".[27]

Since the 1980s, the Islamic Movement has established a network of services that are an alternative to the government network in its efforts to found an autarchic economy. Through the use of associations, and later, companies, they established kindergartens, schools, clinics, and welfare services that are provided at a symbolic cost. The movement also built many mosques that are used as meeting places for religious instruction in which their ideology is instilled into new adherents, sports clubs, and even an Islamic football league. Starting in 1989, the movement began publishing a weekly named *Ṣawt al-*

Haqq wa-al-Hurriyyah (Voice of justice and freedom) and after the split that took place in its ranks in 1996, the weekly became the clarion of the northern branch, while the southern branch of the Islamic Movement had its own weekly called *al-Mithak* (the Charter).

(e) **The Committee of the Heads of Local Authorities.** The first signs of the beginnings of the Committee of the Heads of Local Authorities had already appeared in 1972 when a group of heads of Arab local councils got together to present demands to the Center for Local Government.[28] The founding meeting at which the establishment of the committee was officially announced was in 1974, when the committee was established as a national body whose aim was to advance municipal issues in the Arab sector. During the first years of its activity, the committee tried to advance its goals through dialogue with the government; the members who were active in it prepared working papers in which they itemized their demands – which were the cessation of land appropriation, cancellation of the charges against the people involved in the Land Day incidents of 1976, and the recognition of the Arab minority as a national minority.[29] While at the beginning the committee was established in order to advance civil and municipal issues, more than once the heads of the committee also soon found themselves, as initiators, becoming involved in protest activities amid complaints about civil discrimination or because of their identification with the national demands of the Palestinians. The Committee of the Arab Local Authorities is still active and is part of the general system of the Center for Local Government in Israel. Its leaders maintain ongoing working relations with the different government ministries, and their presence in the public domain has, in practice, served as a negotiating agency between the government and the Arab public. Its areas of activities focus upon efforts to improve the quality of life of the Arab citizens in the State of Israel, but they are not shy about being involved in activities of a nationalist character in the Palestinian context. For its part, the government recognizes the committee as part of the fabric of local government and makes sure that the discussions are about civil and municipal matters and do not spill over into issues connected with nationalist issues.

(f) **The Higher Monitoring Committee.** In the second half of 1982, Arab members of the Knesset from the Labor Party and the communist Party – which during this time changed its name to the Democratic Front for Equality and Peace (Hadash in Hebrew) – initiated the idea of creating a new body that would amalgamate their activities and the activities of the Committee of the Heads of Local Authorities. The immediate catalyst for this was the desire to establish a body that would coordinate the protest activities against Israel in the context of what was called "The War of Annihilation in Lebanon" especially after the Şabra and Shatila events (September 18, 1982).[30] This new body very quickly became an umbrella organization under which representatives of political movements in the Arab sector came together – that is, the highest leadership structure of the Arab minority.

The Higher Monitoring Committee continually deals with improvement of the financial situation of the local authorities in the Arab sector, opposes broadening the area of jurisdiction of the Jewish Misgav local council in the Galilee, and fights to broaden the area of jurisdiction of the Arab villages. The committee has always made sure that its voice is heard protesting the government's policies when, in their view, they were damaging to the Palestinians or the Arab nation. During the 1980s and 1990s, the committee also approached international bodies in order to get assistance for their activities in civil and social areas such as health.[31]

Even today the Higher Monitoring Committee acts as the central leadership body of the Arab minority and convenes as needed, determining the agenda of the protest activities of the sector. At first the head was Ibrahim Nimr Hussein, a man who traditionally tried to carry on an ongoing dialogue with the Israeli government and preferred to avoid violent activity. He was followed by Muhammad Zidan who was seen to be a passive figure who could be influenced; he was appointed to this position from 1999 till 2001 and again in 2013. From 2001 to 2009, Shawki Khatib, who also believed in dialogue with the government, filled the position. Zidan was elected again as head of the committee in 2009 and he was replaced in 2015 by Muhammad Baraka, a veteran activist within the communist party. At every crossroads where the question of the possible use of violence was involved, the character of the chairman of the committee had a crucial influence over the leadership institutions of the minority.

3
Four Possible Choices that can be Made by Protest Groups

The theoretical literature that deal with national minorities and, in fact, with all protest movements, has tried to identify the possible directions that are available for such groups when they are in a confrontation with government policies that they oppose. We suggest that there are four different possibilities that the minority group can choose from to act:

(1) **Separatism.** The meaning of this step is the relinquishment of connection with the government, including receiving resources and services, and the possibility of taking part in the process of decision-making, which includes those that affect the separated group directly.[32] Such a choice encourages the establishment of an autarchic economy that will satisfy all the needs of the minority, the creation of independent political, legal, social, economic, and security institutions (such as a local police force) that will act as alternatives to those supplied to the population by the government.

(2) **Dialogue.** This is, of course, the direct opposite of separatism, and the choice of dialogue means carrying out regular discussions with the various government ministries about civil issues that are of concern to the population – such as education, health, welfare, infrastructure, and municipal administration. These are likely to be issues that touch upon the freedom of religious ritual, including not only the right to carry out religious laws but also the building of houses of prayer, performing religious marriages and divorces, and the appointment of religious people to positions in the houses of prayer. Dialogue can also take place between the minority and the government about national issues as well, in two situations: one, when the minority group has irredentist demands, and two, when the national demands are raised by a third party that has an ethnic-national link to the minority group.

(3) **Protest.** This is carried out by social movements that maintain both formal and informal relations with the government, in order to change the social-political agendas that the latter dictates. Democratic regimes allow widespread expressions of protest in comparison with totalitarian regimes, and in any case, we are talking about activities that have to be carried out within the framework of the laws of the country.

The social protest movements have a very wide range of possible patterns of activity available that they can adopt in order to realize their demands of the government. They can, for example, act with moderation by collecting signatures for petitions, publish notices in the press, hold protest meetings in the field, declare strikes, and apply political pressure through lobbyists in the governmental system.

No matter what approach they take, the protest movements need to possess several components without which they will find it difficult to achieve practical results for their plans. First of all they need material, moral, social-organizational, human, and cultural resources.[33] This mainly means having activists that can advance the desired activities, money to finance the activities, and time and space in which they can publicize their goals. Apart from resources, the protest movements need a collective identity which should preferably be one that is broad enough to allow them to mobilize people towards the social political idea that they are trying to put forward.[34] The identity itself should be a combination of emotional, ethical, and cognitive connections that the individual has with the community, group, institution, or custom.[35] These are the views concerning the common status that can be imagined or real, and in order to produce the same identification with the social-political idea the group has to define itself as a group and its members "have to develop a shared outlook about the social environment, develop common goals and share a common idea about the possibilities of working within its limitations".[36] This same community needs to satisfy two main criteria: the existence of a mutual network of relations between its members and a commitment that relies upon shared values and norms. A group identity does not only sprout from mutual relations within some specific movement, but also as the result of alliances, or following the activities of those who oppose the movement, or sometimes also after observation by factors standing on the sidelines of the activities, for example, the media. The step that follows the development of a collective identity is one in which collective behavior also crystallizes.

Assuming that the social movement possesses the necessary resources for its activities and has also managed to mobilize wide enough support for the idea it is advancing, it needs a third component that is called the exploitation of a political opportunity. The term "political opportunity" refers to a political system which produces opportunities for the movement to act collectively through the presentation of challenges to the government. This means the ability to put its programs into action in different ways, among them the publicizing of its ideas, distributing them through the media, the introduction of a marketing program, and the organization of a public gathering that supports the idea and acts as a forum for protest against the ruling government.

(4) **Violence.** The choice of using violence is found at the extremity of the range of possibilities and includes the use of a variety of activities that are not acceptable from two points of view – one being its lawfulness and the other being its acceptability as a norm in a given society. The definition of the term violence is clearly different from one society to another, as is the way this phenomenon is related to in different kinds of regimes. Violence under one regime, for example in the form of holding a demonstration in Iran or Syria, is not considered to be violence in a democratic regime that allows protest. The use of violence may be the result of a number of factors such as subversion of the political order and exploitation of the opportunity, acting on a decision that has been brewing over a long period of time, despair over

the ability to influence the powers that be in other ways, and the choice of a leadership through the use of violence.[37]

All of the above alternatives have been options for actions for the Israeli Arabs since 1948, when they were transformed into a minority group in the population. From a historical point of view, the relationship between them and the Israeli establishment has moved among four alternatives of which, more than once, in certain situations, several have been used in parallel – such as protest and dialogue, dialogue, protest and violence and separatism and protest. Over recent decades significant events in the internal Israeli arena, the Palestinian arena, and the regional arena have been recorded which have brought the relationship between the Arab minority and the Israeli authorities to the boiling point; some such events have ended with serious violence and each has had an effect upon the relationship between the parties up until today.

4
The 1990 Temple Mount Events

In October 1990, a serious event was recorded on the Temple Mount when Muslim worshippers clashed with security forces. The Temple Mount policemen opened fire upon the worshippers and this resulted in twenty one of the worshippers (twenty Palestinians and one Israeli Arab) being killed. The event took place at the height of the Palestinian Intifada in the territories on the Temple Mount, which is considered to be a holy site for the Muslims. The Arabs in Israel, including Muslims and Christians who declare themselves to be non-religious, attest to its holiness.[38]

The violent events were a surprise to the leadership bodies of the Arab minority in Israel and, when they learned about the magnitude of the event, Ibrahim Nimr Hussein, the chairman of the Higher Monitoring Committee, convened an emergency meeting of the committee in order to decide upon what steps to take in response. During the meeting he declared that those who were killed were not dead people but casualties that had sacrificed themselves for the holiest Muslim site after having been attacked by Jewish extremists. Arab Member of the Knesset ʿAbd al-Wahab Darwasha placed the responsibility for the events on the government of Israel and called the event a crime that had been perpetrated under the protection of government decisions. Sheikh Salah, one of the leaders of the Islamic Movement, argued that the Jews had no right to the Temple Mount and that the whole site was a Muslim sacred compound. Like Darawsha, Salah accused the Israeli government of responsibility for the deaths of the worshippers and rejected the idea of closing the Temple Mount for a number of months and to only open it after a while for Jewish and Muslim worshippers.[39] He proposed several steps of protest be taken, including the declaration of a general strike, the devotion of a week's study in schools to the subject of the importance of the *al-Aqṣa* Mosque, the erection of a monument in memory of those killed, the flying of mourning banners, and dispatching delegations to visit the families of the fallen to offer condolence.

The Monitoring Committee adopted a number of decisions that included the declaration of a general strike in the Arab sector, and the days of strike were declared days of mourning. The committee placed full responsibility for the event and its consequences upon Israel and, taking the long view, they determined that the "Day of Slaughter", as they called it in the announcement, would henceforth be called "Jerusalem Day" and would include visits made to the families of those killed. The Arab minority was called upon to mobilize itself for a campaign to donate blood for those wounded in the incident and demands were made of the Israeli government to release all those who had been arrested during the events. The religious factor was also not left out of the announcement, which warned Israel against doing harm to the sites that were holy to Islam and Christianity in Jerusalem.[40] An analysis of the decisions made shows that the leadership of the Arab sector chose a response that combined indirect dialogue with the establishment through the publication of public notices about the event and quiet protest that included independent activity to commemorate those killed. The option of resorting to violence was not considered in this case mainly because Nimr Hussein, whose leadership at the time was accepted by all the political forces, had been in favor of the traditional soft response.

During the days that followed the events the directives issued by the Higher Monitoring Committee were translated into activities in the Arab villages. Quiet mourning processions took place in a large number of villages in the Arab sector in Israel while protest meetings that took place in Nazareth and Taibeh turned into local clashes between masked youth and forces from the Israeli border police.[41] The organizers of the demonstrations in Nazareth called upon the police not to enter the city and undertook to calm things down, which was a clear expression of their desire to prevent violent confrontations.[42] A large demonstration also took place in Umm el-Fahem, in which the demonstrators carried banners that praised those who had fallen in the Intifada and promised to complete their work. The Northern Branch of the Islamic Movement, which at the time was in control of the municipality, played a special role in the demonstration. The mayor Sheikh Salah, who was carrying out the decisions made by the Higher Monitoring Committee, used his position to go beyond the approach of restraint, including in his speech inflammatory statements that included the blessing of every martyr "who washed the Temple Mount enclosure and the *al-Aqṣa* Mosque with his blood".[43]

The magazine of "the Islamic Movement" called the security forces that were present at the event on the Temple Mount "Arab Killers"[44] and, although in every event that the Islamic Movement held to commemorate those killed there was no direct call to act violently, the tone and content of things said about the responsibility of the government for the deaths of the Palestinians on the Temple Mount represented a step up by the leadership of the Arab sector in terms of the daring they showed in challenging the Israeli government. When viewed historically, one can see these expressions as verbal violence, which, like the declarations made before the Land Day events in 1976, contributed to the public climate of encouraging readiness to protest and act violently over issues of great importance to the Arab sector, such as the mosques on the Temple Mount or the deaths of Israeli Arabs. This, for the Arab minority, was also the budding of the violence based on religion (Islamic) that was led by the Islamic Movement – although not only by them – in the events of October 2000.

5
The Gulf War, 1990–1991

The second event that took place during the period of the Intifada was the crisis in the Persian Gulf that began in August 1990 with Iraq's invasion of Kuwait. The ethnic identity shared by the Arab minority and the peoples of Iraq and Kuwait and their belonging to the Arab nation created the potential for violent behavior from the Arab minority in Israel, even though Israel was a passive observer almost uninvolved in the war. An analysis of the way the Arab minority acted during the war will be made by dividing the period into two parts: the first from the beginning of the crisis in August 1990 up till the beginning of the missile attack on Israel in the middle of January 1991, and the second from this time till the end of the war. The reason for this is the change in position taken by the Arab minority and its leadership towards the war from the moment that Israel, through no fault of its own, became actively involved because of the missile attack launched by Iraq.

With the publication of reports about the Iraqi invasion of Kuwait, the events in the Gulf became the talk of the day for the Arab minority, and the interest shown in this subject was great. To the wider Arab public Saddam Hussein was seen as a national Arab hero because of the courage he showed in standing up to America – but among the Arab leadership the Gulf crisis raised serious differences of opinion among the different political power factions. The Progressive List of for Peace (PLP), the party of Muhammad Mi‘ari, supported the Iraqi invasion of Kuwait and called upon the Arab world to support Saddam Hussein.[45] The "Sons of the Village" movement also supported the of Iraq and a public declaration that they issued called upon the Iraqis not to withdraw from Kuwait and not to surrender to American dictates. These factors within the Arab minority in Israel called the Arab nations to act against the pro-American regimes in their countries, and similar appeals to rise up against Arab rulers also appeared in proclamations and articles in party newspapers – in fact, these were the only expressions of any call to act violently following the Gulf crisis.

The support of the two movements for Iraq was expressed in a number of poorly attended demonstrations, in one of which, in Nazareth, the American flag was set on fire by demonstrators. The police arrested two of the demonstrators and made it clear to them that they would not tolerate any repetition of the incident.[46] In another incident the police prevented activists from the PLP from demonstrating and warned them that if the demonstration did go ahead all of the participants would be arrested. In contrast, Rakah (the communist party) condemned the military invasion of Kuwait by Iraq and viewed it as a catastrophe for both peoples. It warned that Israel and the USA would likely exploit the tension in the gulf to inflame the whole region and stated that the way to solve crises was through diplomatic negotiations.[47] Rakah also expressed criticism of the USSR because of its siding with the USA, which led the campaign against Iraq.

The Islamic Movement also came out against Iraq arguing that violence between two Arab and Muslim nations only served the enemies of Islam. Khaled Mahaneh, one of the leaders of the movement and the editor of its newspaper, wrote that the admiration of Saddam Hussein by the Arab street was not acceptable,[48] and the leader of the movement, Sheikh Darwish, called upon the Muslims to unite in response to the crisis.[49] The two movements also held modest demonstrations, with Rakah organizing a demonstration in Wadi Nisnas in Haifa on August 24, 1990, in which identification with the Iraqi nation was expressed, and another one in Tel Aviv opposite the offices of the Ministry of Defense on August 27 where anti-American placards were held up. The Islamic Movement held a demonstration of identification with the suffering of the Iraqi people in the Bedouin town of Rahat on August 16.

Despite the contrasting positions adopted by the political power groups in the Arab sector, there were a number of common denominators to all of them. First of all, most of the activity was directed at each political body by writing articles in its organ; this was a clear sign of verbal protest side by side with the modest protest that took place in the field. Secondly, at the beginning the blame was directed at the USA, and only later at Israel. Thirdly, in general the factions expressed displeasure with Arab rulers who chose to stand by the USA. Fourthly, in general the factions suspected that Israel was likely to exploit the situation in the gulf in order to advance its goals at the expense of the Palestinians. In this situation of disagreement between the political bodies about the Gulf War together with concerns about the Israeli reaction, the chances of carrying out combined protest activities lessened; this was even truer for the use of widespread violence.

The behavior of the Arab leadership groups changed a little in the middle of January 1991 after the Iraqi missile attacks upon Israel. Nimr Hussein argued that the falling of missiles in Israeli territory showed that there were no safe borders and that all the parties involved in the conflict should end it peacefully. He also praised families from the Arab minority in Israel that were ready to host Jewish families from the center of the country seeking shelter from the missiles, and sent messages of identification to the mayors of Haifa and Tel Aviv.[50] In this way, Nimr Hussein once again made it clear that he opposed violent action and preferred to act towards bringing different groups of people in the population together through dialogue. The Committee of the Heads of Arab Local Authorities adopted his position and expressed sorrow about the victims and destruction that the missiles had caused to Israeli citizens, among whom were also Arabs.[51]

The Communist branch placed the blame for the war on the USA and accused Israel of providing support for the Americans, but even so Rakah condemned the firing of missiles at Israel by Iraq after some citizens were hurt, and Salem Jubran, the editor of *al-Ittihad* newspaper, published an article in which he expressed sorrow over the suffering experienced by Tel Aviv residents as a result of the missile attack on the city of Tel Aviv.[52] The Islamic Movement, whose basic position was against the Iraqi invasion of Kuwait, changed the way it related to the situation in the gulf following the war that took place between the coalition countries and Iraq. The movement marked the fight against the crusaders, leading by the USA, and an editorial printed in their newspaper called upon the Arab and Muslim world to rise up against infidels.[53]

Throughout the whole period of the war, the patterns of activity of the Arab political factions were ultimately characterized by verbal protests accompanied by modest protest demonstrations in a number of central cities. Some of the events did have the nature of protest and others wanted to express identification with the people of Iraq because of their shared ethnic identity. When examined historically, the Persian Gulf War did not engender violent protest, despite potential for it, by the Arab minority for mainly two reasons: Israel was not perceived as being directly responsible for the escalation in the gulf, and a real polarity of views developed within the Arab sector regarding who was to blame for the outbreak of war.

6
The Opening of the Western Wall Tunnel

In September 1996, the Israeli government gave the green light for opening the Western Wall tunnel in the Old City. The decision to open the tunnel, which was close to the Temple Mount, aroused tension in the Arab sector and the potential for a violent reaction. The main headline of the al-*Ittihad,* the day after the opening of the tunnel, dealt with the Palestinian reaction to the Israeli move, and reported that the Palestinian Authority was calling for a general strike and protest demonstrations.[54]

Not until September 26, two days after the opening of the tunnel, did the Monitoring Committee convene to discuss how the Arab public should react to the Israeli move and to the clashes that were taking place in the territories between the Palestinian security forces and the IDF soldiers. The character of the discussion took on a tone of verbal protest and pointed an accusative finger at the Israeli government, based on a scenario in which the opening of the tunnel would do harm to the mosques on the Temple Mount. Nimr Hussein condemned the Israeli activity and viewed it as an attack on the al-*Aqṣa* Mosque, while Hashem Mahamid, the Communist Party representative, warned that Israel wanted to "Judaize" Jerusalem, and he believed that the *al-Aqṣa* Mosque was in real danger. Sheikh Salah warned that under the Temple Mount there were many more tunnels that had not yet been exposed and went on to warn against the collapse of the *al-Aqṣa* Mosque. Ramez Jiraisi, the Christian mayor of Nazareth, called upon Jewish and Arab power factors to unite in order to bring down the Netanyahu government. Azmi Bishara said that the Arab public was at a crossroads because the Israeli government was interested in burying the peace process. He suggested preparing an Arab educational program about the city of Jerusalem which would be taught in schools instead of the "Zionist curricula" that ignored the rights of the Palestinian people in Jerusalem. In all of this not one of the participants issued a call to act violently as a reaction to the opening of the tunnel. On the other hand not one of those present in the discussion suggested entering into a discussion with the Israeli establishment in order to bring about the closing of the tunnel or to at least make sure that opening the tunnel would not actively threaten the safety of the mosques on the Temple Mount.

Ultimately the committee decided to hold a general strike on December 27, 1996 and to declare this day "Jerusalem Day." The Arab public was called upon to hold protest processions on this day in which banners with slogans would be held up, and to organize visits to the *al-Aqṣa* Mosque and the Church of the Holy Sepulcher. The Arab public was also called upon to donate blood for the Palestinians who had been wounded in the territories, and the committee issued a statement calling upon the forces for peace in the Jewish public to join them in their protest activities and to oppose the Israeli government's policy that they maintained was responsible, together with the Jerusalem Municipality, for the deterioration of the situation. A demand was made of the government to cease all diggings that were being carried out under the foundations of the *al-Aqṣa* Mosque;[55] this announcement was, in fact, an expression of indirect dialogue with the government.

The expressions of protest that took place were in line with the spirit of the directives of the Higher Monitoring Committee, and the general strike and demonstrations were carried out in the Arab sector without exceptions. Demonstrations were held in a large number of Arab towns and villages (Kafr Manda, Tamra, Kabul, Shaᶜb, ᶜIlabun, Taibeh, Shfarᶜam, Umm el-Fahem, Acre, Rameh, Majd al-Kurum, Nazareth, Jaffa, Haifa, and in many other places). Banners with slogans condemning what they called the "Israeli slaughter" were waved about in all the demonstrations. At the demonstration in Nazareth Member of the Knesset Bishara declared: "What is happening in the territories happened in South Africa and this is something that was premeditated. The government of Israel thinks that it can spend four years in government making no diplomatic progress and we are standing here united against this government." During the demonstration in Nazareth a small number of cases of disorderly behavior were recorded when some participants blocked the main highway, burned tires, and shattered the glass windows of some shops. Forces from the police and border police dispersed the rioters and arrested 21 people. In Tel Aviv, activists from the Communist Party along with some Jews, demonstrated against the steps taken by the government and called for a Jewish–Arab struggle to bring down the government.[56]

7
The Al-Roha Lands Affair

The fourth incident took place in 1998 and involved the al-Roha Lands west of the city Umm el-Fahem. The affair had already begun in January 1997 when a group of Arab residents of the city and the villages of Mu'awiya and Muşmuş established a popular committee to work to foil the government's intention to turn the lands of al-Roha into an IDF training area. The members of the committee decided to prepare the land for planting and to demand that the land in the area be attached to the jurisdiction of the city of Umm el-Fahem.

After a year and a half, at the end of May 1998, and after more than a year of the subject not being responded to, the battle over the issue began again. Sheikh Salah called upon the residents of his city to resist the plan aimed at appropriating the land. In June, the committee renewed its activities, after the Ministry of Defense announced its intention to declare the area a closed military zone. One of the immediate consequences of this intention was the government's demand that the Arabs would have to obtain permits in order to enter the closed military zone in which the owners of the land were growing different crops. The members of the committee decided to establish a fund to raise money to continue their struggle, and to ask for the emergency convening of the Higher Monitoring Committee to discuss the matter as well. They also decided to continue using the channels of negotiation with the government and asked to meet the Prime Minister, the president of the country, and the Minister of Defense.

About two months later, in August, the committee, encouraged by the Umm el-Fahem municipality, changed its name to the "Committee for the Defense of the al-Roha Lands." The committee called upon the owners of the land to ignore the army order that banned entry into the area, to erect a tent of protest there, to carry out a protest demon-stration at the entrance to Umm el-Fahem every day, to demonstrate outside the Ministry of Defense, and to devote the sermons in the mosques to the subject.[57]

On September 4, 1998, about three weeks before the implementa-tion of the army order, the Friday prayers involving 3,000 participants took place on the al-Roha Lands. Sheikh Salah delivered the central sermon and called upon the public to keep hold of the land "no matter what sacrifices have to be made."[58] He also called upon those striking not to have any fears about the threats being made to them by different government agencies. The sheikh himself and Member of the Knesset ʿAbd al-Malek Dahamshah slept in the protest tent which was a concrete expression of the call to hold onto the land. Three days later, the Higher Monitoring Committee convened in the protest tent; its meeting there was devoted to the issue of the lands. It decided to pave an approach road that would make it easier for the demonstrators to get to the area in dispute. Suleiman Aghbariyyah, one of the leaders of the northern branch of the Islamic Movement said during the meeting that if the government destroyed the protest tent they should erect a new tent and after that another one and so on. He encouraged those present not to hesitate about moving the protest demonstration to the Wadi ʿAra highway in order to block it.[59]

This was the first specific call by a public personage to choose the use of violent activity in order to prevent the appropriation of land. This was also the first time Ibrahim Nimr Hussein, the chairman of the Higher Monitoring Committee, did not add his weight to preventing the call for violent action and, in addition, he complained that the government was restricting any steps that might be taken by the Arab minority and was limiting the area of jurisdiction of the Arab local municipalities. He announced that he would demand that the government attach the lands to the area of jurisdiction of Umm el-Fahem. For its part the government did not remain apathetic to these steps and the police boosted their forces deployed in the place and threatened to arrest those present in the protest tent since this was a closed military zone.

On the day that the appropriation was to be implemented, September 27, 1998, serious clashes took place between the Arab demonstrators and the security forces in the disputed area. These events continued for four days during which Sheikh Salah was observed supporting the disturbances "as he egged on those disturbing the public order with excited exclamations".[60] The police arrested eighteen demonstrators on suspicion of setting fire to forests and throwing Molotov Cocktails at policemen. Charges were brought against seven of them after a brief period of time.[61] Even after the events subsided Sheikh Salah continued to justify the disturbances and, in a newspaper interview, he stressed that "the events were a fortifying experience for the participants and were a first attempt that only added determination and strength to continue to demand our just rights".[62]

The contacts between the government ministries and the relevant factors in the Arab sector continued for months after the violent events in an effort to solve the dispute over the al-Roha Lands but these contacts were unsuccessful since all the compromise suggestions presented by the government to the Arab party were rejected including the possibility of receiving alternate lands in exchange for those designated for appropriation.

Parallel to the discussions over the issue, the Arab leadership factors examined additional steps that could be taken in response among which were appeals to international courts and the mobilization of popular support for their struggle. The northern branch of the Islamic Movement continued to adhere to a defiant approach which was expressed by Sheikh Hashem ʿAbd al-Rahman, the spokesman of the northern branch. He warned that the feeling among the Arabs regarding the al-Roha Lands was "like that of a volcano that would inevitably erupt".[63] These events were the first in sixteen years in which collective political violence was recorded in the Arab minority against the state. The heads of the northern branch of the Islamic Movement felt that they had acquired enough political power and public support to oppose the government through use of violence. The fact that the dispute was over lands near Umm el-Fahem, the stronghold of the branch, also contributed to the decision to act with violence – since the government's moves were perceived as being a direct attack upon their homes.

8
The Events of October 2000

The last and most severe events that marked the last decade of the twentieth century were the October 2000 riots. These were widespread geographically, lasted for two weeks, and were the most serious events to take place in the Arab sector since the establishment of the State of Israel in terms of the number of casualties.[64] They represented the zenith of the continuous escalation that had continued for four years, during which some of the political factions, mainly from the Islamic Movement and Balad, had brought about a permanent state of friction with the government over civil, nationalist and religious issues.

The immediate catalyst for the outbreak was the visit made to the Temple Mount on September 28, 2000 by Member of the Knesset, Ariel Sharon, to inspect the renovations the *waqf* was carrying out in the compound. His visit led to agitation in the Temple Mount area, and confrontations developed between the security forces and the Muslims who had come to the place. Dozens of policemen and demonstrators were injured in these clashes, and the next day, September 29, the confrontations spread to different places in East Jerusalem, in which seven Palestinians were killed and more than a hundred people were injured. In light of the escalation in East Jerusalem, the Higher Monitoring Committee of the Israeli Arabs declared a general strike in the Arab sector and protest processions to be held in the Arab villages. There was a widespread positive response to this call and in some locations violent clashes took place, which were encouraged and directed by political groups. The Monitoring Committee published a declaration in which they praised the rioters, condemned the police, and supported the use of violence which they saw as a pattern of action that should be adopted. Because of this position, the committee did not call upon the rioters to restrain themselves; some of its members confirmed in the evidence they gave to the Orr Commission that in the situation that developed there was a real potential for public disorder.[65] The choice made of the pattern of violent action in response to the policy of the Israeli government – in this case the authorization given to come to the Temple Mount – was something new in the decision-making process of the Higher Monitoring Committee.

Balad issued a statement on September 30 in which they claimed that the events in Jerusalem in which Arabs were killed were "a planned slaughter" carried out by the authorities. The leader of the party, Azmi Bishara, who was asked about this statement and its content when giving evidence before the Orr Commission, at first denied responsibility and claimed that the declaration was distributed by members of Balad in Umm el-Fahem. The protocol of the meeting of the Higher Monitoring Committee that took place on the day the announcement was released proved that at the meeting Bishara stated that "the slaughter and the events were planned," and this was the formulation that appeared in the announcement that was distributed by his party to the public.[66]

On October 1, Balad published a report in which they wrote that as a result of the initiative of its people the previous day (on September 30) dozens of protest demonstrations were carried out in the main streets and junctions in the Galilee and the triangle (a nickname for

Israeli Arab towns and villages adjacent to the Green Line, located in the eastern Sharon plain among the Samarian foothills), protesting the events that took place at the *al-Aqṣa* Mosque. Balad members threw rocks at cars in Kafr Manda and clashed with security forces.[67] Bishara himself attested to the fact that he and all the members of the Balad political bureau were present in every place where serious clashes with the police were taking place, and specifically mentioned Umm el-Fahem and Tamra, and when it became clear that the events were becoming more violent, the leaders of Balad also did not act to calm things down.[68] At the height of the October 2000 events, Bishara declared: "Our file will not be closed as long as the criminals and murderers remain in power. Our fallen did not die for budgets. This time we came out to declare our political position and this is our right".[69]

On October 2, Balad published an additional declaration that called upon the Arab public to continue to take part in the events. This declaration included expressions praising the harsh clashes that had taken place on October 1 it defined the serious clashes as an "Intifada" – that is, widespread violent rebellious action that challenges the authorities. This was done as part of Balad's attempt to advance its political goals through pushing forward violent patterns of activity, and Bishara did not consider it worthwhile to deviate from the violent line he had taken. During the meetings held by the Orr Commission he explained that he did not usually try to mediate between the police and the public and explained this by claiming: "We know that our legal activity in parliament, in the Knesset committees, in elections, in licensed mass assemblies, in demonstrations outside the Prime Minister's Office – all end up as blind alleys and the inability to influence the process of decision making. As a result a dynamic develops between the population and the leadership that leads to more radical forms of protest." He agreed that calls made of the kind he made encouraged violent demonstrations against the government.[70]

Balad did not change the violent line it had adopted even after the events had ended. Declarations that it published about two weeks after the end of the riots expressed unreserved admiration and praise for the October events that it called "supreme acts of courage" and a "just uprising." In January 2001, Bishara himself said that "regarding participation in the Intifada, some think that participation is in sending rice, chick peas and sugar. This is excellent and good but participating in the battle is the foundation . . . I think that raising the level of the battle of the Arabs from 'inside' (the nickname for Israel Arab citizens) not only in the provision of food products, but also in the battle in different ways is fundamental." The general secretary of

Balad, wad ʿAbd al-Fattaḥ, explained to the Orr Commission that he saw it as an obligation to call upon the Arab public to join the battle.[71]

In contrast to the leaders of Balad, when the heads of the Islamic Movement gave their evidence to the Orr Commission, they did not admit that they had taken an active part in the harsh events of October 2000. Along with this, the day after the beginning of the events, the northern branch of the movement published a declaration that praised the sacrificing of blood for the *al-Aqṣa* Mosque. Sheikh Salah confirmed to the Commission that it was he who formulated the declaration.[72]

In another declaration, the northern branch, like Balad, defined the Temple Mount events as "planned slaughter" and Sheikh Salah blamed the outbreak of the events on the government, claiming that this was a conspiracy concocted by the security forces. The first edition of their newspaper after Member of the Knesset Sharon went up to the Temple Mount opened with the headline "Sharon breaks into *al-Aqṣa*".[73]

When the events were taking place, the Umm el-Fahem munici-pality, which was then headed by Sheikh Salah, issued an announcement which thanked "all the residents of the cities and villages throughout the homeland that have proven their loyalty and unity in the matter of *al-Aqṣa.*" In the announcement there were words of praise and admiration for the violence that the rioters had used against the security forces[74]. Sheikh Salah himself made a public state-ment in which he defined the events as the "*al-Aqṣa* Intifada"; the Orr Commission interpreted his words as meaning that the sheikh held the opinion that the nature of these events was rebellion rather than just demonstration. Another declaration made by the northern branch connected the event of Land Day in 1976, whose goal was to defend land, with the October 2000 events – whose goal was to defend the *al-Aqṣa* Mosque.

Like Balad, Sheikh Salah and his colleagues in the northern branch did nothing to calm down the area, and did not call upon the public to stop their violent actions. From the moment the first signs of violence appeared until they ended two weeks later, the Islamic Movement presented a single and continuous line that justified the use of violent actions and encouraged the people to continue them in order to protect the religious and political interests of the Arab minority. Sheikh Kamal Kahtib accused Prime Minister Barak of being respon-sible for the deaths of the Muslim worshippers and he published an article in which he wrote: "Barak, just wait for the payback for what you have done with your own hands. Barak can expect to have a black year." Sheikh Salah explained that there was a need to document the divine revelations that surrounded the events and that he intended to devote his coming articles to describing what had taken place.[75]

Historically, this was the most serious clash that had taken place between the Arab minority and the government of Israel since 1948. The events continued unstopped for fourteen days, were spread over seventy Arab villages, and thirteen Arabs (twelve Israelis, one Palestinian) and one Jew were killed. This was the result of a decision made by the Arab minority's leadership to use force and violence in an attempt to improve its civil status as a national minority, which was what Balad was striving for, and to defend the sites that were holy to Islam according to the Islamic Movement viewpoint. The violence-mongers such as Sheikh Raᶜid Salah and Members of the Knesset Bishara and ᶜAbd al-Malek Dahamshah, did not express any regret over the pattern of action that they had adopted, which included encouraging young Arabs to fight with the police and security forces. These events came as the direct continuation of the experimental balloon that was the al-Roha Lands affair two years earlier, and reflected the concoction created of nationalist and religious violence and the striving for civil integration. The factions that led the events – Balad and the Islamic Movement – stressed nationalist and religious motifs, even though the ultimate goal of each was completely different. The other Arab political factions exploited the wave of violent protest and joined it in an attempt to extract benefits in civil matters from the government.

9
The Political System after the October Events

The decade following the October events was marked by learning the lessons of the tragic events. These events actually made the rift between Jews and Arabs more profound, at the end of a decade in which the government had changed its policy and was active in a variety of civil areas to reduce the gaps between the minority and the Jewish majority. From the point of view of the Arab side, the upgrades made by the government through the increase of resources for the Arab minority and the legislation of laws that would make it easier for Arab citizens to be integrated into the civil service were too little and too late, when one takes into consideration the feelings of deprivation that had been felt by the Arab public for more than four decades. The immediate political reaction of the Arab minority to the harsh events of 2000 was the sweeping boycott of the direct elections for the Prime Minister in

February 2001 when only 19 percent of those with the right to vote in the Arab sector used this right.[76]

As part of the lessons learned from the violent clashes, the government's policy after the October 2000 events was marked by an increase in attempts to reduce the gaps. This policy in civil areas created a division into two in the Arab population's political system. On a continuum between dialogue and separatism, some of the power factors chose to continue the process of dialogue with the government, while others chose a policy of separatism and rejectionism along with continuing to criticize the State of Israel and striving to change its character.

The power factors that supported dialogue did so in two ways. In civil issues, there was direct dialogue between the heads of the local authorities and the governmental ministries; this included matters involving the municipalities, the attempt to reduce the demolition of illegally built structures and land appropriation, the arrangement of master plans, increasing development budgets, and enlarging the number of Arabs employed in the civil service. For national issues, indirect discussions took place with Arab public figures using the situation in Judea and Samaria and the Gaza Strip in order to express identification with the Palestinians and to call for solutions to their problems. This included subjects such as the IDF's activities in the territories, protesting the killing of Palestinians, organizing humanitarian aid campaigns, and visits to express identification with leadership bodies and local residents. From the declarative point of view and activity in the field, all the political power groups in the Arab sector presented one front in nationalist issues. They all made sure to carry out similar activities, sometimes cooperatively, and demanded that the Israeli government be more flexible in their policies so as to end the historical conflict.

As noted earlier, activity in civil areas created a division between the integration camp and the separatist camps. The integration camp was nationalistically identified with the Palestinian struggle, but saw its home within the State of Israel whose existence it accepted, and those who belonged to this camp fought to improve the situation of the Arab minority in various civil issues while also trying to garner support from the Jewish public. Social and political frameworks such as the communists (Hadash), Ra'am Ta'al (including the southern branch of the Islamic Movement) and the Higher Monitoring Committee were in this camp with the two political parties active both within parliament and outside it, while the Higher Monitoring Committee, as a roof leadership framework, was also interested in improving the situation of the Arab minority and did not dismiss having contacts with the government. The Committee of the Heads of Local Authorities, which was recognized by the government with which it carried on an ongoing dialogue, was also in this camp.

The other camp was the separatist camp, and the pattern of activity of this camp arose out of a nationalistic and religious ideology that dictated its relations with the government regarding civil issues. This ideology strived to establish an Islamic Sharia state in the territory or to establish a "state for all its citizens" which would eliminate the Jewish characteristics from the state. The political powers that belonged to this camp operated in a manner detached from the state, while exploiting the state's democratic regime. This camp included the northern branch of the Islamic Movement, the Sons of the Village Movement, and Balad, whose platform, which called for turning Israel into a state for all its citizens, sank its roots into the Arab public; it is, in fact, the ideological foundation upon which the vision published by the Committee of the Heads of Local Authorities was written in 2006.[77] Balad, in contrast to the northern branch of the Islamic Movement and the Sons of the Village, tries to enjoy the benefits of two worlds. On the practical and principled level it wants to receive aid from the government – as long as this fits with its goals – and so it takes part in the parliamentary game, but from a political and declarative point of view, it acts to change the existing political reality and tries to establish structures that are separated from the state.[78]

The two camps have not ideologically given up on the vision to improve the situation of the Arab minority, and some of their members are interested in changing the character of the state – whether this would mean movement toward a state for all its citizens or change in the direction of a religious Islamic state. The political and declarative activity on the part of all the political bodies regarding these matters reached its peak during the 1990s and the first decade of the 21st century. In addition, the activity furthered the process of empowering Arab civil society.[79] Despite this, the consensus around the vision has not matured into creation of a monolithic political framework with an ideology and orderly operations capable of leading to the mobilization of resources and creation of a broad collective identity for the Arab public – that is, a structure that could result in effective protest activity against the Israeli establishment. The different political frameworks did put together a common list that participated in the Knesset general elections in 2015, which was a step that led to a rise of seven percent in the number of Arab voters compared with the 2013 elections; beyond this, since they won 13 seats in the Knesset (out of 120) there has been no protest (or violent) activity identified in the Arab minority which has been led by this list in any united fashion.[80] Moreover, since

2015, various forms of activity by Arab members in the Knesset have been in response to political, civil and security topics.

During the decade following October 2000, a number of events with the potential for clashes between the government and the Arab minority were recorded, the most prominent of which was the IDF Defensive Shield Campaign in Judea and Samaria in 2002. There were also the three rounds of military campaigns in Gaza Strip (Cast Lead/2008, Pillar of Cloud/2012, and Protective Edge/2014) – as well as the Gaza flotilla of the Turkish ship (Marmara) in an attempt to break the siege imposed on Hamas (May 2010), which was an event in which two of the prominent leaders of the Arab sector (Sheikh Salah and MK Hanin Zuᶜbi) took an active part.

Inside the Israeli arena, the following significant steps were taken by the government to frustrate moves taken by public personages and leaders of the Arab sector: Sheikh Salah was charged (2005) with having contact with a foreign agent (Iran), and Bishara fled Israel (2007) after it was revealed that he had allegedly spied for Hizbullah. Steps taken to frustrate the actions of these people, like the severe line adopted towards Israeli Arabs who had been involved in terror, were part of the message of deterrence being spread by the government. The cumulative result of the lessons learned from October 2000 and the uncompromising stance taken by the government led to the political factions in the Arab sector reacting with restraint towards steps taken by the government. In all the above cases, reactions took the form of verbal protest and the expression of identification with the Palestinians. Some of the Arab public figures expressed condemnation of the perpetrators mainly when terror was involved.[81]

The vision papers that were published in 2006 were an expression of new ideas that had not matured into any political reality. This was an initiative taken by the Committee of the Heads of Local Arab Authorities and was a document that galvanized the Arab minority into actions and toward goals they had been aspiring to achieve. The document was written by forty intellectuals from the Arab sector who reflected the broad political consciousness of the Arab educated class. It received the authorization of The Higher Monitoring Committee – which was a step that significantly reduced criticism by political groups with different ideologies from that proposed by the document.[82]

The vision document proposed a strategic plan of action in eight areas based upon the assessment that this program could be achieved within a period of two decades. The areas dealt with were: (1) the relationship with the state; (2) the legal status of the minority; (3) the question of lands and planning of building; (4) economic development

(5) social development; (6) education; (7) culture; (8) political and public endeavor.[83] During the decade since its publication, the document has interested only a small number of intellectuals in the Arab sector of Israel, and it is difficult to assess the amount of influence that this text, which supports dialogue with the government, has had on the quality of the dialogue – since such dialogue has continually existed and even significantly broadened since the beginning of the 1990s. The document did not succeed in leading to the establishment of a new political framework that would put the proposals into action, perhaps because most of its contents were similar to or identical with the ideology of Balad. Moreover, this document did not take root in the Arab population or arouse the interest of the public as the authors had hoped it would. Instead, Arab society in Israel, which is mostly made up of young people under twenty, has undergone social changes in the last two decades that have steered most of that population into activities that are not political – and this will be analyzed below.

10
Changes in the Arab Public Demography and Main Characteristics

In contrast to the 875,000 Arabs living in Israel in 1990, at the end of 2015 there were 1,757,800 Arab people (300,000 of whom were living in East Jerusalem, which is a group that has not been included in this study).[84] The percentage of Muslims in the Arab population reached 83 percent and the proportion of Arabs living in the Negev reached 16 percent. In 2010 the Arab public lived in 123 Arab population centers and seven mixed urban centers.

The Arab population is very young, with 55 percent of them under the age of 24 and a median age of 19.1 years among the Muslims, while the median age of the Bedouin living in the Negev is under 14. The median age for bridegrooms is 26 and for brides 21, which is significantly younger than the median age for Jews. There has been a significant rise in the number of unmarried men and women, including Bedouin women in the Negev between the ages of 35 and 44 (about 22 percent). As a rule the size of the Arab household has dropped from five members in 2001 to 4.5 in 2010, while the drop in the number of household members in the Negev has been greater.[85]

These figures make it abundantly clear that during the years of the large immigration from the former Soviet Union, which was parallel to the outbreak of radical Islam into the political arena and the eruption of the Intifada, the rise in the relative number of the minorities in the population dropped very significantly. Also during the decade that followed, in which there was a dramatic drop in the number of Jewish immigrants, there was no significant rise in the percentage of minority residents in the overall population as the result of the modernization processes[86] that had accelerated among them and the continuing drop in birthrate.

Dealing with the demographic data is necessary if only because such changes have an effect upon the character of any given society, the kind of dwellings lived in, the work market, the number of educated people, economic development, social changes, and participation in politics. In Israel there is another aspect to the demographic question that is relevant to the relations between the Jewish majority and non-Jewish minority (Muslims, Christians and others who perceived as Arabs) populations because of the character of the country which combines the values "Jewish" and "democratic."

There can be no argument over the fact that the relative percentage of the Arab population in the general population has, since the 1990s, remained stable with fluctuations of fractional percentages. If, however, this is also the way the continuing reality looks, does this information suggest that in the foreseeable future, in a decade or in the next generation, the democratic balance among the Israeli citizens will significantly change so that the Arab population and its electors will become a central and important factor in the election campaigns and in the forming of coalitions? An analysis of the data and forecasts published by the Central Bureau of Statistics since 1978 show that, if the forecasts had been realized, then Israel would already have been living in the demographic reality of being a bi-national state. In different publications, the Bureau (in its lowest prediction) and other researchers expected that by 2000 the proportion of Arabs would be 20.1 percent of the general population while in fact it was 18.7 percent. The gap between the forecast and reality grew once again in 2003 with the forecast being 21.2 percent as opposed to the reality of 19.3 percent.

These forecasts and others failed because it is difficult to almost impossible to construct a credible predictive model in a heterogeneous society such as Israel. The natural population growth of the Israeli Arabs is decreasing, and except for the Bedouin population in the Negev, is approaching a rate parallel to that of the Jewish population, whose growth rate is continuing to increase. There are many reasons for this: the growth in the number of ultra-orthodox families in the Jewish majority group, the socialization of the former USSR immigrants into Israeli society, which includes their adoption of similar patterns of natural population growth to those of the veteran Israelis – and especially, the Israeli government's longstanding practice of preventing uncontrolled Palestinian immigration into the sovereign borders of the state in order to avoid any subversion of the demographic balance. The relative number of Israeli Arabs has grown somewhat since 1967, but since then and for the foreseeable future, has had no significant influence upon the general Israeli demographic balance.

11
The Israeli Arab: Sociological Characteristics and Political Participation

Who is the Israel Arab of the end of the 20th century and the beginning of the 21st? There is no doubt that this is not the first generation that experienced the *Nakba* back in 1948 and not even about the second generation that was educated in the light of the catastrophe that befell the Arabs when their parents saw the State of Israel being established. The third generation, along with the beginning of the fourth, is seeking a new way to realize itself in a world in turmoil and in a complex reality from the point of view of being an Israeli citizen who belongs to a different national group from that of the Jewish majority. The complexity does not, however, end by distinguishing between what is civil and what is national, as has been the conventional thinking in previous studies made of the Arabs in Israel. This is a new generation that moves between preserving tradition and adjusting to the innovations that come with modernization. We are going to argue regarding this point that the Israeli Arabs, 60 percent of whom are younger than nineteen, are combining the preservation of traditional values with a new concept that we suggest calling functional and instrumental modernization.

The Arab Israelis are adopting innovations such as technological developments, consumer practices, and dress codes that serve their existential needs (both men and women), and are making use of them instrumentally in order to position their status in Arab society and in the shared Israeli space. Thus, for example, they adorn themselves with new cars clothes with prestigious labels, they often sit in bars and visit shopping malls to buy from large chain stores instead of buying in the village, and they use credit cards, which were a kind of rare fantasy up till the beginning of the 1990s in the Arab sector. One of the owners of a food store chain in the Arab sector attested thus:

"There are Arab yuppies that mainly consist of young couples and singles that habitually use credit cards."[87] Another expression of the desire to be part of society is the adoption of the habits of the majority group, as was demonstrated by Arab workers who dressed in fancy costumes for the festival of Purim – even though this was a clearly Jewish festival.[88] In contrast to adoption of modern characteristic, the Arab citizen preserves a traditional lifestyle that, for example, expresses itself in a modest dress code for women, in a lack of tolerance for sexual freedom, and stubborn barriers to the full liberation of women in the widespread, comprehensive way that it exists in the societies of western countries. These patterns of behavior have, among other things, brought about changes in the nature of what goes on in the household, in the Arab work market, and the involvement of the Arab sector in political issues. Looked at from a broader point of view, one can argue that the Arab public has adjusted to the civil society lifestyle that has dug roots in Israeli society over the last two decades.[89]

In order to understand the depth of the changes that have taken place in Arab society in Israel since 1990, we have chosen an approach that combines the analysis of the voting in election campaigns in democratic countries [90]and public opinion polls, together with a qualitative analysis of texts written by public figures and leading social bodies in the Arab sector. This approach has allowed us to provide a basis for drawing conclusions about whether the Arab minority is headed towards separatism, dialogue, protest or violence.

Previous studies and public opinion polls have tried to explore what has been happening in the Arab public and to understand what directions they have chosen for their activities in the last two decades. One can learn from these surveys that the younger generation has undergone significant changes which have also influenced the patterns of its reaction to steps taken by the government. The demographic aspect in the case of the Israeli Arabs is also important because the younger generation has traditionally been involved in demonstrations, clashes, and confrontations with the security elements in Israel and, in fact, throughout the world. In the research literature, the tendency of the younger generation towards militancy and the readiness to adopt radical positions is considered to be one of the keys to analyzing the demonstration of violent protest.[91]

A survey that was published in the middle of 2010 and which included interviewees between 18 and 24 years old has provided us with several relevant conclusions for our discussion. First of all, most of the young Arabs, like the Jews, place personal goals at the top of their order of priorities. More than 40 percent want to establish a happy family and 35 percent aspire towards higher education, which they see as the key to getting a job after their studies, whether this is in the private or public sector. According to this survey and other studies, the key to this is the transition to being a young educated society that prefers individualism.[92] This reality, which is mainly devoted to self-realization, significantly reduces the ability and spare time available to become deeply involved in political issues and to try to influence things through dialogue, protest or violence. Most free time is spent browsing internet sites and surfing social networks such as Facebook so that politics, in its different varieties, is viewed as something distasteful that is controlled by corrupt people who are only concerned about themselves.[93] It appears that when there is plenty of spare time and the economic possibility the Arab public prefers travelling overseas, mainly to summer vacations in Egypt, Jordan and Turkey. The reasons for this are the low cost, their knowledge of Arabic, the availability and the ethnic and religious connections.[94]

These findings are directly related to the basic questions about the way these young people see their relationship with the country. Here we can distinguish between great political consciousness about their status as a minority compared to the majority group and their readiness to involve themselves in militancy. A decisive percentage of the interviewees, more than 90 percent, believe that it is important that Israel is a democratic country, and in another survey almost 80 percent of the interviewees responded that they would support the adoption of a constitution that defines Israel as a Jewish and democratic state that guarantees full equality to Arabs.[95] These findings are supported by other surveys which also show a large majority of the Arab public are interested in assimilating into Israeli society. Thus, for example, 68 percent are prepared to live in Jewish neighborhoods and 60 percent want to spend time in parks and swimming pools with Jews.[96] In addition to the above, 20,000 young Arabs throughout the country have been members of the *Hanoar Haoved Vehalomed* which is a youth movement and have been exposed to shared activities with Jewish youth.[97] These expressions of consciousness about democratic values were, among other things, expressed in the rise in the number of Arab voters in the 2015 general elections. From the point of view of being able to identify the quandaries experienced by the Arab voter who, on the one hand, as noted above, has contempt for the political system that is infected by negative influences, and on the other hand, wants to have an influence through taking an active part in the democratic process, it seems that a common list that includes all the political power factors in the

Arab sector has solved the quandary for some of the voters. This is because it includes public figures who want to advance the civil assimilation of the minority, as part of the essence of democracy, together with figures who want to sharpen the national divide, who are mainly those that represent Balad.

There are a number of explanations for these findings, as there are for the lack of readiness to turn to protest or violence. First of all we are talking about a generation that was educated towards democratic values which were in practice translated into aspects of human rights (certainly basic rights), freedom of religious ritual, the right to elect and be elected to state institutions, and the clear separation of powers. It is natural that young people who have been educated in this way and have learned what the advantages are for the individual obviously support the preservation of the existing situation. There are, however, at least two other reasons for the lack of readiness to go out and actively fight the establishment. One of these is the desire to ensure that the activities of the government ministries to close the gaps and encourage the development of the Arab population, as being analyzed in Part Two of the book, be preserved. The linear and ongoing improvement – sometimes quick and sometimes slower – has been continuous and has even strengthened since the beginning of the 21st century. Violent confrontations with the authorities lead, almost naturally, to a worsening of the rifts and possibly even to freezing off initiatives and projects to advance the sector, until the public atmosphere makes them possible again. Another reason is the lack of desire to give legitimacy to and provide proof of the claims that are regularly broadcast to the public in the media by entities in the Jewish majority against the Arab population. In contrast to the integrative civil policy of the Israeli governments, it is actually the parliamentary dialogue, including legislative steps taken, and the public climate that have, since 2000, been characterized by increasing hostility towards the Arabs – and this includes feelings of hatred.

There is also another way of looking at the aspiration to preserve a policy that has a democratic character. More than 90 percent of the Arabs support full equality regarding political rights for the different groups; the significance of this is twofold – it reflects the desire to be part of the country through dialogue with the government, while at the same time expressing complete agreement with Balad's platform which calls for transforming Israel into a state of all its citizens.[98] This internalization has not been translated into political action since almost half of the young people do not politically identify with any particular party. The analysis indicates that despite the high level of political consciousness, there has been no rush to join Arab political parties probably because of the disenchantment with politics that is perceived to be a corrupt arena.

The feeling of disenchantment did not come from nowhere. A historical analysis shows that personal and political disputes prevented the Arab political parties from signing a preferential vote agreement that would have been likely to increase their electoral strength. In preparation for the elections to the sixteen Knesset in 2003, however, the Democratic Front for Peace and Equality (The Israeli Communist Party and public groups of Jews and Arabs), the Arab Renewal Movement, and the National Democratic Alliance (Balad) did make such an agreement. In the elections for the seventeen Knesset in 2006 they once again signed a preferential vote agreement, and these agreements garnered one more mandate for the Arab factions in both cases. From the point of view of the Arab public this was too little too late, because the personal and ideological factionalism had been engraved in its collective memory – as had the understanding that the unification of their forces would not create a political power capable of influencing the public agenda within the parliament. Looking to the future, at this point one does not see the Arab public flocking into the political arena, and it does not look like the disenchantment with politics and the focusing on individualism [99]as part of the process that all Israeli society is experiencing will lead to the development of new political frameworks in the Arab sector. The political fact that in the 2015 general elections, although a single list made up of representatives of existing parties was put together no new political framework emerged – only strengthens this argument.

If the direction being taken by the Arab public is not towards the political field then one has to ask what its other channels of activity are, and how it uses them to realize the goals it wants to achieve. To put it another way, what is the young Arab looking for and what is he ready to do to achieve, first of all, his personal goals and, if possible, his collective ones? In this we can see a picture developing in which most of those asked oppose both violent and non-violent civil rebellion as a reaction to government policy that does harm to the interests of the Arab minority.[100] Another survey revealed that 17 percent are ready to use violence in order to change the situation of the Arab minority;[101] these findings are consistent with the patterns of actions taken by the Arab minority since the October 2000 events. In the periods of escalation in which there was the potential for violent protest, this did not take place even when there was an attack carried out by Jews that led to the deaths of Arab citizens;[102] the reason for this cannot only be found in the political apathy of most of the Arab public. Additional reasons that prevented the use of violent protest were the memory of the harsh response of the security forces against Arab demonstrators in October 2000, and the deterrence created by the establishment when it charged Arab figures with security offences.

Also, a new phenomenon has developed in Israeli public life during the last decade, characterized by attacks being made by Jews upon minority members in public places where there has been a lot of friction between the groups, such as in places of leisure activities and shopping, the seaside and sports arenas. The possibility that they may be hurt by young Jews is taken into account by young Arabs before they choose to use force. One survey that asked a specific question about this issue in 2003 found that 70 percent of the Arab interviewees were afraid of physical violence used by Jews. A later survey found that a third of the Arabs were afraid to get close to the Jewish population because they might be hurt.[103]

The social and demographic changes along with civil and security steps taken by the government therefore explain the lack of exhibitions of protest and violence. Since the beginning of the twenty first century, the Arabs have, as a whole, been busy with issues that are not political and have preferred to enjoy the benefits of modernization and technological innovation. Browsing internet sites, social network activities and trying to acquire status symbols such as prestigious cars and clothes with fancy labels have all been preferable to political activity which has not guaranteed fruitful results as far as the younger generation is concerned. The cumulative result of the conduct of the public has been the avoidance of violence, reduced participation in protest events (but greater participation in memorial events) and attempts to assimilate into Israeli society along with activity of some to advance independent projects of their own within it.

In light of these findings and their meaning for the democratic process in the State of Israel, are the minorities likely to achieve the status in which their votes will allow their representatives to become balancing factors without whom it would be impossible to form a workable coalition? The demographic data presented above do not support this possibility, but there are two other issues along with this that arise from them. One is the question of whether those Arabs who have the right to vote in Israel are capable of using the electoral power they have gained by uniting their political forces and bringing all their voters to the voting booth. The experience of many other countries shows that the stronger the process of modernization and globalization, the greater the involvement of the citizens in political activity in their countries. Accordingly, in light of these processes that are powerfully present in Arab society, the second issue is whether it is therefore possible to expect that we will be hearing the clear and loud voice of the Israeli Arabs in the election campaigns in the State of Israel?

One should not underestimate the influence the political power groups in the Arab minority had over the way things have been managed with the government since 1948 and certainly over and since the 1990s. It appears, however, that an analysis of the Arab population would not be complete without examining the political, social, economic, and cultural changes that have taken place in Arab society, since these changes, among other things, have been the outcomes of Israeli policies, external influences upon the Palestinian, regional and international networks, technological innovations, and demographic changes.

During the 1990s, when the change in the government's policy was first felt, there were three election campaigns. In 1992, 70 percent of those with the right to vote in the Arab minority voted, four years in 1996 later 77 percent voted, and almost the same thing happened in the 1999 elections. The conclusion that can be reached here is that this was the Arab public's reaction to the changes in the government's policy – which included dialogue, the provision of increased resources to the Arab minority, and legislation of laws aimed at closing traditional gaps. This trend reversed itself in the following decade after the October 2000 events, and in the direct elections for Prime Minister in February 2001 only 19 percent of those with the right to vote in the Arab minority took part, while the overwhelming majority boycotted the elections as a protest against the October 2000 events. This, however, was not a passing episode, since in the 2003 general elections the number of Arab voters was 62 percent, about 15 percent fewer than in the 1999 elections, and the lower number of Arabs using their democratic right to vote persisted in the elections that took place in 2006 and 2009.

As we understand it, there were several, both internal and external, reasons that, over a period of time, led to the drop in the number of Arab voters in the last decade. First, there was indeed a real rise in the political consciousness of the Arab minority – but this was almost completely steered towards independent activity and detached from the basic democratic process of electing representatives to the Parliament. This activity included the establishment of associations, some of which tried to advance separatist initiatives.[104] This phenomenon was also the result of a strengthening of Arab consciousness that ran parallel to the denial of Israel's right to exist at all and certainly not as a Zionist state.[105] These positions led to a minority of people voting in the general elections while, paradoxically, on the municipal stage, high levels of voting were recorded. This was because the Arab minority perceived the municipal arena to be a political one whose agenda it could influence.[106]

Second, the understanding grew that improvements could be acquired from the establishment without actually voting in the Knesset elections, where their representatives' ability to have any effect was highly limited. Turning to the courts for assistance, together with protests in the field, forced the Israeli establishment to respond to the demands of the Arab minority. Some of those researching the Arab society in Israel believe that due to the events of October 2000, they overcame the barrier of fear and began to display readiness to take unconventional steps, including confronting the Israeli system of running the country.[107] One assumption which time showed to be mistaken is that events of the size of those that took place in October 2000 would not be repeated, even when there was the potential in several other events for renewed outbreaks.

Apart from these reasons, there are other explanations for the low numbers of Arab voters. The Arab public has been disappointed in the quality of the Arab candidates and their inability to unite and establish a list that represents the consensus, despite the great similarity in the platforms of the parties regarding the two core issues: the peaceful solution to the Palestinian question and the achievement of equality for all the country's citizens. The source of this failure, according to some of the Arab researchers, is in the battle for prestige that results from the political battles.[108] This point shows how the political maturity of the Arab public has deepened since it no longer blindly follows its leaders. The patterns of activity of these leaders, who have been focused upon self-aggrandizement instead of worrying about the needs of the Arab population, have increased the feelings of disenchantment among the voters. This disappointment with their leaders arose parallel to a process in which the Arab parties were providing study stipends to students who expressed the desire to study in Jordan, despite the blunt interference of the Palestinian Authority which was encouraging the Arab voters to go and vote.[109]

Different surveys that have been carried out in the Arab sector have tried to examine how satisfied the Arab citizens are with the functioning of the sector's leadership bodies. One of these surveys, in which 756 Arabs took part, was carried out in November 2002 before the general elections to the Knesset. Forty-two percent of them gave an intermediate grade to the functioning of the Arab leadership, 37 percent rated their functioning in matters concerning the Arab population as bad or very bad and only 20 percent indicated that their functioning was good or excellent. A survey that was carried out a decade later found that the trend had not changed. Most of the Arab public (more than 60 percent) had no trust in the Arab leadership and the public also believed that they were not finding practical solutions to the problems and needs of the Arab minority.[110]

The cumulative result of the analysis is that despite the increases in the Arab population, both numbers and percentages, this has not led to any rise in the rate of people voting in the general elections. Political rivalries, the increased disenchantment with anachronistic leaders, and the search for something new and fresh – which at the moment is missing in the realm of politics – has led to a growing number of Arabs who are giving up on their basic democratic right to elect their representatives to Parliament.

12
The Arab Associations:
A Mixture of Integration and Separatism

Above we have discussed one of the prominent phenomena of the last two decades whose purpose has been internal, sectorial empowerment. One of its most concrete expressions has been the real increase in the number of civil society organizations in Israel which are part of the third sector that includes bodies that are not part of the public or business sectors. This phenomenon has not bypassed the Arab population, in which there has been a real growth in the number of associations that aim to influence the social and political agenda of the Arab minority because of interest in improving its status. Discussing the growth of the phenomenon, the areas of activity of the associations, and the number of people employed by them can also assist us in our analysis of the question of whether the Arab public is turning towards separatism, integration, protest, or violence in the attitude it takes towards the Israeli establishment. Our central argument is that the phenomenon itself consumes significant resources due to the minority's involvement in the considerable number of activities of the associations, which reduces its ability to act violently against the government. When they ask to change the status quo or raise demands to improve the status of the citizens, most of the associations turn to legal channels. Another argument we make is that the segmentation of the areas of activity shows that certain associations declare that they are striving towards integration, while a smaller number, mainly those connected with the Islamic Movement, focus on activities whose purpose is separation from the state.

Arab social organizations already existed at the beginning of the twentieth century but there were not many of them, and they had a Christian or Muslim orientation.[111] Organizations like these existed throughout the previous century, and according to at least one study they did not succeed in influencing the government until the eighties. Some of those, who research Arab society, claim that the Israeli government prevented the Arab minority from establishing independent Arab associations. Others believe that it was in fact the Arab political culture which believed that it was the central authority's task to take care of the citizen's needs, which prevented the establishment of the associations. A third group of scholars believe that these associations, instead of the government, focused on providing services to the population and thus contributed to the perpetuation of the gaps between the majority and minority groups and made the role of the state superfluous.[112] We believe that the Arab minority did not release the establishment from its responsibility to provide it with services. The clear proof of this was the activity of the associations in the areas of law and education which appealed to the judiciary to ask for help to obligate the state to provide resources to the Arab population.

From 1989 on, there was a sharp increase in the number of associations registered in the Arab sector, largely because the Law of Associations, which was legislated in 1980, made registration better organized. Up until 1988 there had been more than 650 new Arab associations registered that represented 65 percent of all the Arab associations registered, and in 2004 this number was doubled to 1,300. Most of the political factions were involved in the establishment of associations, but there were also new social organizations which did not necessarily have any political links. The reasons for the sharp increase in the number of social organizations and associations are partly internal for the sector and partly external for other reasons.

The first external explanation was the distress of the Arab population, which was the direct outcome of the government's policy up until the nineties. This policy, which was analyzed above in Part One, was the mixture of a tough security approach accompanied by the provision of basic democratic rights and minimal dialogue which expressed itself in areas such as health, welfare, education, religion, building and housing, and economics. Other aspects of this discriminating reality were the very small number of Arabs who found employment in government service and the low level of budgets provided to the Arab local authorities. The Arab population's feelings of being discriminated against and deprivation were key factors for these organizational steps being taken in order to provide alternative services for the Arab minority.[113] One can therefore see these factors as steering the activity into channels that separated it from the state, on the basis of the virtual uselessness of asking the government to provide the Arab citizens with the things they needed.

The second external reason as indicated above is the Associations Law that was legislated in 1980 and which regulated the registration process for associations and made it easier. The Israeli establishment used to carefully examine requests made by associations that were politically identified with parties and groups that were perceived as being security threats, such as the northern branch of the Islamic Movement or Balad. Thus, for example, at the beginning of 2000 the registrar of associations decided to close seventy-five Arab associations and refused to register thirty new ones.[114]

Another reason for the rise in the number of Arab associations was the increased activity of both branches of the Islamic Movement which were influenced by the Islamic revival in the Middle East. The leaders of the movement established dozens of charities devoted to education, welfare, and sports, including an Islamic football league, as well as arts and religious organizations. The goal of all this was to establish an autarchic economy and this activity, which was introduced for the benefit of the Arab community, significantly strengthened the power of the movement and provided it with widespread support. Some of the people who were involved in establishing the associations and the introduction of the activities in the field leveraged their involvement into political dividends mostly on the municipality level.[115] Some of the associations were involved in activities that led to security violations, mainly for providing assistance to the Hamas terror organization in the West Bank and the Gaza Strip, and the government reacted by closing some of these down.

Regarding the internal reasons, it is worthwhile taking time to look at the significant growth in the number of highly educated people and the rise of the young people as a group. From the time education became a central value in Arab society a layer of young academics developed who wanted to utilize what they had learned in their everyday reality. The bureaucratic barriers that had once prevented easy integration into government service, despite the significant steps the government took to improve the situation, led many of them to get administrative positions within the Arab community; the result was the entry of better educated people into the frameworks of the associations, in order to bring about change through their own efforts.[116] The growth of the associations also directly led to the development of research work on women in the Arab minority which was something that had been absent in the academic dialogue of earlier decades. Among the associations that were established were also those that contributed to the public discourse about women and gender issues, initiated applied research projects, and aroused interest in research themselves. Some of the studies were also carried out by women researchers.[117] This directly led to some of the associations being especially established to improve the status of women in the Arab minority. There was one association that especially stood out because of its special activity of looking into new interpretations of the Muslim holy book (the Quran) that made it possible for Arab women to learn about their rights and to demand them.

There are thousands of Arab associations in the Arab sector in Israel that have been functioning during the past few decades; most are active in six main areas: religion, culture, housing and development, welfare, education, and research and the protection of civil rights, but there are also associations that are active in the areas of health and the quality of the environment. The following table shows the different areas of activity for 2010 and is based upon a division of the activities of 260 associations that are a representative sample of all the associations in the Arab sector.[118]

Table 4 The main areas of activity of social and civil organizations in 2010[1]

Religion	42%
Culture	13%
Housing and Development	5%
Welfare	9.5%
Civil rights	6%
Education and Research	17.5%
Others	7%

[1] Yitzhak Gal-Nur et al., *The Committee for the Examination of the Roles of the Third Sector in Israel and the Policy Taken Towards – A Summary Report* (Ben-Gurion University: The Israeli Institute for Research into the Third Sector, 2003), p. 47.

An analysis of the findings shows the great importance the Muslim and Christian religious identity has in the Arab society in Israel despite the changes that this society has experienced during the process of modernization and technological development. This is of course not the only explanation for the large number of religious associations, since the dynamic activity of the Islamic Movement in this area has also made a contribution to this through its associations that deal with religious matters, welfare, education, and health. Most of these associations were established as part of the vision to establish an independent, achievement-oriented community that would not be dependent on the government, as part of the approach of the northern branch of the Islamic Movement that believed in separatism. The activities of these associations stand out in two ways that are relevant to the framework of our discussion when compared to other associations. They are the only associations that have declared that they have chosen to operate independently of the state and have not tried to integrate into different public frameworks. They are also the only examples of organizations in Israel which carry out some activities in order to arouse protest, even violent at times, against the establishment. Especially involving claims, which over time, have proven to be unsubstantiated, that the mosques on the Temple Mount are in danger of being demolished or of collapse as a result of the steps taken by the Israeli government.[119]

In the legal sphere, what stands out is the tendency to be active in the protection of civil rights through a number of associations – claiming equal rights for the Arab minority and its increased integration into the state's public life. The most prominent of these are *Adalah* and *Musawa*. The *Adalah* association was founded in 1996 and since then has been active in protecting the human rights of the Arab citizens of Israel and the rights of the Palestinians in the occupied territories. The association works to gain both personal and collective rights for the Arab minority in areas such as land and planning rights, political and civil rights, economic, social and cultural rights, and the rights of prisoners. *Adalah* does this through presenting complaints and appeals on the principle issues to the Israeli courts and state authorities and by turning to international institutions and forums.[120] The content of the petitions that the association has made include striving for equality between Jews and Arabs and the integration of the Arab minority into Israeli society. The association also found itself indirectly involved in politics when one of its appellants asked the court to protect the right of Knesset Member Hanin Zuʿbi to take part in the Knesset elections in 2015. Other issues have included: the demand to pave a road from the village of Jisr al-Zarka to the Coastal Highway (route 2) in order to make accessibility to places of work easier for the village's residents; opposition to demolition orders in the village of Husainiyya and the provision of services to its residents; demanding that the Haifa municipality publicize notices about available positions in Arabic to make it easier for Arabs to gain employment in its departments; the creation of free educational organizations for children from unrecognized villages in the Negev; and the cancellation of certain impending employment criteria by Israel Railways whose introduction would have threatened the future continued employment of members of the Arab minority. According to some of the Arab researchers, these petitions and others play a central role in the efforts made by the Arab minority to achieve equality, and owing to the activities of the association the voices demanding affirmative action have grown and these benefit the minority.[121]

13
Adalah: The Legal Center for Arab Minority Rights in Israel and Other NGOs

The *Adalah* Center is a non-governmental, non-partisan and non-profit civil social organization registered in Israel. In fact, this is the first Arab center in Israel that is an independent legal organization which operates, according to its founders, "to protect human rights in general and the rights of the 'Arab Palestinian' minority in particular."[122] In *Adalah*'s view every human being is entitled to liberty, dignity and equality as the basic rights of an individual, and although these rights are protected in every democratic society, in a society that includes a (ethno-national, religious, cultural, etc.) minority group, a condition for enjoying these rights is society's acknowledgment of its collective rights as a minority. Such an acknowledgment guarantees the realization of the individual's basic liberties – otherwise, *Adalah*'s activists argue, the result will be recognition of the majority group and the repression of the minority group's rights, or discrimination based on collective affiliation. The organization's main goals, therefore, are to achieve equal individual and collective rights for the Arab minority in Israel in fields that include: land rights; planning and housing rights; civil and political rights; cultural, social, and economic rights; religious rights; women's rights; and prisoners' rights.

On the official website one can learn about *Adalah*'s activities in the past and present; the site lists publications and press releases and provides links to various Israeli, Palestinian and international organizations that deal with minority rights. In addition there are links to sites that deal with the Middle East, human rights organizations, and periodicals. From the above and the references to the organization's activity in the media and in academic research, one can learn about the actions and strategies used by the organization to achieve its objectives, which include the following:

1. Presenting cases before various legal institutions and state authorities in Israel regarding the rights of the Arab minority.
2. Advocating for legislation that will ensure equal individual and collective rights for the Arab minority.
3. Providing legal consultation to individuals, Non-Governmental Organizations and Arab institutions in Israel.
4. Making appeals based on legal precedents to international institutions and forums in order to promote the rights of the Arab minority and human rights in general.
5. Organizing study days, seminars and workshops, and publishing periodicals and reports on legal issues concerning the rights of the Arab minority.
6. Training legal apprentices, law students, and young Arab lawyers in the field of human rights.

The legal activity of the *Adalah* organization has been the foundation of its work since its establishment. In order to realize equality and protect the individual and collective rights of the Arab minority in Israel, *Adalah* presents appeals to Israeli courts, enters pleas and represents individuals in civil and criminal suits – while relying on Israeli law and precedence, international law, and the literature available on human and minority rights. *Adalah* is active on both the international and local levels. Its international activity includes participation in various UN committee meetings, primarily The United Nations Commission on Human Rights (UNCHR), international conferences that deal with human and minority rights, submitting reports to international bodies on the implementation of a range of international covenants that are relevant to human and minority rights issues in Israel and fostering contacts with international human rights organizations to inform about *Adalah*'s work and activities.

An analysis of *Adalah*'s petitions to the Supreme Court of Justice regarding the Arab minority's rights reveals that the organization follows an orderly plan which covers the full range of topics related to the individual and collective lives of the Arab minority in the State of Israel, including the following groups of issues:

1. Land, planning and construction. The organization has filed dozens of petitions directed at government authorities, such as that filed against the Israel Land Administration, which challenges policies that prevent Arab citizens from participating in tenders published for marketing Jewish National Fund land and that grant a 90 percent discount on the leasing of land only to people who have served in the military.[123]

2. The right to participate in political events, freedom of expression, freedom of movement, the findings of the Orr Commission, and family unification issues. The following are selected examples:

    (A) *Adalah* represented the Balad party and its leader, Bishara, against the attempt to disqualify them from participation in the Sixteenth Knesset elections. On January 9, 2003, the court accepted the appeals and thus ratified the legality of the nomination and participation of the above.

    (B) Extensive activity by *Adalah* regarding freedom of speech, such as in the petition to allow marking the day of *Nakba*, which was rejected, and the petition made against the attempt to prevent a procession protesting the war in Iraq, which succeeded.[124]

    (C) The organization's activity regarding the State Commission of Inquiry into the Events of October 2000 – the Orr Commission. The Commission summoned dozens of people to appear to give evidence, and requested expert opinions from specialists in Arab society in Israel. Seven professional expert opinions were presented, some initiated by the Commission and others by *Adalah*. On July 21, 2002, *Adalah* filed a petition with the Supreme Court of Justice in its own name and on behalf of the Higher Monitoring Committee for the Arab Citizens in Israel, the three Arab public representatives, and the Committee of the Bereaved Families of the October Riots. The petition sought to cancel the warnings issued against MK ʿAbd al-Malek Dahamshah, MK Bishara, and Sheikh Salah, and claimed that the Orr Commission had exceeded the scope of its mandate, had discriminated against the Arab public representatives and had violated their right to due process. The Supreme Court rejected the petition in August 2002.[125]

    (D) Activity regarding the unification of families. *Adalah*'s Review Volume 4 (2004) entitled "In the Name of Security" discusses the issue of security as a cultural, social, political and military concept. A prime example of *Adalah*'s activity in this area revolves around the new Citizenship Law, passed in the Knesset in July 2003. The law imposes restrictions on "granting citizenship to the area's [Arab] residents . . . including by way of family unification and on granting residence permits based on the Entry into Israel Law." *Adalah* claimed that the law was discriminatory and inequitable and directly violated Israeli citizens' constitutional right to personal liberty which is the foundation of personal autonomy, including their right to self-determination in the construction of a family life and fulfilling their most basic human needs.

3. Cultural, social and economic rights. *Adalah* has been intensively active in this sphere regarding the Arabic language, rights to education, health, and water, economic and religious rights, women's rights, prisoners' rights, and what they term "rights regarding the occupied territories."

4. Women's rights. The Convention for the Elimination of all Forms of Discrimination against Women (CEDAW) published under the auspices of the United Nations in 1978 was the first human rights convention targeted at protecting the rights of women. The resulting document was ratified by 178 countries including Israel (in 1998). *Adalah*, however, claimed that the convention's clauses had not been implemented in Israel's internal laws. In its online newsletter volume 10 (February 2005) *Adalah* claimed that: "due to the fact that Israel's report does not refer to the case of Palestinian women in the State of Israel, who are discriminated against for their national affiliation and for being women in general and women in Palestinian society in particular, the acting committee (including *Adalah*) had submitted a parallel report by Non-Governmental Organizations in order to emphasize the status of Palestinian women in Israel."

5. Human rights in the "occupied territories" and prisoners' rights. *Adalah* has been active in these issues – as well as reactive against what is perceived as violations of basic individual and collective rights. For example:

(A) Demanding that the children of security prisoners be allowed physical contact with their incarcerated parents during their visits at the penitentiary.[126]

(B) Petitioning for the right of attorneys to meet with the security prisoners on hunger strikes.[127] The Supreme Court of Justice accepted the petition. This is a precedent ruling by the Supreme Court of Justice.

(C) Demanding that the legal term "immediate military need," which the army uses as a basis for home demolition in the "occupied territories"[128] be defined. This petition against the demolition policy in the "occupied territories" was submitted on behalf of *Adalah*, the Palestinian Center for Human Rights in Gaza, and al-Haq Human Rights Legal

Advocacy Organization of Ramallah. It rests on the claim that international law and humanitarian law forbid home demolition, which constitutes a severe breach of the Fourth Geneva Convention and the rules of war.

(D) Uncompromising activity against the use of Palestinian civilians as "human shields".[129] The petition was submitted in May 2002 by six human rights organizations in addition to *Adalah*.

The *Musawa* (equality) association also deals with legal issues, and made an appeal to the Supreme Court of Justice to demand that the Ministry of Culture pay to carry out a survey that would map the cultural needs in Arab villages so that they could be budgeted for by the government. By doing this, they were expressing a clear interest in integration into Israeli society, but in contrast, the association provided teachers to independently teach children, unconnected to the state system, in the village of Ein Hud, after the Ministry of Education closed the village school and the pupils had to go to a school that was more than 20 kilometers away. In this case the temporary separatism paid off after the appeal made to the Supreme Court of Justice to reopen the school was approved. Similar activity performed separately from the state was carried out by the association in the non-recognized Bedouin villages in the Negev, which ultimately rewarded them with the financing of solar panels that allowed them to independently produce electricity after the government had refused to provide the infrastructure that would supply them with regular electricity.[130]

The associations that operate in the area of education reflect the complexity of the mixture of separatism and integration, and in practice prove that the two options can be simultaneously applied as the outcome of the religious and ideological heterogeneity that makes up the mosaic that is the Arab minority in Israel. One outstanding example of this can be found in the study that accused the Ministry of Education of attempting to carry out the de-legitimization of the Arab minority's group identity in Israel and exclude it from the public domain at a time when the Arab education system was, according to the research, waiting for two parallel developments – one being "the systematic and sincere involvement of the Ministry of Education in the progress being made towards the equalization of its status to that of Jewish education," and the other being "the broader and deeper involvement of the local Arab authorities and the local social organizations (the associations) in the progress being made with the program that would have the power to improve its deteriorated status." These were not the only things, since this double gift was being given while expressions of protest were taking place against the establishment's policy.[131] The clear message being expressed was that steps had to be taken to integrate the Arab minority, with equality, and to demand programs that would reduce the gaps between the majority and minority groups. If necessary, people would have to fight for this equality and integration by protesting, while at the same time, also acting independently and separately from the establishment, in order to strengthen the Arab education system in which the largest age group of Arabs in Israel, in fact the majority, were learning. This kind of experiment continued from 2008 on to establish an independent pedagogical council for the Arab education system.

The Center for Alternative Planning, a body whose name suggests the search for alternatives to the state, and which deals with representing the interests and needs of the Palestinian population in Israel in the areas of planning, lands, housing, growth and development, also seeks cooperation with the Israeli establishment. The organization asked to be recognized by the Ministry of the Interior for its activities as a public body, and received this in 2004. The goals of the center, as they were formulated when it was founded, also combine integration and independent activity: equality in the allocation of land resources and planning and development, cooperation in planning processes, and Jewish–Arab cooperation in economic and social development for all of the population. The center strives for the empowerment of the Arab population in order to protect its basic rights. In spite of the introduction by the Ministry of the Interior of master plans for Arab villages in the first decade of the 21st century, the center regularly publishes independent studies in which it attacks the government policies and sets out recommendations for the development of these villages, which it wants to execute in cooperation with the government.[132]

As a whole, most of the associations operate through turning to the establishment, and the readiness to enter into direct negotiations exists for most of them – except for those of the Islamic Movement that, having no other alternative, turns to the authorities for permits for their activities, which is the sum total of their connection with the establishment. Appeals for legal help are made when associations feel the channels of communication have been exhausted and are no longer useful. There is no organization whose main public activity focuses on public-political protest; it is possible that this is because of the historical fact that traditionally protest has been organized by political groups that already exist in the Israeli public arena, such as the Arab Committee for the Protection of the Lands, the National Students Union, The Islamic Movement, Balad, the communist faction, and others. Moreover, it is doubtful that the authorities would register an association that wrote on its registration forms that it would be focusing upon the expression of protest.

Since the beginning of the millennium, the associations have contributed to the advancement of the rights of the Arab minority in Israel and to the increase in this public's consciousness about its rights, especially among the younger generation. Even though this is the case, we are mainly talking about symbolic achievements that are less significant, at least according to some of the researchers, and what we have here is more of a media halo effect than a real long-time influence.[133] Being symbolic, these achievements do help to form the political consciousness of a minority that demands broader rights for itself; thus the potential for conflicts of interest with the government is created as an understanding of the gaps between the groups grows.

The multiplicity of associations in the Arab sector also revealed negative phenomena, such as the ideological factionalism that characterized the political activity in the Arab sector for many decades, which prevented cooperation that, according to some of the researchers, might have improved the situation of the Arab minority even more, and hastened the process of internal empowerment. Because of this, for example, the associations that were striving for integration and equality did not manage to present a united front in the demands presented to the establishment. A unification of the associations that were dealing with identical issues might have given greater weight to the demands being made, because this would have been done by a number of associations that represented a larger collective. Another difficulty the associations faced was the extravagant expenditures on publicity instead of on projects for the benefit of the community.[134]

14
Social Aspects and Employment in the Arab Sector

The central area that can help us solve the question of what the Arab public wants for itself and how its relations with the establishment (and the Jewish majority) function is revealed in the analysis of the work market in Israel. The structure of employment of the whole Israeli economy, including that of the Arab economy, has undergone significant changes during the last two decades. There has been a drastic drop in the number of people employed in agriculture, both

Jews and Arabs, for whom this field was their main source of income up until the eighties. There has also been a drop in the number of Arabs employed in manual works, industry, and construction, while the work market has been characterized by a growth in the number of those employed in education, commerce, banking, transportation, communications, and financial services.[135] These changes are only one expression of the process of modernization that the Israeli Arabs have been experiencing during the last two decades.

From 1970 until 1990 the relative presence of the Israeli Arabs in the Israeli workforce rose from 9 percent to 12 percent, and during these two decades there was also a real growth in the entry of Arab women into the workforce, although their number in 1990 was very low in absolute terms. Among the main reasons for the increase in women were the changes taking place in the structure of households, which were becoming less reliant upon agriculture and more upon external sources of income, and because of the greater accessibility to the large cities, a rise in the number of the highly educated, and a rising desire to integrate into the civilian work market.

The trend towards the integration of Arabs into the workforce also continued after 1990, with one of the outstanding trends being the change that was taking place in the employment sectors composition of the Arab workforce in Israel.[136] In 2010 the rate of employment in the workforce of the Arab population in Israel was 42.4 percent, while the rate of Arabs employed in the first decade of the twenty first century jumped by 52 percent (107,000 additional employees) compared to the 22 percent growth for the Jews. The number of employed Arab women rose by 76 percent (about 37,000 additional employees), which was a concrete expression of the changes Arab society was experiencing. Another significant finding was that 59 percent of the employees were in the 25–34 age range, the same age group that has traditionally been involved in protest activity against the establishment whenever this took place in the Arab minority.

The level of education is a key factor in the determination of the rate of participation in the workforce. The more the level of education rises the more the participation in the work cycle rises, and among the Israeli Arabs, there has been a constant growth in the number of highly educated people during the last two decades. Between 1997 and 2007 there was a growth of 45 percent in the number of Arabs who received a matriculation certificate. In the context of seeking integration, there was also a significant rise in the number of Arab students who chose technological studies and in 2004, 41 percent of them chose this track (as opposed to 26 percent in 1995) and there was an almost two-fold rise (33 percent as opposed to 19 percent) recorded for young women.[137]

There has also been a growth in the number of Arabs holding academic degrees during the last two decades. At the end of 2005 there were 60,000 Arab university graduates, 79 percent of whom were working as teachers in the civil workforce, but others were also working as chemists, engineers, physicists, doctors, accountants, psychologists and lecturers in academic institutions.[138] An outcome of this was the leap in the percentage of Arab graduates to close to 88 percent in 2012 and a slightly smaller percentage of Arab women graduates employed.[139] Altogether, at the end of 2012, the number of employed reached 348,000, and the changes that had taken place in the characteristics of the work market led to Arabs being integrated into professions that demanded higher education so that they also found themselves working in medicine, engineering, social work and teaching.

These figures clearly indicate the integration of a high percentage of Arabs; moreover, the overwhelming majority of the highly educated who had developed political awareness about the situation in the Arab minority chose to join the workforce and not turn to protest or violence. The fundamental desire to have a permanent place of work and, based upon this, to integrate into Israeli society reduced their participation in political organizations and the danger that they might turn to physical opposition to the establishment. "The Israeli Arabs want to work, but nobody wants to employ them" was the headline of an opinion piece that was published by an Arab Israeli in the middle of 2012 on one of the leading internet sites.[140] This was supported by findings in a survey that had appeared a year earlier which reported that 88 percent of the Arabs were interested in economic integration and 78 percent in civil integration.[141]

An even more fascinating finding showed that 70 percent of the Jews supported the economic integration of the Arab minority and an almost identical finding supported their social integration. The findings themselves indicate an identity of interests between Jews and Arabs when joint economic projects are being discussed and the potential to create a combined work market that would lead to a growth in the Israeli economy. An analysis of the Arab work market, however, has shown that the reality is not what is suggested by the findings of the survey, and that the Arab employment market is suffering from a number of basic maladies. It is important to raise these in the context of any discussion, not only because of the gap between the desire of the Arabs to integrate into the workforce and the existing situation, but also because the solutions that are being proposed might become part of the government's policy that will lead to a reduction in the gaps and in the unrest that might otherwise accelerate into ferment and protest among the Arab minority.

The Arab work market in Israel suffers from traditional problems, some of which are internal, while others, such as the following, are external:

1. The lack of equal opportunity for work between Jews and Arabs. The cultural barrier that exists in the employment of minority members makes it difficult for Jewish employers in the private sector to hire Arab candidates for jobs even if they find that they satisfy all the criteria and have abilities suitable to the job. Arabs who have tried to be hired by Jewish employers have come up against the presence of a glass ceiling, and the cumulative result is that well-educated Arabs find themselves being employed in positions that are not suited to their level of education.[142]

2. The limited accessibility to places of work. The physical infrastructures in the Arab villages and the lack of accessibility to great regularity in public transportation, despite improvements that have taken place, make gaining employment outside the villages difficult. The result is fewer or a total lack of opportunities to find suitable employment that is readily accessible.

3. The lack of suitable work opportunities in the Arab villages. Only in recent years, as the result of the efforts made by the Israeli establishment, has there been a certain amount of growth in the number of workplaces in these villages, but the number that exists does not satisfy the demand by young Arab men and women for jobs in the workforce. Obviously, work in the villages is preferable because of the proximity to their homes which makes the need for public transport unnecessary.

4. The entry of foreign workers into the work market in Israel. There has been a sharp rise in the number of foreign workers in Israel during the decades between 1990 and 2010 that compete with the Israeli Arabs for jobs in areas that do not demand higher education – such as building, agriculture and work in restaurants and hotels. The attractiveness for Jewish employers of hiring foreign workers is great for two reasons: since they are not Arabs, they are not branded as being potential security threats, while at the same time, the wages they earn are lower than those asked for by Israeli Arabs who know what the salary scales are in the Israeli economy.

5. The rise in the rate of unemployment in the Arab sector. There are a number of basic reasons for this phenomenon, among

which are the changes that have taken place in the Israeli work market, which needs fewer professional (and non-professional) workers in jobs requiring physical labor because of the accelerated transition to electronic mechanization. This situation has created a gap between the work abilities of some people in the (less-educated) Arab population and the minimal requirements needed for many jobs. Another reason for the rise in the number of unemployed is the high level of unemployment benefits paid by Israel to the unemployed, which is a situation that reduces the motivation to go out and find work that pays the minimum wage.

Two central problems can be identified as internal barriers to the development of the Arab work market and the increased integration into the Israeli economy in particular and Israeli society in general. One is the difficulty in understanding Hebrew, which was a significant barrier, and even when the motivation to go out and work has been high, it appears that this has been the barrier that prevented many minority members from doing it. According to at least one study, Arabs looking for work have avoided seeking to fill certain positions because of the language barrier. The fact that they have been forced to leave the village to work in a large factory was not as great a deterrent as the difficulty of handling a language that they did not speak well.[143] This phenomenon is especially severe among women who are interested in working in chain stores and service centers such as banks, credit companies and health funds, as they may come up against the language barrier.

The second difficulty also involved the employment of women. This has been a significant internal barrier and, despite the constant increase in the rate of employment of Arab women during the last two decades, which was the result of enlightened social values and the need for an additional wage earner in the Arab household, the number of Arab women who are employed is still low. In 2002 the population of Arab women of working age (over 15) was 369,000, of whom 63,000 were working. The number of those employed climbed to 22 percent in 2010, which was still low compared to the percentage of employed Jewish women which reached 67 percent at that time.[144] Two years later, at the end of 2012, the number of Arab women of working age stood at 410,000, and the percentage of those employed jumped to 30 percent, and in 2014, to 33 percent. The continuous growth in the number of employed demonstrates the profound social change undergone by the Arab population, including the women, which was seeking the golden path into Israeli society while preserving their traditions and adopting the components of functional modernism. The rise in the number of employed Arab women, which is impressive even in comparison with the rise registered in the number of employed Jewish women,[145] has mainly been in the 18–34 years age group, which is the dominant age group for those involved in protest or violence. The significance of the findings is that these same women are constantly striving to become part of the work market and do not turn to non-establishment political activity whose main purpose is protest and at times, violence.

The result of the growth in the number of Arab women working also created a new social phenomenon in the Arab sector, which was the establishment of day care centers for children and infants. The number of such centers has grown constantly during the last few years, although not enough to make it possible for every Arab woman who wants to do this to go out and work.[146] Despite this, at least among the Muslims who constitute the majority of Arabs in Israel, there is still a traditional cultural barrier according to which the woman's place is in the home and she should mainly concentrate on the raising of children. This barrier prevents Arab women, who value peace in the home over additional income, from going out to work when they get real opportunities to do so outside the village.[147]

These barriers are well-known to the decision-makers in Israel and are regularly presented to them. One of the lessons learned has been the need to make the work market more accessible to the Arab minority by creating physical infrastructures such as roads and public transportation, but also by creating more places of employment both in Arab villages and outside of them. Grants and incentives are given on a permanent basis by the government to encourage initiatives in different areas and to absorb Arab workers. Together with this, the Economic and Social Authority in the Prime Minister's Office handles a series of programs to increase the number of places of employment for Arabs with the goal of removing social barriers, creating mixed employment spaces, and creating compatibility between the skills of the Arab workers and the existing areas of employment.

15
The Arab Minority and the Issue of National/Civilian Service

The question of army service for the Arab minority is an issue that has been at the center of public discourse in Israel since the beginning of statehood. The Israeli government during the Ben-Gurion period exempted the Arab population from the rules governed by the security service law, according to which every boy and girl who reaches the age of eighteen is obligated to serve in the Army. It was only in the seventies that civilian service was introduced as an alternative to serving in the IDF for religious young women, and not until 2007, after continuous public pressure, did the government adopt the recommendation made by the Ivri Committee to require other groups that had been exempted from army service to be mobilized for civilian service – and this included the Arab population.

The idea of civilian service was as follows: every young Israeli who received an exemption from army service or was not called up for army service would be able to volunteer for a period of one or two years. At the end of this period of service, he/she would be eligible for recognition as someone who has performed national service and would be granted the same payments and benefits granted to demobilized soldiers. These included a demobilization grant, a temporary exemption from taxation, discounts in tuition fees, and the right to receive larger mortgages.[148]

While the government finally authorized civilian service for Arabs in 2007, the public debate about it had already begun in the middle of the nineties. This debate led to conducting a number of surveys which showed that about half of the Arab young men and women were interested in doing national service.[149] The question about when this would begin for the Arab minority, however, very quickly became a controversial public issue in the Arab sector; the debate revolved not only around the content of the service but even its name. The national context led to radicalization of the position taken by leadership factions in the Arab sector – they objected strongly to the idea by arguing that Israeli Arabs, whose national identity was Palestinian, would not be able to serve the Jewish national homeland. The semantic, but significant, solution that was found was the change of the name of the project from national service to civilian service, while the organizational idea of the Israeli establishment was that the members of the minority would do their time in service to the Arab community. This also did not satisfy the Arab leadership that was afraid that the realization of the project would lead to the imposition of compulsory civilian or army service upon young Arabs, which was a step that might create a split in their national allegiance to the Palestinian people. Part of the basis of this opposition lay in the personal interests of Arab public figures who were offended by the fact that they had not been participants in the decision-making process about the issue.

The Arab leadership was not satisfied with expressing verbal opposition, and different political groups, such as the Communist party and Higher Monitoring Committee, organized protest demonstrations through which they wanted to pass on a double message that consisted mainly of opposition to civil or national service and a demand to obtain rights from the state that would allow the creation of equality between the minority and majority groups. Editorials were published in the Arab press that called upon the Arab public not to participate in the project, and a number of efforts were made to get people to sign petitions against the government. The main arguments raised by the protesters were that rights and obligations should not be linked in a democratic country and that the government should adopt a policy that would bring about equality between the majority and the minority.[150]

The Arab public did not rush to take part in the protest demonstrations against national (or civil) service and we believe there were three reasons for this. First, some people did not know about the project so that they were not in a position to decide whether to participate in the protest or not; second, those who had heard about the project were well aware of its advantages and chose to join it and not protest; thirdly, it seems that the potential threat that it presented to the Arab minority in the form of a loss of national identity was abstract and not the concrete threat posed by the appropriation of land or the demolition of houses. A collective mobilization based upon the idea of opposing national service did not put down roots in the Arab minority and the opposition ultimately remained the province of the interested parties that were trying to extract personal benefits from it. Moreover, an analysis of findings since national service was opened up to include members of the Arab minority has shown a continuous rise in the numbers each year, with the number of Arabs taking part in the project in 2015 reaching 4,500 (for the 18-year-old group) compared to 500 in its first year.[151]

There are several reasonable explanations for the rise in the number of Arabs interested in participating in the national service program. First, the program was marketed aggressively by the Israeli government in a campaign that highlighted the benefits it was offering to Arab participants. Second were the possibilities offered to young Arabs to do their national service in the social and educational frameworks of the communities in which they had grown up. The result was the mobilization of a large number of Christian and Bedouin young women, most of whom found themselves doing civil service tasks in the areas of health, education and welfare in their own communities and continuing to live at home. Third, the civil service was viewed as something instrumental by many of the young people, since one could gain professional experience, enjoy benefits heretofore only provided to those who served in the IDF and, in addition, be helped to form an independent and responsible character.

On a more general level, as we learned from the responses of Arabs who had completed their civil service, it was clear that they had gained much from the period of their service, which had helped them to realize their plans in their fields of study and their entry into the world of work.[152] These findings also support the main argument of this discussion, which claims that these young people are moving themselves away from the sphere of politics, including participation in protest demonstrations – not to mention removing themselves from violent incidents. The provision of places where young Arab men and women could do their service that were opened up by the authorities, which included hospitals, schools, centers for the aged, welfare institutes and others, not only served the purpose of the participants but also helped to break down cultural barriers, since it created dialogue in the common spaces shared with Jews with whom they worked. The mutual exposure to each other has created another reality in the shared space, and in the long run the service has served these young people as an entry pass into institutes of learning and work in the civil service.

No less interesting or relevant to the discussion about where the young Arab is striving to get is also the examination of the findings that arise from the way Arabs who have completed their civil service and have entered the work market relate to their experience. In general most of them were satisfied with their civilian service, were proud of it, did not regret their volunteering, and would support the volunteering of a brother or sister. They feel that their civilian service strengthened their commitment and the feeling of not only belonging to Arab society but to Israeli society in general. The interaction with Jews in the shared public space more than once helped them to remove cultural blocks and barriers and to dispel prejudgments. This trend has been supported by another survey that was published in 2012 which included 1000 interviewees, half of whom were Arabs. Its findings indicate that most Arabs want to integrate into the country, including participating in civilian service. Sixty-two percent of the Arab interviewees agreed to Arab citizens doing civilian service on a voluntary basis and that this should become compulsory within five years. This finding clearly stands in contradiction to the position taken by the Arab leadership which has already exploited the issue of national-civilian service to attack the government. Another interesting point is the fact that the survey made it clear that if the management of the recruitment of the Arabs to civilian service moves from the Prime

Minister's Office to another government ministry or to shared responsibility for this with Arab representatives, the percentage of those agreeing to do compulsory civilian service would jump to 74 percent of all the interviewees.[153]

The trends that can be identified from the analysis of the subject of civilian service for the Arab minority are clear:

1. There was a continuous growth in the number of volunteers each year and this continued after 2010 as well.
2. The graduates of the service program more easily found their way into work and study situations.
2. The authorities cannot handle the growing demand which is the result of the aggressive publicity and the positive messages passed on by the graduates and those serving within family and social circles.
4. There is a clear gap in the perceptions of the Arab public about the project and those of the leadership actors that oppose it for personal and ideological reasons.

Young Arab men and women see the work market and the civilian/national service program as entry passes that also cement their position inside Arab society. The process of personal empowerment that they experience as they move between tradition and modernity also includes progress in their individuation ("my personal self") and less in their collectivization. The Arab does see himself as having a Palestinian identity, but his everyday life and the various possibilities that the country offers him in the areas of education, employment and housing push the involvement in national issues aside, and this is the paradox that has characterized Arab society in Israel for the last two decades. On the one hand there is a leadership that has a nationalist orientation, which is also forced to deal with civil issues – and on the other hand, there is a public that is looking towards instrumental and functional Israeli citizenship, while continuing to mainly express identification with nationalist issues, especially in times of escalating security problems in Judea and Samaria or the Gaza Strip, but which is not prepared to mobilize itself and invest resources in protest.

Most of the ways in which the Arab public has conducted itself in civilian affairs, expressing itself in striving for integration into the work cycle, learning structures, projects that the government has provided, and a process of self-empowerment, has had an effect on the directions the Arab leadership has taken. In a reality in which government ministries have been working towards the reduction of the gaps and increased civilian integration, the Arab public has been choosing to take what it can from the government. Turning to the use of protest against the government, and even more so to the use of violence against its representatives and institutions, does not only involve breaking the law but also the loss of opportunities that have opened up for members of the minority during the last two decades. The result has been a paucity of participants in protest events, a reduction in violent acts, and a satisfaction with holding memorial and nationalist identification days in which political activists take part in old style traditional activities. On a continuum that moves from separatism to violence, most of the Arab public has been choosing the option of integration, even if it is differential and does not, for example, include integration into security structures, over other options that are more oppositional and which can lead to disconnection from the country in the best case and negative escalation in relations in the worst case.

The classic Arab leadership, which is made up of members of the Knesset, the heads of Arab villages, religious figures, and others, now finds itself experiencing internal conflict. This national leadership wants to keep nationalist subjects on its agenda based on the assumption that they will rouse the public to act as a collective against the Israeli establishment. Thus Israeli actions in the Palestinian arena, or in the context of this arena such as military campaigns or the prevention of international assistance to terror organizations such as Hamas, arouse the leadership to acts of identification and protest into which they wish to rein the Arab population. An analysis of such exhibitions of protest since the October 2000 events has shown that the Arab public is not in a hurry to demonstrate in the streets, and has discovered the solution of expressing identification from a distance by expressing its responses in the social networks. In such a situation the Arab leadership is "forced" to adapt itself to the demands of the population – for clearly political reasons – and finds itself involved in dealing with civilian issues even if these do not necessarily lead to strengthening the nationalist collective component of the Arab minority. In this way it finds itself trying to help Arabs whose houses have been designated for demolition, solving budgetary crises in the local authorities, and finding ways to increase the resources available for the initiatives of citizens – all of which are activities that distract its attention from issues that have a clearly nationalist character.

Conclusions

This study has tried to identify the changes that have begun in the relations between the majority and minority in Israel during the last two decades, on the basis of the processes that have taken place in the fifty years that preceded it since the establishment of the State of Israel. A historical examination of these relations requires a point of view that is based upon three basic components that will continue to characterize the complex relationship between the parties: religion, citizenship and nationalism.

The historical examination shows that in the Declaration of Independence Israel already obligated itself to the assurance of freedom of religion and the preservation of the holy sites of all the religions. In the area of personal rights the state chose to preserve the Millet approach of the Ottoman Empire, which determined that in matters concerning family law and religious law each person would be subject to the laws of the group to which he/she belonged. As a result of this decision, the Muslims in the State of Israel, who are the overwhelming majority in the Arab minority, are subject to the laws governing the legal courts of Sharia (Islamic Law) which provides broad and exclusive judicial authority to the Islamic religious courts in these matters.

The state has not yet fully determined its relations with the Arab minority beyond the religious component; this study indicates that there has been a change from a security approach to an integrative (civil-security) approach over the last three decades as a result of the understanding that the Arab minority is both similar and different from the Palestinians in the territories in the way that they act towards Israel. As analyzed in the second half of the study, the series of decisions taken (and applied) by the government and the legislative steps taken have expressed the policy changes in practical terms. Together with these changes, however, a hostile, exclusionist and sometimes hateful public and parliamentary discourse has developed within the Jewish majority society against the Arab minority. The contradiction between a policy of reducing the gaps and a rise in the level of hostility in the Jewish public towards the Arabs demands more governmental attention and the intelligent management of this relationship. It is also clear that every development in the Palestinian arena – whether it is some political arrangement or security escalation – will both directly and indirectly influence the Israeli government's attitude towards the Arab minority group.

The establishment of an authority for the economic development of the Arab, Druze, and Circassian sectors in the Prime Minister's Office (2007), like the establishment of a state administrative center for national/civic service (2005), and the continuous rise of the rate of the number of Arabs employed in the civil service, were steps taken in the direction of integrating the majority and minority. Although more than a few government initiatives came up against cultural and bureaucratic barriers, as shown in the body of the study, adherence to continuing with these initiatives and broadening the basket of civil opportunities for the Arab minority could contribute to an improvement in the relations between the parties. If these are accompanied by a public dialogue that is characterized by the readiness to listen to each other, one can expect that the friction between the parties will lessen and the appearances of violence will be likely to take place less frequently, if at all, in the Arab minority.

For the Arab minority the civil and national aspects are more complicated. The main components of identity for the Arab minority are anchored in the Palestinian national identity and the social and familial links they have with the Palestinians in the West Bank and the Gaza Strip. The constant contiguity with the Jewish majority group has caused Arab society to develop accommodations with the majority group and it is precisely here that the paradox we are trying to unravel in this study lies. Together with powerful Palestinian national feelings, which are mainly characterized by identification expressed at times of escalation of security problems between Israel and the Palestinians in the territories, the Arab minority emphasizes its existence as part of the country it is living in. The changes that took place in the policy of the Israeli government from the beginning of the 1990s significantly increased the possibilities of integrating the Arab minority into the public life of the state. The processes of integration of the Arab minority into the different areas of life in the state have continued despite the new legislative initiatives and the expressions of hatred and racism in the Jewish society.

One of the results of these processes is the fact that, among the Jews and Arabs, there is no complete agreement about how the Arab minority's status should be defined or what alternative they should choose to determine their future existence. Despite this, there is wide agreement that the majority of the Arab sector would prefer not to give up their Israeli citizenship for any alternative. It seems that this citizenship provides them with the hopes and possibilities that they prefer over other models put forward by the extremist streams. The idea of the nationalist stream to establish a state for all its citizens and the idea of the religious-Islamist stream to establish an Islamist state are not perceived by the Arab minority as being practical goals whose realization is worth mobilizing themselves to work towards. The fact is that the vision documents publicized in 2006 were received with disinterest in the Arab community and, shortly after the first discussions they aroused with their publication, interest in them ended as did any real activity involving their content. The attitude of this minority towards the state is also not unanimous, as opinion polls have shown differences about the question of Israel's right to exist as an independent democratic state in which Arabs and Jews live.

From a sociological point of view, it is possible to identify a process of cumulative change in the Arab minority since 1948, from being a compliant generation to being a generation that "stood tall" – and which today has become a generation that dares to claim its place in the public, social, and political space of the state. During the first two decades since the establishment of the state, the leaders of the Arab public were dealing with the effort to reduce the damage being done by the authorities that saw this group as a security threat for ethnonational and religious reasons. The decision to establish a military government was a concrete expression of this view, which was based upon the potential security threats that might emanate from the Arab minority. The first generation of the Arab minority experienced the defeat in the 1948 war with the Zionists, its conversion from being a majority to being a minority, and the loss of ownership of the land. All of these induced the feelings of victimization and engraved the term *Nakba* into the consciousness of this generation's children.

The awakening of Palestinian nationalism among the Arab minority in Israel was a major focus of research conducted during the period after the June 1967 War, which indicated that this national feeling became politically established from the beginning of the 1970s and was expressed in violent protests that took place from the 1970s onwards. The generation of its children, who had not personally experienced the *Nakba*, "stood tall" and emphasized the components of the Palestinian national identity as part of its support for the battle being waged by the PLO against Israel. This support included continuous expressions of identification and protest during these years, a miniscule part of which also overflowed into violence against the Israeli government. This was almost a Catch-22 situation in which it was, in fact, the national "standing tall" of the Israeli Arabs that determined the harsh political and security policies of the Israeli establishment during the 1970s and 1980s. Only at the end of the 1980s, as a result of the escalation of the security situation in the territories and a changing of the guard in the Israeli government to include public figures with liberal orientations did the transition from a security point of view to a point of view that favored integration, take place.

The last two generations, from the 1990s onwards, have been characterized by the presence of a younger generation (60 percent of Israeli Arabs are aged 0–24) that is more daring and more demanding of its personal and collective rights. An addition to the struggle to preserve its Palestinian heritage (and the memory of the *Nakba*) was the civil dimension of the demand to recognize the Arab population in Israel as a national minority that deserves to have collective rights in the areas of religion, language, education and culture, lands and communications. Although the vision documents did not take root in the Arab society, in Israel the practical reality of the ongoing contact between the minority and majority groups, the opening of employment in the civil service to the younger generation of the Arab population, and the existence of a widespread civil dialogue (the result as well of an active civil society) did fashion a new generation that is Palestinian in its nationality and Israeli in its citizenship.

All of the above present the Arab minority and the State of Israel with a series of complex challenges going forward. In the tension that exists between nationality and citizenship (assuming that there is no intention to do damage to the freedom of religious rituals of the non-Jewish minorities), both parties will have to determine what their positions are vis-à-vis each other. There are a number of scenarios in the spectrum of possibilities that are worth sketching out for the readers that they might find useful for an analysis of the complex relations between the majority and minority groups:

Institutional autonomy, which means the establishment of a shadow government (an improved version of the Higher Monitoring Committee) that, will concern itself with the needs of the Arab minority without being dependent on services from the state (the vision of the northern branch of the Islamic Movement). This is an approach that is essentially separatist, which can in the long run express the demand for an irredentist entity. The interim stages could form a kind of cultural autonomy in the areas of education, culture, and communications, and autonomy in the areas of health and welfare.

A state of all its citizens according to Balad platform. This means that only citizens who are living in the political community have the right to influence their future. This kind of state is not identified with only one national group and provides complete equality between all the national groups living in it. This equality is expressed in the symbols, institutions and laws of the state, and emphasizes the identity that is common to all.

A de facto bi-national state (within the Green Line). In principle this is a preservation of the present situation in Israel. Theoretically the definition of the state is that it is Jewish and democratic but, in reality, two ethno-national (and religious) communities live side by side. The shared public space – in the parliamentary, judicial, economic, sports etc. arenas – does not bridge the gaps in attitude towards the questions of identity and character of the political entity in Israel. Israel, as a Jewish and democratic state, is not prepared to give up its distinctly Jewish character (and thus does not completely include the Arab minority), and the militant declarations made against the Arab minority is perpetuating the separate national identities of the two groups. The Arabs neither can nor want to identify with the Zionist symbols and thus remain hanging suspended between their Palestinian nationality and their Israeli citizenship.

Finally, this study has tried to examine the changes in Israeli policy towards the Arab minority and the sociological changes that have taken place in the Arab minority since 1990. It has not included an analysis of the Bedouin who are living in Israel (over 300,000 people, most of whom live in the Negev, which is in the south of Israel). This sector, which is a kind of sub-sector of the Arab minority group, is worth its own investigation since it has also not only undergone developmental changes throughout history but also changes in culture and various customs.

Notes

Preface

1 The determination of policy is defined as a process of judgment made by public bodies that choose between alternative directions in which action can be taken. The process consists of the definition of the problem that needs to be decided about, the presentation of a series of goals, the location of alternatives that can be acted upon, forecasting the expected results, comparing the alternatives and joining/selecting the most preferable. For more see: Yehezkel Dror, Improving Policy Making and Administration in Israel (Tel Aviv: Sifriyat ha-Minhal, 1978).

2 Francesco Capotorti, Study on the Rights of Persons Belonging to Ethnic, Religious and Linguistic Minorities (New York: United Nations, 1991), p. 96.

3 Whether the sovereignty of the original minority over the territory has been confirmed by international factors or not, in reality this minority was the sovereign power over the territory up until the presence of the new foreign factor and, from its point of view, it was the sovereign power over the land.

4 Council of Europe, Framework Convention for the Protection of National Minorities, 1995.

5 The Israeli Declaration of Independence, the official gazette of the Temporary Israeli Government: no. 1, Tel Aviv, Iyyar 5, 5708, May 14, 1948.

Part One The Historical Background

1 Sammy Smooha, "Approaches to Arab–Jewish Relations and the October 2000 Riots," in Jewish–Arab Relations in Israel: Dream or Broken Dream?" Studies in National Security (2001), issue no. 1 [Hebrew], pp. 17–32.

2 Whether the sovereignty of the original minority over the territory was authorized by international factors or not this minority was, in reality, the sovereign factor in the territory up until the appearance of a new and foreign factor which saw itself as sovereign over the territory. From the point of view of this research, there was no sovereignty over the country during the period of the British Mandate for either Arabs or Jews.

3 Amal Jamal, "Collective Rights for Original Minorities: Theoretical and Normative Views," in: Eli Rekhess and Sarah Osatsky-Lazar (eds.), The Status of the Arab Minority in the Country of the Jewish Nation (Tel Aviv University: The Ziv Centre, 2005), pp. 27–45 [Hebrew].

4 *The State Committee of Inquiry into the clashes between the security forces and Israeli citizens in October 2000* – Hereafter, The Orr Commission, named after Supreme Court Judge Theodore Orr who headed the committee.

5 Rasem Khamaisi, "The al-*Aqṣa* Intifada among the Palestinian Arabs in Israel: Processes, Motivations and Factors," in *The Orr Testimonies*, 2003 [Hebrew].

6 Ted R. Gurr, *Why Men Rebel* (Princeton: Princeton University, 1970).

7 After the 1948 war the Lebanese writer and academic Constantine Zureik published a book entitled "The Significance of the Defeat" in which he discussed the reasons for the failure of the Arab side in the war. After the June 1967 War Zureik wrote another book entitled "The Renewed Significance of Defeat."

8 The Orr Commission, p. 28.

9 The Israeli Declaration of Independence, *The Official Gazette of the Temporary Israeli Government* (Iyyar 5, 5708, May 14, 1948), issue no. 1.

10 Uzi Benziman and Atallah Mansour, *Sub-tenants: The Arab Israeli Citizens – Their Status and the Policy toward Them* (Jerusalem: Keter, 1992), p. 211 [Hebrew].

11 Eli Rekhess, "The policy principles towards the Arab population I Israel," in Varda Pilavsky (ed.), *The Passage from the Yishuv to Statehood 1947–1949: Continuity and Change* (University of Haifa, The Herzl Institute for Zionist Research, 1990), p. 295 [Hebrew].

12 Ra'anan Cohen, *In the Tangle of Loyalties – Society and Politics in the Arab Sector* (Tel Aviv: Am Oved, 1986), p. 43 [Hebrew].

13 Yair Boimel, *Blue White Shadow* (Tel Aviv: Pardess, 2007), pp. 17–69 [Hebrew].

14 The Provisional Government Covenant, 13, Sections 15–16 [Hebrew].

15 Yossi Amitai, "The Arab Minority in Israel during the Military Government period: 1948–1966," in: Anita Shapira (ed.), *Independence – The First Fifty Years* (Jerusalem: The Zalman Shazar Centre, 1998) [Hebrew].

16 Pinhas Lavon, the official site, www.pinhas-lavon.com, retrieved April 29, 2014.

17 *al-ha-Mishmar*, Daily, Hebrew, January 15, 1948.

18 Amitai, *The Arab Minority*, p. 130.

19 Israel State Archive (ISA)/L/303/21; 307/56.

20 ISA/FM/A/2401/19.

21 ISA/L/308/4.

22 ISA/L/308/20, memorandum from January 28, 1949.

23 *al-ha-Mishmar*, December 1, 1948.

24 ISA/L/304/8, From Yehoshua Palmon to the governors, June 12, 1949.

25 IDF archives, 53/28/1960, Avigur letter.

26 *Ben-Gurion Diary*, October 27, 1952.

27 The Ratner Committee included the head of the committee, Yohanan

Ratner, who was the head of the first national command of the Hagana and the Palmach, Daniel Oster, who was the first mayor of Jerusalem after the Declaration of Independence, and Yaakov Salomon. The report was written in 1955 and presented to the political level at the end of the same year. The citation is taken from page 6 of the committee report.

28 *The Ratner Committee Report*, 1957, pp. 7–10.

29 Yigal Alon, *A Screen of Sand* (Tel Aviv: Am Oved, 1960), p. 327 onwards [Hebrew].

30 *Ben-Gurion Diary*, November 14, 1958.

31 Pinhas Rozen, who was head of one of the committees examining the necessity of the military government, was one of them.

32 The Central Bureau of Statistics, annual no. 15, 1967.

33 On May Day 1958 riots broke out in Nazareth and spilled over into Wadi ᶜAra. The Arab Communist Party members of the Knesset, aided by locals, instituted a violent protest demonstration to demand the improvement of the situation of the Arab citizens. The reaction of the government was harsh and hundreds of rioters were arrested while dozens of people were injured in clashes with the security forces. See more on this event in: Gadi Hitman, *Israel and Its Arab Minority, 1948–2008: Dialogue, Protest, Violence* (Baltimore, MD: Lexington, 2016), pp. 77–97.

34 The Knesset protocols, February 22, 1960, p. 663.

35 The Knesset protocols, February 20, 1962, p. 1316.

36 *Maᶜariv*, Daily, Hebrew, February 18, 1962.

37 ISA/G/6397 /3944/2.

38 Knesset minutes, February 20, 1962:1326. Ben-Gurion did not just announce the easements to the Knesset for nothing since he wanted to neutralize the appearance of a growing opposition in the legislature that was calling for the cancellation of the mechanism of the military government.

39 ISA/G/6337/1653.

40 Knesset minutes, October 23, 1963, p. 51.

41 ISA/L/313/11.

42 Boimal, 2002, p. 149.

43 The Knesset protocols, November 8, 1966, pp. 228–242.

44 ISA/FM/2451/13.

45 *Ben-Gurion Diary*, October 26, 1948.

46 ISA/FM/2401/22.

47 Alexander Bligh, "Israel and the refugee problem: from exodus to resettlement 1948–52," *Middle Eastern Studies* 34(1998), Issue 1, 1998.

48 There is no room in this work to deal with the various significant issues of both these laws. The very brief mention made of them here is essential to the study because of the vote on the policy carried out by the government in which there were elements that created a distinction in the way the government related to the Jews on the one hand and to the non-Jews on the other.

49 ISA/G/297/59.

50 ISA/FM/2451/13.

51 The department was established as the result of the integration of the Committee for Arab Property that had been created by the Higher Command of the Hagana in March 1948 and the attachment of additional clerks that had been attached to Ben-Gurion. See Arnon Golan, "The seizing of Arab lands by Jewish settlements in the War of Independence", *Cathedra* 63 (5752), pp. 124–125.

52 Details of all the laws were published in *Davar,* Daily, Hebrew, November 15, 1958.

53 Ṣabri Jiryis, *The Arabs in Israel* (Haifa: The ha-Mehaber publication, 1966). The book deals with the everyday hardships that the Arab citizens had to endure during the military government in everything concerned with traffic, employment, education and other areas. They had contact with the military government officers who were the operative arm of the central government. Jiryis, who is a Greek-Catholic, born in the village of Fasuta in the Western Galilee, was one of the founding members of the "al-Arḍ " movement which was outlawed in the middle of the 1960s after it tried to take part in the Knesset elections. He left the country after this and became a prominent member of the PLO.

54 Yosef Vashitz, "Majority and Minority," *Bashaᶜar* (1966), p. 6.

55 ISA/GL/17037/25.

56 Jiryis, *The Arabs in Israel*, pp. 28–29.

57 Khalil Kaoughi, *The Arabs under the Israeli Occupation since 1948* (Beirut: PLO Research Center, 1973), pp. 142–152 [Arabic].

58 *al-ha-Mishmar*, May 23, 1949.

59 Ahmad Saᶜdi, "Social Conceptions, Citizenship Rights and Protest: The Road to the October Events," *Orr Testimonies* (Hebrew), (2003), p. 185

60 The list of the towns and villages that were destroyed or damaged during the war in 1948 appears according to a geographical distribution on the internet site www.nakba-on line.tripod.com.

61 ISA/GL/17108/28.

62 Charles Kayman, "After the Catastrophe: The Arabs in the State of Israel, 1948–1950", *Research and Review Notes*, booklet 10, (Haifa, 1984) [Hebrew].

63 Yitzhak Oded, "Land Losses among Israel's Arab Villagers," *New Outlook* 7 (1964), No. 7, p. 14.

64 Following the appropriation of lands for the construction of Upper Nazareth an appeal was made to the Supreme Court of Justice in 1955. The state responded by arguing that, among other things, what was involved was the construction of a government complex that would be populated by clerks and that the government had the right to choose the site as it saw fit. The court accepted this argument. For more on this see: The Supreme Court of Justice 30/55, The Committee for the Protection of Appropriated and Other Lands in Nazareth vs. The Minister of Finance and Others., Rulings, 9 (2), p. 261 onwards.

65   Benziman and Mansour, *Sub-tenants*, p. 73.

66   Ibid., p. 74.

67   ISA/GL/17019/3.

68   Benziman & Mansour, *Sub-tenants*, p. 77.

69   Toledano document, cited from Benziman & Mansour, *Sub-tenants*, p. 76.

70   *Ha'aretz* , Daily, Hebrew, May 24, 1976.

71   The Prime Minister's Office. The Bureau of the Advisor on Arab Affairs, "The detailed plan of operations" (1979), pp. 10–11.

72   Benziman & Mansour, *Sub-tenants*, p. 94.

73   The detailed plan of operation, p. 17.

74   Prime Minister's Office, the Bureau of the Advisor on Arab Affairs, *The plan of operations* (1979).

75   Benziman and Mansour, *Sub-tenants*, p. 84.

76   The Prime Minister's Office, The Israeli Arabs – An assessment of the situation, goals and policy suggestions, the Advisor's Bureau 1978, pp. 5–6.

77   Benziman & Mansour, *Sub-tenants*, p. 86.

78   The Prime Minister's Office, The Bureau of the Advisor on Arab Affairs. Prime Minister's Office, the Bureau of the Advisor on Arab Affairs, Selection of Events in the Sector 2, March 1981, pp. 13–14. The data about classrooms do not include construction for pupils in Bedouin settlements in the north of the country.

79   Ibid., April 3, 1981, p. 31.

80   Prime Minister's Office, *The Policy towards the Arab Israeli Citizens* (1985), pp. 2–5.

81   Benziman & Mansour, *Sub-tenants*, p. 86.

82   Arnon Sofer, *A Proposal for Policy towards the Arab Sector in Israel.* The document was presented to the Prime Minister's Advisor on Arab Affairs in 1987. The citation appears on p. 48 of the document.

83   Ibid., p. 38.

84   The Prime Minister's Office, The Bureau of the Advisor on Arab Affairs, *A Proposal for the Israeli Government's Policy Towards the Arab Sector* (1987), p. 14.

85   Minister Moshe Arens resigned from the government following the decision to cancel the Lavi airplane project which he opposed.

86   Benziman and Mansour, *Sub-tenants*, p. 93.

87   Selection of Events in the Arab Sector 22, November 1982, p. 1.

88   Israel Koenig – Head of the northern branch of the Ministry of the Interior – oversaw the contacts with the heads of the Arab villages. The agreements that were made between the government and the heads of the Arab villages were of great significance not only because of the reaching of an agreement but because of the involvement of Koenig who was perceived in the Arab community as a hostile figure after he wrote the 1976 report in which he claimed that the Arabs in the Galilee were a security risk and that they should be encouraged to emi-

grate from the country. See in: *al-Anba*, Daily, Arabic, April 2, 1984.

89 Selection of Events in the Arab Sector 27–28, May 1983; Collection 35–36, December 1983–January 1984.

90 Benziman and Mansour, *Sub-tenants*, pp. 76–90. Sami Smooha also found a similar pattern of behavior by the Israeli establishment at the end of the 1970s and, according to him, the establishment had no interest or time to deal with the question of the Israeli Arabs. See: Sami Smooha, "The existing policy and alternatives towards the Arabs in Israel." *Megamot* (September 1980), p. 14 [Hebrew].

91 Ibid., pp. 14–18. See also: Ian Lustik, *Arabs in the Jewish State* (Haifa: Mifras, 1985).

92 Adham Saouli, "Arab Organizations within the Israeli State" *Journal of Social, Political and Economic Studies* 26 (2001), no. 2, p. 444.

93 Azmi Bishara, "The Israeli Arab: A study in a mutilated political discourse." In: Ruth Gabizon and Dafna Hacker (eds.), *The Arab–Israeli Rift in Israel: An Anthology* (Jerusalem: The Israeli Institute of Democracy, 2000), p. 36.

94 The Orr Commission, p. 27.

95 Rasem Khamaisi, *The al-Aqṣa Intifada*, p. 56.

96 The Mufti Hajj Amin Al-Husseini, for example, left for France already after the Second World War. For more see: Tsilla Hershko, *Between Paris and Jerusalem: Zionism and the Establishment of the State of Israel 1945–1949* (Tel Aviv: The Defense Ministry, 2000); Yuval Arnon Ohana, *The Arab Revolt in the Land of Israel 1936–1939* (Jerusalem: Ariel, 2013), pp. 185–198.

97 Benny Morris, for example, argues that the weakness of the Arab leadership was due to a number of reasons, the main one being the small number of national institutions that was essential for the stage prior to the establishment of a state. Other reasons he gives are: the split between the Muslims and the Christians and clashes between clans. For more see: Benny Morris, *The Birth of the Palestinian Refugee Problem 1947–1949* (Tel Aviv: Am Oved, 1986), pp. 27–37 [Hebrew].

98 *Ha'aretz* , February 4, 1966.

99 Rustam Bastuni, "The Arab Society in Israel," *The New Orient* 15 (1965), p. 3 [Hebrew].

100 The categorization of the leadership was done by Salam Jubran, one of the Maki leaders in the past and editor of the newspaper *al-Ittihad* in February 1993. For more see: Hezi Kalo, "The development of the national leadership of the Israeli Arabs – trends and directions," The National Security College (1993) [Hebrew].

101 ISA/GL/17037/25.

102 Ibid.

103 ISA/GL/17037/20.

104 ISA/GL/17029/20.

105 Knesset minutes, Vol. 1–2, December 1951.

106 Knesset minutes ,Vol. 17–18, May 16, 1955.

107 The Program of the Communist Party. The document was written in the Communist Party during the 1950s and is not dated. The citation appears on p. 17 in the pamphlet that can be found in the library of the Givat Haviva Information Center [Arabic].

108 ISA/L/307/56, May 5, 1954, the Zayyad letter.

109 On May 28, 1953 a delegation of the Union for the Protection of Arab Rights in Israel, a body that was established by Maki and that demanded the cancellation of the military government, which it defined as "national discrimination," came to the Knesset.

110 In June 1953 about 12,000 citizens signed a petition on this subject. This is recorded in the Knesset minutes, 13–14, June 8, 1953, p. 1521.

111 In this context the Maki newspaper *al-Ittihad* stood out as did the *al-ha-Mishmar*, the Mapam newspaper.

112 One of these was the appeal made to the consciences of the Israeli public by the Committee for the People Uprooted from the Village of Birᶜam on June 8, 1949 when it called upon them to make it possible for them to return to their homes. This letter was also sent to the Prime Minister's Office from which they received an answer in which Yehoshua Palmon, the Prime Minister's Advisor on Arab Affairs informed them that, because of security considerations, it would not be possible to return them to their homes.

113 The protocols of all the evidence given can be found in the files of the military government in the Information Centre of Givat Haviva.

114 *al-Ittihad*, Daily, Arabic, November 2, 1956.

115 Knesset minutes, December 12, 1956.

116 Judge Binyamin Zohar was chairman of the committee and its members were Abba Hushi, the mayor of Haifa and the lawyer Aharon Khoter-Yishai.

117 *al-Ittihad*, November 13, 1956.

118 Meir Vilner, one of the prominent Jewish members of Rakah, verified it in his article under the title: The first Land Day. Seen at www.icf.org.il, June 20, 2008.

119 Shira Robinson, "Local Struggle, National Struggle: Palestinian Responses to the Kafr Qassem Massacre and its Aftermath, 1956–1966," *International Journal of Middle East Studies* 35 (2003), no. 3, p. 400.

120 Documents and papers from the Maki archives, manifesto published on the anniversary of the Kafr Qasem massacre. A collection of documents and papers about Maki that were collected in the archives of the party in Yad Tabenkin was found in the library of Givat Haviva.

121 *al-Ittihad*, October 24, 1957; November 1, 1957.

122 Yair Boimel, "The Military Administration and its Cancellation Process 1958–1968," *The New East* 43 (2002), pp. 138–139 [Hebrew].

123 Berl Belti, *The Struggle for Jewish Existence* (Jerusalem: Magnes, 1981), pp. 49–50 [Hebrew].

124 Maki 13 Conference Minutes, Tuma's speech, p. 180.

125 *Maaᶜriv*, February 3, 1958.
126 *Zo Haderekh*, Weekly, Hebrew, February 9, 1958.
127 Belti, p. 62.
128 *al-Ittihad*, May 6, 1958.
129 Belti, p. 63.
130 Knesset minutes, 27, March–September 1958, p. 1900.
131 The importance of Member of the Knesset Vilenska's remark is not in what she said but that she was the only person that found it necessary to interrupt what Ben-Gurion was saying. Her Arab friends preferred to remain silent during the Knesset discussion.
132 Knesset minutes 27, March–September 1958, p. 1901.
133 Belti, p. 87.
134 *Qol ha-ᶜAm*, Daily, Hebrew, April 13, 1962.
135 Belti, p. 103.
136 For more about the split in the ranks of Maki that led to the establishment of Hadash alongside Maki see Balti, pp. 110–114.
137 *Ha'aretz* , December 12, 1959.
138 *Kifa al-Arḍ* , monthly, Arabic, December 7, 1959.
139 Supreme Court of Justice 241/60, Kardush vs. The Registrar of Companies.
140 Ori Stendahl, *Between the Hammer and the Anvil* (Jerusalem: Academon, 1992) p. 237.
141 Israel High Court sitting as the Supreme Court of Justice, Elections appeal 1/65, Yaᶜakov Yerador vs. the head of the Central Elections Committee for the Sixth Knesset. Ruling, vol. 19 (1965), part 3, pp. 365–390.
142 ISA/G/382/15/l, 6243/30.
143 *al-Ittihad*, December 2, 1966.
144 Knesset minutes, November 8, 1966, p. 234.
145 *al-Ittihad*, June 6,1967.
146 Knesset protocols, July 31, 1967: 2781.
147 Kahougi, pp. 553–555; *al-Ittihad,* June 20, 1967.
148 ISA/L/13/ 289.
149 Stendahl, pp. 296–302.
150 Ibid., p. 303.
151 Rustam Bastuni, "Socialism and the Israeli Arabs," in Zeev Goldberg (ed.), *Western Socialism – Anthology 16* (Beit Berl, 1971), pp. 65–71.
152 Zuᶜbi, ᶜAbd al-ᶜAziz, *The Arab Citizens of Israel and Their Dilemma of Double Loyalty* (Macalot, 1971); Khalil Nakhleh, "Cultural Determination of Palestinian Collective Identity: The Case of the Arabs in Israel," *New Outlook* 18 (1975), no. 7, pp. 31–40.
153 *al-Mirṣad*, Weekly, Arabic, August 31, 1972.
154 During the 1960s undisturbed Egyptian, Syrian and Lebanese television broadcasts could be received in Israel (also because of the absence of Israeli television until 1968). These broadcasts were a direct channel of communication for the Israeli Arabs who were exposed to anti-Israel

content that was broadcast and which placed an emphasis on Arab national issues. For more see: Yaakov M. Landau, *The Arabs in Israel: Political Studies* (Tel Aviv: Maᶜarkhot, The Ministry of Defense, 1971), pp. 45–46.

155 Lustick, *The Arabs in the Jewish State*, pp. 241–242.

156 This was the expression given to the harsh expressions of violence that took place in the Hashemite Kingdom of Jordan during September 1970, a month during which the Jordanian army were hunting down the PLO's terrorist organizations that had established themselves in the kingdom.

157 Gideon Shiloh, *The Arab Citizens of Israel in the Eyes of the Arab Countries and the PLO* (Jerusalem: The Harry Truman Institute of Research into the Middle East, series of research and studies, 1982), p. 75, p. 78.

158 Landau, *The Arabs in Israel*, p. 256.

159 Alexander Bligh," Political trends in the Israeli Arab population and its vote in parliamentary elections," *Israel Affairs* 19 (2013), no. 1, pp. 21–50.

160 The concept of "relative participation" becomes even more relevant from the research point of view when one examines the participation of the Arab voter in later elections. This is because a comparative analysis of the percentage of voters shows a consistent drop in the numbers. In the 2006 elections 56% of eligible voters voted in the Arab sector and in 2009 and 2013 the rate of voters was 54%.

161 *al-Dustur*, Daily, Arabic, November 26, 1979.

162 Stendahl, *Between the Hammer and the Anvil*, p. 254.

163 *al-Ittihad*, October 23, 1973, p. 6.

164 The poem first appeared in *al-Ittihad* on December 23, 1973. When it was published again on October 4, 1974 it created a great controversy because of its content which expressed complete identification with the Egyptian successes on the battlefield. For more on this see: Avraham Yinon. "Tawfik Ziad: We are the majority here," in Aharon Layish (ed.), *The Arabs in Israel – Continuity and Change* (Jerusalem: Magnes Publications, 1981).

165 A comparative analysis of involvement in terrorist activity shows a decrease in the rate of involvement of Arab Israelis. Fifty-five were involved in the period between 1973 and mid-1976, an average of 14 per year, as opposed to 320 Arab Israelis involved between 1967 and 1973, an average of 54 per year.

166 *al-Ittihad*, June 27, 1975.

167 *al-Ittihad*, August 19, 1975.

168 *al-Ittihad*, February 24, 1976.

169 Ibid., March 2, 1976, p. 1.

170 Ibid., March 9, 1976.

171 www.icf.org.il/landday25.

172 *al-Ittihad*, February 20, 1976, p. 2.

173 *al-Dustur*, February 26, 1979.

174 Eli Rekhess, "The Educated," p. 188.

175 *Maʿariv*, March 2, 1978.

176 Ibid., January 24, 1979.

177 Ṣabri Jiryis, "The Arabs in Israel: 1973–79," *Journal of Palestine Studies* 8 (1979), no. 4, pp. 34–35.

178 *Haʿolam ha-Zeh*, Weekly, Hebrew, April 22, 1981.

179 Nadim N. Rouhana, "The Political Transformation of the Palestinians in Israel: from Acquiescence to Challenge," *Journal of Palestine Studies* 18 (1989), no. 3, p. 45.

180 The nine bodies were "The Sons of the Village," The Progressive National Movement, (PNM) that was made up of students, "ha-Thiya (Resurrection) Taibeh", "The Dir el Assad Front," "The Union in Memory of Rashad Hussein" (an Arab Israeli intellectual), "The Voice Association" (publisher of books and poems in Arabic), "The Anis Kardush Fund" (named after the uncle of Mansur Kardush), "The Friends of Prisoners Association" and "The Nazareth Academics Association."

181 Up until 1980, when the law governing associations was legislated, a variety of organizations, including political ones, registered themselves as Ottoman associations.

182 Selection of Events in the Sector 2, March 1981, p. 30.

183 *The Jerusalem Post*, Daily, English, September 14, 1980; *al-Anba*, September 14, 1980.

184 *al-Ittihad*, April 19, 1982.

185 Selection of Events in the Sector 14, March 1982, pp. 17–18.

186 Selection of Events in the Sector, 17–18, June–July 1982, p. 1.

187 *al-Anba* newspaper, July 2, 1982.

188 Selection of Events in the Sector, June 1982, 17–18.

189 *Haʿolam ha-Zeh*, July 14, 1982.

190 Eli Rekhess, *Challenges for Rakah in the Arab Sector* (Tel Aviv, 1983), p. 95.

191 *Haʿolam ha-Zeh*, August 4, 1982; Selection of Events in the Sector 19, August 1982, p. 13.

192 Selection of Events in the Sector, June 1982 17–18, p. 11.

193 *al-Ittihad*, September 21, 1982, p. 1.

194 *Ha'aretz* , September 22, 1982; Atallah Mansour, *Haaretz*, October 5, 1982.

195 Selection of Events in the Sector 20–21, September–October 1982, pp. 4–6.

196 *Ha'aretz*, November 16, 1982.

197 Eli Rekhess, *The Eleventh* Knesset *Elections in the Arab Sector* (The Dayan Center for Studies of the Middle East and Africa, Tel Aviv University, August 1984).

198 *al-Ittihad*, December 28, 1982; *al-Fajr Weekly*, March 4, 1985.

199 Selection of Events in the Sector 37–38, March–April 1984, pp. 11–14.

200 Selection of Events in the Sector 41–42, August–September 1984, p. 21.

201 *al-Ittihad*, October 1, 1985; *al-Watan*, September 26, 1986.

202 *al-Ittihad*, February 4, 1986.

203 *al-Fajr*, October 8, 1985.

204 *al-Ittihad*, November 22, 1985.

205 *al-Ittihad*, December 17, 1985, p. 2.

206 The government claimed that this was a military area and the Sakhnin council claimed that this was in its area.

207 The First Intifada took place during 1936–1939, and in other publications was called the Great Arab Revolt.

208 The strike that took place on "Equality Day" took place on the day that the government had slated for providing a solution to the distress of Jewish sectors in the country. The fact that the government had also decided to allocate funds to the Arab local authorities was perceived by the Arab leadership as an achievement of the strike.

209 *al-Watan*, Weekly, Arabic, December 11, 1987, p. 1.

210 *al-Ittihad*, December 12, 1987, p. 8.

211 Ibid.

212 Ibid.

213 Ibid. December 15, 1987, p. 1.

214 *al-Ittihad*, December 18, 1987, p. 1.

215 *al-Watan*, December 18, 1987, p. 1.

216 *al-Sirat*, Weekly, Arabic, March 10, 1988, pp. 9–10.

217 *al-Ittihad*, December 18, 1987, p. 7.

218 *al-Ittihad*, December 20, 1987, p. 7.

219 *Zo-ha-derekh*, December 23, 1987, p. 1.

220 Stendahl, p. 13.

221 *al-Ittihad*, December 31, 1987, p. 1. In his address Milo did not reveal the information that Zayyad had given the instructions for the throwing of stones.

222 The Knesset Minutes, December 30, 1987.

223 Khamaisi, "The al-*Aqsa* Intifada," p. 66.

Part Two   The Government's Policy, 1987–2010

1 *al-Ittihad*, August 29, 1990.

2 *al-Ittihad*, November 11, 1988.

3 *Ha'aretz*, February 21, 1989.

4 *Ma'ariv*, November 15, 1988.

5 Prime Minister's Office, Arab Affairs Bureau, Topics for a Radio Interview, December 30, 1991.

6 The Markowitz Committee examined the issue of illegal building in the Arab sector and, in August 1986, presented its findings to the Minister of the Interior. Its members made the following recommendations: to grant building permits retroactively to buildings illegally built in areas that were included in the master plan for the Arab villages; to impose limitations upon other buildings; to be satisfied with a limited amount of the demolition of offending buildings. For more see: Inter-Ministerial

Committee for illegal construction within the Arab sector, August 1986.

7   The State of Israel, Ministry of Interior, *A Progress Report Regarding Illegal Building*, March 14, 1989, p. 2.

8   *The Master Plan for Arabs in Israel: Situation Report* (The Arab Center for Alternative Planning, 2012), p. 26.

9   Kais Nasser, Housing Shortage and Illegal Building within the Arab Society in Israel: Current Obstructs and Recommendations for a Change (*Dirasat Center*, Nazareth, 2011), p. 8.

10 Research Center of the Israeli Parliament, *Local Planning in the Arab Sector* (Jerusalem, 2010).

11 Ibid., p. 4.

12 Aziz Haidar, *The Collapse of the Local Arab Municipalities: A New Offer for Reconstructing* (Jerusalem: Van Leer Institution, 2010).

13 Ministry of Interior, a Letter from the General Manger to the Mayor of Shfarᶜam, June 24, 1988.

14 Prime Minister's Office, *Budgets for Arab Sector*, March 8, 1992.

15 Prime Minister's Office, Deputy Minister Roni Milo's Letter, December 30, 1987.

16 Benziman and Mansour, Sub-tenant, p. 90.

17 *Ha'aretz*, May 1, 1989.

18 Minister Olmert's interview with Benziman and Mansour, p. 95.

19 *al-ha-Mishmar*, January 27, 1989.

20 Ministry of Minorities, A Multi-Year Plan for the Minority Population, June 1990.

21 Benziman and Mansour, *Sub-tenants*, pp. 96–97.

22 *al-Ittihad*, March 18, 1991.

23 This decision was implemented in 1994.

24 Prime Minister's Office, *The Arabs in Israel: An Effort to Equality* (August 1992), p. 2.

25 Ibid., pp. 3–9.

26 *al-ha-Mishmar*, November 20, 1992.

27 *Davar*, January 26, 1993.

28 *Yediot ha-Galil*, Weekly, Hebrew, July 2, 1993.

29 *Davar*, July 14, 1993.

30 *Kull al-Arab*, Weekly, Arabic Newspaper, August 26, 1993.

31 *Sikkuy Voluntary Association* (Annual Report 1993), p. 1.

32 *Civil Rights Association*, Annual Report, 1996.

33 Orr commission, p. 50.

34 Ibid., p. 1.

35 The Guidelines of the twenty seventh Government of Israel, 1996–1999.

36 Knesset minutes, July 2, 9, 22, 1996.

37 Ibid., December 18, 1996.

38 *al-Ittihad*, August 13, 1996.

39 Knesset minutes, July 8, 1996.

40 Knesset minutes, July 23, 1996.

41 Knesset minutes, January 13, 1997.

42 Knesset minutes, March 5, 1997.
43 Knesset minutes, March 26, 1997.
44 Knesset minutes, May 28, 1997.
45 *Ṣawt al-Ḥaqq wal-Ḥurriyyah*, Weekly, Arabic, November 29, 1997.
46 Knesset minutes, July 23, 1997.
47 The seven villages were: Husainiyya, Ras el-ᶜAyn, Kamane, Humeirah, al-Arian, Ein Hud, Dmeideh.
48 Knesset minutes, July 15, 1997.
49 Knesset minutes, December 1, 1987.
50 *al-Ittihad*, January 8, 1998.
51 Knesset minutes, March 24, 1998
52 Knesset minutes, May 20, 1998.
53 Knesset minutes, July 21, 1998.
54 Arab citizens were always entitled to appeal to the Supreme Court and since 1990 the number of petitions had increased consistently.
55 Muhammad Dahleh, "The Demand for Collective Rights to Arab Minority," in Elie Rekhess and Sara Osatzcy-Lazar (eds.), *The Status of Arab Minority in Jewish Nation State* (Tel Aviv: Tel Aviv University, 2005), pp. 84–90.
56 Knesset minutes, December 16, 1998.
57 *Ṣawt al-Ḥaqq wal-Ḥurriyyah*, January 5, 1999.
58 Knesset minutes, January 27, 1999.
59 The Committee of Forty is a body that is carrying out a struggle against the government to receive their recognition for 40 Arab villages throughout the country that are not recognized or legal.
60 *al-Ittihad*, March 30, 1999.
61 Knesset minutes, November 11, 1998
62 Knesset minutes, December 23, 1998.
63 Knesset minutes, January 18, 1999.
64 *Sikkuy Voluntary Association* (Annual Report 1998), pp. 16–19.
65 Knesset minutes, June 23, 1999.
66 Prime Minister's Office, *A Multiyear Plan for Arab Settlements 2000*, p. 13.
67 Knesset minutes, October 13, 1999.
68 Knesset minutes, October 18, 1999.
69 *Ṣawt al-Ḥaqq wal-Ḥurriyyah*, February 4, 2000.
70 Knesset minutes, January 26, 2000.
71 Ministry of Education, Annual Report 1999–2000.
72 Knesset minutes, March 28, 2000.
73 Gadi Hitman, *Israel and Its Arab Minority, 1948–2008: Dialogue, Protest, Violence* (Lanham, MD: Rowman & Littlefield, 2016), pp. 45–51.
74 *Kull al-Arab*, February 26, 1999.
75 *Ha'aretz*, January 4, 1999.
76 *al-Ṣinara*, Weekly, Arabic, September 10, 1999.
77 Knesset minutes, September 14, 1999.

78 Knesset minutes, January 1, 2002.
79 Government's resolution 2467 (October 22, 2000).
80 Prime Minister's Office, Coordination and Monitoring Department, August 2005.
81 Michal Belikof, "Government's resolutions regarding Arab Citizens: Development Plans 1999–2005", in: *Sikkuy Annual Report 2004–2005*, pp. 17–18.
82 Sikkuy Voluntary Association, *Annual Report 2000–2001* (Jerusalem, 2002).
83 The plan was discussed here succinctly. For full details see: Prime Minister's Office, *Multi-year Plan for Social-economic Developing of Arab Settlements* (October 2000).
84 Knesset minutes, December 18, 2000.
85 Between June 1999 and December 2000, another 428 Arabs were joined the public service.
86 Based on *Sikkuy* Voluntary Association (Annual Report 2000–2001).
87 Ibid., p. 18.
88 Ministry of Education, Five Year Plan: Resource Allocation and its Influence on entitlement for matriculation certificate (2002).
89 Prime Minister's Office, Government's Guidelines of Ariel Sharon, March 6, 2001.
90 Nasser, p. 8.
91 Research Center of the Israeli Parliament: Local Planning in the Arab Sector (Jerusalem, 2010).
92 Belikof, p. 27.
93 Prime Minister's Office, Appropriate Representation for Arabs (including Druze and Circassian) in the Public Service (Jerusalem: Civil Service Commission, 2008).
94 Prime Minister's Office, Government Resolution 1402 (January 27, 2004).
95 Prime Minister's Office, Government Resolution 414 (August 31, 2006).
96 Minister's Office, Government Resolution 3855 (July 28, 2008).
97 Prime Minister's Office, Final Announcement of Prime Minister's Conference for Arab Sector 2008.
98 Prime Minister's Office, A Program for Economic Development of Arab Sector (January 2009).
99 Government Resolution 1204 (February 15, 2007).
100 Ahia Raved, "Olmert: There is a Discrimination against Israeli Arabs," www.ynet.co.il (July 10, 2008).
101 Prime Minister Olmert Speech. July 10, 2008, at www.pmo.gov.il.
102 Prime Minister Office, The Authority for Economic Development within the Arab Sector (Annual Report 2009–2010), p. 9.
103 Ibid., pp. 15–16.
104 Prime Minister Office, A Five-Year Plan for Economic Developing for Arab Sector (June 2013), p. 15.
105 Talia Shtainer, *Breaking Inequality: Competing with Arab*

Discrimination in the Israeli Labor Market, Policy Paper 97 (The Israel Democracy Institution, 2013), p. 2.

106 Prime Minister Office, The Authority for Economic Development within the Arab Sector (Annual Report 2011), p. 8.

107 Ibid., p. 10.

108 Prime Minister's Speech in "The Partnership's Conference" (March 22, 2011), at http://www.youtube.com/watch?v=BvQGM-eSyTA.

109 Prime Minister Office, Government's resolution 4432 (March 18, 2012).

110 Prime Minister Office, The Authority for Economic Development within the Arab Sector (Annual Report 2009), pp. 11–12.

111 Ibid., p. 12.

112 Prime Minister Office, The Authority for Economic Development within the Arab Sector (Annual Report 2012), p. 2.

113 Ibid., p. 7.

114 Cabinet Secretary, resolution 4193 (January 29, 2012).

115 Research Center of the Israeli Parliament, The Civil-National Service in Israel, p. 1.

116 Ibid., p. 3.

117 Thabet Abu Ras, "Arab-Bedouin Population in Unrecognized Villages in the Negev: Between the Hammer of Prayer and the Anvil of Goldberg," Electronic Monthly of *Adalah*, 81 (April 2011), pp. 1–2.

118 Shlomo Svirsky and Yael Hasson, *Transparent Citizen: Government's Policy towards the Bedouin in the Negev* (Tel Aviv: Adva Center, 2005), p. 10.

119 Government's resolution 5345 (January 27, 2013).

120 Government proposal of law 761 in order to organize Bedouins Settlements in the Negev 2013 (May 27, 2013).

121 Eli Rekhess and Doron Navot, "Equal Policy and Arab Politics: Paradigmatic and Pragmatic Obstructions," in: Shlomo Hasson and Michael Kraini (eds.), *The Arabs in Israel Facing Obstacles towards Equality* (Jerusalem: Florensheiner Institution for Policy, 2006), pp. 145–148.

122 Ibid., p. 147.

123 Prime Minister Office, The Authority for Economic Development within the Arab Sector (Annual Report 2011), p. 12.

124 Belikof, p. 25.

125 See below in the next chapter.

126 www.nrg.co.il, August 10, 2012.

127 The Commission of Second Lebanese War 2006, p. 47.

128 One of many examples was presented publicly in 2004 during the annual conference in Herzliyya city. One of the salient findings in a survey which was conducted with 15,000 participants, was that a crucial majority defined the security situation as "bad" or "very bad."

129 MK Issam Makhul's declaration in the Knesset (June 4, 2002).

130 Meeting number 268 of the Fifteenth Knesset, January 2, 2002, p. 4.

131 Ibid., p. 10.

132 *Opinion Survey: Rights of the Palestinian Citizens of Israel, the Association for Civil Rights in Israel* (December 2007), pp. 19–20.

133 Ibid., p. 19.

134 The authors had faced methodological obstacles to identify who were behind these publications. However, the contents led us to the conclusion that the publishers are Jews. For more see: Aviram Zino, Racism 2007: Most of the Jews refuse to accept an Arab neighbor, www.ynet.co.il (December 8, 2007).

135 Ofra Idelman, Most of the Jews support in Loyalty Declaration to a Jewish State in condition for voting right, *Ha'aretz*, December 1, 2010.

136 Israel Democracy Index 2011, at www.idi.org.il.

137 Einat Horowitz "*Love thy neighbor as thyself – Racism in the name of the Halacha: An incitement by Rabbis,*" ([New York]: The Reform Center for Religion and State, November 2011).

138 Ibid., p, 5.

139 Aviram Zino, A Conviction: Rabbi Batzri and his Son incited against Arabs, at www.ynet.co.il (January 10, 2008).

140 Eight Jews were murdered by Palestinian terrorist in Talmudic College in Jerusalem (March 2008).

141 A Draft Law (Correction: Prohibition to mourn in response to Independence Day of Israel (2009).

142 The Association for Civil Rights in Israel: Anti-Democracy Legislation (August 1, 2012), at www.acri.org.il, p. 2.

143 Ibid., p. 3.

Part Three   Political and Social Changes within the Arab Minority

1   Muhammad Amara, "The Collective Identity of the Arabs in Israel in an Era of Peace," *Israel Affairs* 9 (2003), no. 1–2, p. 253.

2   Reuven Aharoni and Yosef Ginat, "The Arab Citizens of Israel: From a Struggle for Equality to Political Separatism," in David Mensheri (ed.), *Religion and State in the Middle East* (Tel Aviv University, The Dayan Center for Middle Eastern and African Studies, 2006), p. 278.

3   As‘ad Ghanem, "The Palestinian Minority in Israel: the Challenge of the Jewish State and its Ramifications," *Studies in the Revival of Israel* 9 (1998), p. 422.

4   Issam Abu Raya, "The Northern Branch of the Islamic Movement and the Israeli Establishment: A Security Confrontation and/or a Political and Ideological Confrontation" in *Dilemmas of Identity* (Tel Aviv: The Dayan Center for Middle Eastern and African Studies, 1998), pp. 257–271.

5   The Balad Platform for the Elections to the Seventeenth Knesset (2006).

6   Marwan Dalal, "National rights for the Arab minority," *Ha'aretz*, May 14, 2000.

7   As‘ad Ghanem, Nadim N. Rouhana and Oren Yiftachel, "Questioning 'Ethnic Democracy': A Response to Sammy Smooha," *Israel Studies* 3 (1998) no. 2, pp. 253–267.

8   Lior Greenbaum, "And their Independence," *Globes,* Daily, Hebrew, May 10–11, 2005, p. 2.

9   Oded Haklai, "Palestinian NGOs in Israel: A Campaign for Civic Equality or Ethnic Civic Society", *Israel Studies,* 2004, Vol. 9, No. 3, p. 157.

10   Eli Rekhess, *Between Communism and Arab Nationalism: Rakah and the Arab Minority in Israel* (1965–1973), (Tel Aviv, Tel Aviv University, 1993) p. 24.

11   About the committee – see below.

12   Stendahl, Between the Hammer and the Anvil, p. 253. See also: Muhammad Darwish, *The Palestinian in Israel: the Arab Voice and the Knesset's Elections* (Nablus: Palestinian Research Centre, 1996), p. 10 [in Arabic].

13   Yitzhak Reiter and Reuven Aharoni, *The Political World of the Israeli Arabs* (Beit Berl: The Center for the Study of Arab Society in Israel, 1992) p. 21.

14   Darwish, p. 20.

15   A Jewish–Arab movement, that was established in 1989 by Azmi Bishara and Jamal Zahalka, which supported a bi-national state.

16   The Committee of Forty is a body that is carrying out a struggle against the authorities in order to gain the recognition of forty scattered Arab centers of population throughout the country that have no legal recognition.

17   The party's platform appears in the official site of the party, January 2007, www.tajamoa.org. It can also be found at http://m-meee.blogspot.co.il, retrieved November 11, 2013.

18   Ibid., p. 13.

19   Balad brochure of November 1999 is containing the platform, the principles and the goals, p. 3. These things also appeared in Balad's platform booklet for the Knesset elections of 2006.

20   The Balad booklet. The platform, principles and goals, November 1999, appeared in the official site of the party, www.tajamoa.org.

21   *Orr Commission Report,* 2003, pp. 522–523.

22   Itamar Inbari and Tal Volvovitch, "The suspicion: Bishara aided the enemy during wartime," www.nrg.co.il.

23   Nachman Nachman, "The Islamic Movement in Israel," *Strategic Bulletin* (February 2000), no. 4, pp. 8–12.

24   Rafi Yisraeli, *Muslim Fundamentalism in Israel* (London, 1993), p. 26.

25   Tal, "The Islamic Movement," p. 8.

26   The Orr Commission was asked to deal with this issue and provided its conclusions in its final report, p. 76.

27   Abu Raya, The Northern Branch of the Islamic Movement, pp. 263–264.

28   Reiter & Aharoni, *Their Political World,* p. 29.

29   Avner Regev, *Israeli Arabs: Political Issues,* (Jerusalem: Jerusalem Institute for Israel Studies, 1989), pp. 28–32. Also see: Stendahl, *Between the Hammer and the Anvil,* pp. 276–277.

30 Regev, *Israeli Arabs*, p. 14.

31 Reiter & Aharoni, *Their Political World*, pp. 30–31.

32 In the USA, for example, this kind of separatism is interpreted as detachment from another race and the establishment of a political framework that is made up of one race. See, for example: Lester K. Spence, Todd C. Shaw and Robert A. Brown, "True to Our Native Land," *Du Bois Review* 2 (2005), no. 1, p. 103.

33 Bob Edwards and John D. McCarthy, "Chapter 6: Resources and Social Movement Mobilization", in: D. A. Snow, S. A. Soule, and H. Kriesi (eds.), *The Blackwell Companion to Social Movements* (Malden, MA: Blackwell Publishing, 2004), pp. 116–152.

34 Nancy Whittier, *Feminist Generations: The Persistence of the Radical Women's Movement* (Philadelphia: Temple University Press, 1995).

35 Francesca Polletta and James. M. Jasper, "Collective identity and social movements," *Annual Review of Sociology* (2001), Vol. 27, p. 284.

36 Bert Klandermans, "The social construction of protest and multi organizational fields in Frontiers in *Social Movement Theory*," ed. Aldon D. Morris and Carrol McClurg Mueller (New Haven: Yale University Press, 1992), p. 81.

37 The research literature contains at least eight theoretical approaches that can be used to explain and analyze group violence in political contexts. See: Conteh-Morgan, Earl. *Collective Political Violence: An Introduction to the Theories and Cases of Violent Conflicts* (Hove, UK: Psychology Press, 2004).

38 Nimrod Luz, *al-Haram al-Sharif in the Palestinian Arab Dialogue in Israel: A Collective Identity Memory and the Ways to Construct It* (Jerusalem: The Florsheimer Institute for Political Research, 2004), p. 8 [Hebrew].

39 *al-Şirat*, October 12, 1990.

40 *al-Ittihad*, October 9, 1990.

41 *al-Şirat*, October 12, 1990.

42 *al-Ittihad*, October 11, 1990.

43 Ibid., p. 3.

44 Ibid., October 26. 1990, p. 8.

45 *al-Waţan*, August 3, 1990.

46 *al-Ittihad*, August 22, 1990.

47 Ibid., August 3, 1990; August 10, 1990.

48 *al-Şirat*, August 3, 1990.

49 Ibid., September 14, 1990.

50 *Kull al-Arab*, January 25, 1991.

51 *al-Ittihad*, January 30, 1991.

52 Ibid., January 25, 1991.

53 *al-Ittihad*, January 25, 1991.

54 *al-Ittihad*, September 27, 1996.

55 Ibid., p. 8.

56 Ibid., pp. 3, 6–7.

57 *Ṣawt al- Haqq wa-al-Hurriyyah*, August 28, 1998.
58 *al-Ayyam*, Daily, Arabic, September 7, 1998.
59 Ibid.
60 *The Orr Commission*, p. 542.
61 The Knesset protocols, December 1, 1998. The meeting can be found on the internet site of the Knesset.
62 *Kull al-Arab*, October 9, 1998, p. 7.
63 *Ṣawt al- Haqq wa-al-Hurriyyah*, December 25, 1998.
64 To make it clear: we refer to the number of victims within a harsh conflict between the Arab population and security forces. The tragic event of the Kafr Qassem massacre is not part of the discussion here.
65 *The Orr Commission*, pp. 515, 517.
66 Ibid., pp. 527–528.
67 *Ayyam al-Arab*, Weekly, Arabic, October 1, 2000.
68 *The Orr Commission*, p. 529.
69 The use here is of the word *Shuhadah*, which means a holy martyr who fell in the name of a supreme goal. The words appeared in *Ṣawt al-Haqq wa-al-Hurriyyah* on October 6, 2000, p. 6.
70 *The Orr Commission*, pp. 524–525.
71 Ibid., pp. 424; 529–530.
72 Ibid., p. 547.
73 *Ṣawt al-Haqq wa-al-Hurriyyah*, September 29, 2000.
74 *The Orr Commission*, p. 548.
75 *Ṣawt al- Haqq wa-al-Hurriyyah*, October 6, 2000.
76 Aharoni and Ginat, "The Arab Citizens of Israel," p. 287.
77 *The Future Vision of the Arab Palestinians in Israel* (The National Committee of the Heads of Local Authorities in Israel, 2006).
78 Gadi Hitman, "Israel's Arab leadership in the decade attending the October 2000 events." *Israel Affairs* 19 (2013), no. 1, 121–138.
79 Oded Haklai, *Palestinian Ethnonationalism in Israel* (Philadelphia: University of Pennsylvania, 2011), pp. 1–7.
80 *al-Bayan* brochure, (Tel Aviv University: The Dayan Center, 2015), Issue 5, pp. 9–10.
81 This is, for example, what happened when two brothers who were *Balad* activists were charged with terrorist activity. See: *Ha'aretz*, March 14, 2005.
82 Three other documents were written after the Vision Document: A Constitution Equal to All by the *Musawa* Center, A Constitution for Everybody by the *Adalah* Center, and the Haifa Declaration. These documents mainly dealt with the legal rights of national minorities and the establishment of similar goals to those of the Vision Document.
83 *The Future Vision*, p. 8.
84 Israeli Central Bureau of Statistic, annual 2015.
85 Israeli Central Bureau of Statistic, annual 2011.
86 Previous sources defined the term "modernization" to mean a change in concept or the transition of people from something that has been defined

by their culture as a norm and moral value to something else that has been defined as a modern norm and value. See: J.B. Stephenson, "Everyone going modern? A critique and a suggestion for measuring modernism," *American Journal of Sociology*, (1969) 74, pp. 265–275. Other researchers have been more detailed in their discussion of "modernization" as a process of change that takes place following the transition from a rural-traditional society into an industrial-modern society. See: D. Cowgill, "Aging and Modernization: A Revision of Theory." Ch. 19 in J. Gubrium (ed.), *Later Life: Community and Environmental Policies* (New York: Basic Books, 1974). According to this explanation, which is still widespread in the literature today, in societies that are undergoing the processes of transition from rural agricultural societies to urban industrial societies changes take place in the social, cultural and economic structures. In this way, according to the sources, for example, societies in transition find themselves in an intensified process of urbanization that is accompanied by technological and medical development as a result of which, on the one hand, these societies experience demographic changes such as a rise in longevity, the splitting up of the extended family into independent nuclear families, a reduction of the availability of women in the home because of their going out to study and work outside their homes and the strengthening of the status of the young in society because of their higher level of education.

87 Yusuf Alashkar, one of the owners of the "Big" marketing chain, in an interview with Meirav Crystal, 68% of Israeli Arabs prefer blue-white products, www.ynet.co.il, May 23, 2010. Retrieved February 28, 2014.

88 Interview with Arab workers in a large food chain, March 14, 2014.

89 Yoav Peled & Adi Ophir (eds.), *Israel: From a Mobilized State to a Civil Society?* (Tel Aviv and Jerusalem: Hakibbutz Hamehuad and the Van Leer Institute, 2001) [Hebrew].

90 When we use the term "democratic" we mean the holistic understanding of the term which includes the process of clean elections, a multiplicity of parties, free elections, the absence of forgeries, human rights and the separation of powers.

91 *The Orr Commission*, p. 78. The involvement of youths in violent events in the Arab sector in Israel since the establishment of the state, for example on Land Day in 1976 and in the October events in 2000.

92 Khaled Abu Aşba,"Young Arabs in Israel in the Whirlpool of Social-Cultural Change" in: Eli Rekhess & Arik Rodnitsky (eds.), *Young Arabs in Israel: Between Opportunity and Risk* (Tel Aviv: Tel Aviv University, The Dayan Center, 2008), p. 18 [Hebrew].

93 Tajrid Yahye Yunis, "Political and Social Views and Positions of Palestinian-Arab Youths in Israel" in: Hagar Tsameret-Kercher (ed.), *Both This and That: Identity Contradictions in Young People in Israel* (The Friedrich Ebert Fund, 2010), p. 13; p. 230 [Hebrew].

94 Lior Greenbaum, "The Consumer Feast," *Globes*, October 11–12, 2004, pp. 12–13.

95 Survey of the Arab survey institute Yafa, appeared in *Ha'aretz*, Yoaz Yovel, "Three out of four Arabs agree to a Jewish-Democratic Israel," October 8, 2004 [Hebrew].

96 Yair Ettinger, "Extremists Have No Fear," *Ha'aretz*, May 25, 2004.

97 David Ratner, "The Alternative to the Islamic Movement: The Youth Movement *ha-Noar ha-oved ve-ha-Lomed*" (Working, Studying Youth), *Ha'aretz*, January 12, 2004 [Hebrew].

98 A public opinion poll that was carried out in 1997 with 1,000 interviewees in the Arab sector found that 66% of them supported the changing of the Jewish character of country to "a state of all its citizens." See in Eli Rekhess.

99 Oz Almog, "The Ruling Nerds: A Historical and Sociological Background to the Growth of the Y Generation in the World," at www.peopleil.org, retrieved March 3, 2014.

100 Younis Yahyah, Views and Positions, p. 220.

101 Smooha, *Don't Break the Rules – Measuring the Arab–Jewish Relations in Israel* (Haifa University and the Israeli Institute for Democracy, 2012), p. 118.

102 Prominent cases in this context: in August 2005, an IDF soldier shot and killed four minority group members; in November 2014 police killed a young Arab in Kafr Kana after he approached the police patrol car with a knife; in July 2016 Jews burned a young Arab from East Jerusalem.

103 Survey: A third of the Arabs are afraid to move about among the Jewish population, in http://news.nana10.co.il/Article/?ArticleID=1111388.

104 For the phenomenon of the associations in the Arab sector see the following analysis.

105 Aharoni and Ginat, "The Arab Citizens of Israel," p. 281.

106 Majed el Hajj, "Arab voting trends for the Knesset in Israel," in Eli Rekhess (ed.), *The Arab Minority in Israel and the 17th Knesset Elections* (Tel Aviv University: The Dayan Center, 2006), pp. 18–19.

107 Amal Jamal, "Avoiding participation: On the illusions of Arab politics in Israel" in Asher Iran & Michal Shamir (eds.), *The 2001 Elections in Israel*, pp. 57–100.

108 al-Haj, "Trends in the voting of Arabs," p. 19. See also Aziz Haider, "The boycott of elections by the Arab public: the perspective of a decade (1996–2006)," in Eli Rekhess (ed.), *The Arab Minority in Israel and the 17th Knesset Elections* (Tel Aviv: Tel Aviv University, the Dayan Center, 2006), p. 89.

109 Ibid. Another clear example of political factionalism took place in April 2004 when differences of opinion between public personages prevented the participation of a single delegation to the conference on the subject of the Arab minority which was organized by the Arab League in its base in Cairo. See: *Ha'aretz*, Yair Ettinger, "Intrigues and Factionalism will leave the leaders at home." April 20, 2004.

110 Sami Smooha, "Don't Break the Rules," p. 105.

111 Elias Zidan & Asᶜad Ghanem, "Contribution and Voluntarism in the Arab-Palestinian Society in Israel," *The Israeli Center for Research into the Third Sector* (Beer Sheva, Ben-Gurion University, 2000), p. 8.

112 Shany Payes, *Palestinian NGOs in Israel: The Politics of Civil Society, Library of Modern Middle East Studies* (New York: Taurus Academic Studies, 2005).

113 The feelings of deprivation felt by the Arab minority since 1948 have three dimensions: its present situation as opposed to its situation in 1948, its present situation compared to the situation it would like to be in and its situation as opposed to that of the Jewish majority. For theories of relative depravation see: Robert T. Gurr, *Minorities at Risk: A Global View of Ethnopolitical Conflict* (Washington D.C: United States Institution of Peace, 1993).

114 *Faşl al-Makal*, Weekly, Arabic, January 20, 2000; January 27, 2000.

115 Omar Masalha, "The Islamic Movement in Israel," at http://www.articles.co.il/article (August 2009).

116 Zidan & Ghanem, "Contribution and Volunteerism," p. 14.

117 Tajrid Yahyeh-Yunis, "Changes in the research dialogue about Palestinian-Arab women in Israel" in Uzi Rabi & Arik Rodnitsky (eds.), *Women in Arab Society in Israel* (Tel Aviv University: The Dayan Center, 2011) pp. 12–13.

118 It was not possible to get the exact number of associations in the Arab sector from the Ministry of Justice. As a result the analysis is based on a sample of 262 Arab associations by NPTECH Records which is an association that defines itself as "an association for associations."

119 For this see, for example: *The Orr Commission Report*, pp. 522–529.

120 *Adalah* association homepage, http://adalah.org.

121 Jamil Dakwar, "The Challenge Presented by the Arab Palestinian Minority in Israel," at
http://www.wcl.american.edu/hrbrief/ 05/2dakwar.pdf, p. 9.

122 https://www.adalah.org/he/content/view/4135.

123 Supreme Court of Justice 9289/03; 9205/04.

124 Supreme Court of Justice, 4130/03; 3479/03.

125 Supreme Court of Justice 6342/02.

126 Supreme Court of Justice 7585/04.

127 Supreme Court of Justice 7864/04.

128 Supreme Court of Justice 4969/04.

129 Supreme Court of Justice 3799/02.

130 www.mossawacenter.org; retrieved February 10, 2014.

131 Yussef Jabarin and Iman Aghabariyyah, "Awaiting Education," in: *Dirasat* (The Arab Center for Legal and Political Affairs), (Nazareth, 2010), pp. 9, 13.

132 The Master Plans for the Arab Villages in Israel: An Update, The Arab Center for Alternative Planning (2012), pp. 78–84.

133 *Ibid.*, pp. 96–97. On the ability to make profound changes and not be dazzled by symbolic legal aid see also: Gerald Rosenberg, The Hollow

Hope: Can Courts Bring About Social Change? (Chicago: University of Chicago Press, 1991), p. 340.

134 Asᶜad Ghanem, "Review on Shany Payes: NGOs in Israel," *Middle East Journal*, Vol. 59, No. 4 (Autumn, 2005), p. 682.

135 Yussuf Jabarin, Strategies for the Development of Employment for Arabs in Israel: The Vision of Broadening the Arab Middle Class (Haifa: The Shmuel Neeman Institute, 2007), p. 22.

136 Noah Levin-Epstein, Majid Alhaj & Mosheh Semyunov, *Arabs in the Work Market in Israel* (Jerusalem: The Florsheimer Institute for Policy Research, 1994), pp. 4, 5.

137 Yussef Jibarin, *A Strategy for the Development of Employment of Arabs in Israel: a Vision for the Broadening of the Status of the Arab Middle Class* (Haifa: The Shmuel Neeman Institute, 2007), p. 17.

138 Ibid., pp. 17–18.

139 Ramses Gera (ed.), *The Book of Arab Society* 7, The Van Leer Institute (2015), p. 59.

140 Thaᶜar Abu Ras, "Arabs want to work but nobody wants to employ them," www.themarker.com. May 7, 2012. Retrieved March 2, 2014.

141 Nuhad Ali & Shai Inbar, *Who is for Equality? Equality between Jews and Arabs in Israel: Summary of Research*. Emdot (Positions), Sikkuy Association (2011), p. 8.

142 Levin-Epstein, Alhaj & Saminov, *The Israeli Arabs in the Work Market*. See also: Dan Ben Dor, Avner Ahitov, Noah Levin-Epstein & Haya Shteier, *A Master Plan for the Improvement of the State of Employment in Israel* (Tel Aviv University: The Department of Public Policy, 2004). See also: Bank of Israel, Research Department, 2004 Report, pp. 127–128.

143 Shirli Merom, *The Importance of the Arab Language for the Integration and Advancement of the Arab Population in the Employment Market*, The Joint Organization Israel, (2012), pp. 120–121.

144 *Pluralism and Equality of Opportunity in Higher Education: The Broadening of Accessibility to Academia for Arabs, Druze and Circassians in Israel, The Council for Higher Learning*, 2013, p. 25.

145 *The participation of Arab women in the workforce during the last decade*, The Ministry for Labor and Welfare (2002), p. 1.

146 Orly Almagor-Lotan, *Recognized day and family centers in the Arab sector,* The Knesset Research Center (July 2008), p. 1.

147 *Women's employment and initiatives in the Arab sector*, The Knesset Center for Research and Information (July 2005) p. 1.

148 Reuven Gal, *The Perception of the Rights and Obligations of Arab Israeli Citizens as Reflected in the Idea of Civil Service* (Tel Aviv: Tel Aviv University, May 2008), p. 11.

149 Ibid., p. 21. The findings are surprising because the high rate of response already in the 1990s were received without the Israeli government embarking on an organized information campaign to emphasize the advantages of the project. It is possible that one of the explanations for

this can be found in the public atmosphere that existed during this time in the Arab sector which saw the Rabin government (1992–1995) as having a positive approach that was expressed in the diplomatic dialogue being carried on between Israel and the Palestinians.

150 Reuven Gal, *The Perception*, p. 24. See also: MK Basel Ghattas: "We will not give our hand to make Arabs Zionists," in *Ha'aretz*, June 6, 2014.

151 See for example: Because of the Arab women: a rise of 30% in the number of volunteers for national-civil service (*The Marker*, December 15, 2015), on the site http://www.themarker.com/career/1.2798482.

152 Susan Diab: Those who oppose civil service to Arabs are wrong, in *Ma'ariv*, November 9, 2007, at
http://www.nrg.co.il/online/1/ART1/656/804.html.

153 Rafi Smith & Olga Paniel, *The findings of the opinion poll on the subject of inclusive citizenship* (April 2012), p. 3. Appears on the internet site: http://www.fnst-jerusalem.org, retrieved March 13, 2014.

Bibliography

Primary Sources

Bank of Israel, Research Department, *2004 Report* (Jerusalem, 2005).

Civil Rights Association, *Annual Report* (1996).

Council of Europe Strasbourg, *Framework Convention for the Protection of National Minorities 1995*, (February 1, 1995).

[Gilbocᵃa, Amos]. *A Proposal for the Israeli Government's Policy Towards the Arab Sector* (March 1987).

[Policy paper:] *Budgets for Arab Sector*, March 8, 1992.

Sharon, Moshe. *The Plan of Operations* (1978).

[Sharon, Moshe.] *The Israeli Arabs – An assessment of the situation, goals and policy suggestions* (Jerusalem: Prime Minister's Office, 1979).

Sikkuy Voluntary Association, *Annual Report 1992* (Jerusalem, 1993).

Sikkuy Voluntary Association, *Annual Report 2000–2001* (Jerusalem, 2002).

Sofer, Arnon, *A Proposal for Policy towards the Arab Sector in Israel*. Policy paper presented to the Prime Minister's Office (1987).

The Arab Center for Alternative Planning, *The Master Plans for the Arab Villages in Israel: An Update* (2012).

The Balad Platform for the Elections to the 17th Knesset (2006).

The Future Vision of the Arab Palestinians in Israel (The National Committee of the Heads of Local Authorities in Israel, 2006).

The Governmental Commission of Inquiry for The Second Lebanon War (2007). The Israeli Declaration of Independence, *The official gazette of the Temporary Israeli Government* (Iyyar 5, 5708, May 14, 1948), issue no. 1.

The Knesset protocols, 1951–2005.

The Master Plan for Arabs in Israel: Situation Report (The Arab Center for Alternative Planning, 2012).

The Policy towards the Arab Israeli Citizens (1985).

The political platforms of the Communist Party [n.d.].

The Provisional Government Covenant, 13, Sections 15–16.

The Ratner Committee Report, 1956.

The State Commission of Inquiry into the clashes between the security forces and Israeli citizens in October 2000 (The Orr Commission), http://uri.mitkadem.co.il/vaadat-or/.

Topics for a Radio Interview, December 30, 1991.

Cabinet Resolutions

No. 2467 (October 22, 2000).
No. 1402 (January 27, 2004).
No. 414 (August 31, 2006).
No. 1204 (February 15, 2007).
No. 3855 (July 28, 2008).
No. 4432 (March 18, 2012).
No. 5345 (January 27, 2013).
No. 761 proposal of Law Organizing the Bedouins Settlements in the Negev 2013 (May 27, 2013).

David Ben Gurion Archive (BGA)

10/101/Diaries/164/Correspondence Files, 26/10/1948–09/12/1948.

Israel Defense Forces (IDF) archives

53/28/1960.

Israel State Archives

FM/A/2401/19.
FM/2451/13.
FM/2401/22.
FM/2451/13.
G/6397 /3944/2.
G/6337/1653.
G/297/59.
G/382/15/l.
G/6243/30.
GL/17019/3.
GL/17029/20.
GL/17037/25.
GL/17108/28.
L/289/13.
L/303/21.
L/307/56.
L/308/4.
L/313/11.

Ministry of Interior

A Letter from the Director General to the Mayor of Shfarᶜam, June 24, 1988.
A Progress Report regarding Illegal Building, March 14, 1989.

Ministry of Education

Ministry of Education, *Five Year Plan: Resource Allocation and its Influence on Entitlement for Matriculation Certificate* (2002).

Ministry of Labor and Welfare

The Ministry of Labor and Welfare, *The participation of Arab women in the workforce during the last decade* [n.d.].

Ministry in charge of Minorities

A Multi-Year Plan for the Minority Population, June 1990.

Other Government Publications

Final Announcement of Prime Minister's Conference for Arab Sector (2008).
Appropriate Representation for Arabs (including Druze and Circassian) in the Public Service (Jerusalem: Civil Service Commission, 2008).
A Program for Economic Development of Arab Sector (January 2009).
The Authority for Economic Development within the Arab Sector (Annual Reports 2009, 2011, 2012).

Prime Minister's Office

A Multiyear Plan for the Arab Settlements, 2000.
Coordination and Monitoring Department, *[no topic]*, (August 2005).
Deputy Minister Roni Milo's Letter, December 30, 1987.
Israel Central Bureau of Statistic 1967, 2011, 2015.
Selection of Events in the Arab Sector (1981–1984).
The Arabs in Israel: An Effort for Equality (August 1992).

Supreme Court of Justice Cases

30/55; 241/60; 1/65; 9289/03; 9205/04; 4130/03; 3479/03; 6342/02; 7585/04; 7864/04; 4969/04; 3799/02.

Newspapers and Periodicals

Arabic

al-Anba (Israel, weekly)
al-Ayyam (Palestinian Authority, daily)
Ayyam al-Arab (Israel, weekly)
al-Dustur (Jordan, daily)
al-Fajr (Israel, weekly)
al-Ittihad (Israel, daily)
al-Mirṣad (Israel, weekly)
al-Ṣirat (Israel, weekly)
al-Ṣinara (Israel, weekly)
al-Waṭan (Israel, weekly)
Faṣl al-Makal (Israel, weekly)
Kifaḥ al-Arḍ (Israel, monthly)
Kull al-Arab (Israel, weekly)
Ṣawt al-Ḥaqq wa-al-Ḥurriyyah (Israel, weekly)

English

The Jerusalem Post (Israel, daily)

Hebrew

al-ha-Mishmar (Israel, daily)
Davar (Israel, daily)
Ha'aretz (Israel, daily)
Haᶜolam ha-Zeh (Israel, weekly)
Qol ha-ᶜAm (Israel, daily)
Maᶜariv (Israel, daily)
Yediot ha-Galil (Israel, weekly)
Zo ha-Derekh (Israel, Weekly)

Internet Sites

www.pinhas-lavon.com
www.icf.org.il/landday25
www.nrg.co.il
www.idi.org.il
www.acri.org.il
www.peopleil.org
www.news.nana10.co.il
www.articles.co.il
http://adalah.org
www.wcl.american.edu
www.mossawacenter.org
www.themarker.com
http://www.fnst-jerusalem.org

Secondary Literature

Books

Arabic

Darwish, Muhammad, *The Palestinian in Israel: The Arab Voice and the Knesset's Elections* (Nablus: Palestinian Research Centre, 1996).
Kaoughi, Khalil, *Al-Arab taḥt al-Iḥtilal al-Israili mundhu 1948* [The Arabs under the Israeli Occupation since 1948] (Arabic), (Beirut: PLO Research Center, 1973).

English

Capotorti, Francesco, *Study on the Rights of Persons Belonging to Ethnic, Religious and Linguistic Minorities* (New York: United Nations, 1991).
Conteh-Morgan, Earl, *Collective Political Violence: An Introduction to the Theories and Cases of Violent Conflicts* (Hove, UK: Psychology Press, 2004).
Gurr, Ted R., *Why Men Rebel* (Princeton: Princeton University, 1970).

Haklai, Oded, *Palestinian Ethnonationalism in Israel* (Philadelphia: University of Pennsylvania, 2011).

Hitman, Gadi, *Israel and Its Arab Minority, 1948–2008: Dialogue, Protest, Violence* (Lanham, MD: Rowman & Littlefield, 2016).

Payes, Shany, *Palestinian NGOs in Israel: The Politics of Civil Society, Library of Modern Middle East Studies* (New York: Taurus Academic Studies, 2005).

Rosenberg, Gerald, *The Hollow Hope: Can Courts Bring About Social Change?* (Chicago: University of Chicago Press, 1991).

Whittier, Nancy, *Feminist Generations: The Persistence of the Radical Women's Movement* (Philadelphia: Temple University Press, 1995).

Yisraeli, Rafi, *Muslim Fundamentalism in Israel* (London, 1993).

Hebrew

Alon, Yigal, *A Screen of Sand* (Tel Aviv: Am Oved, 1960).

Belti, Berl, *The Struggle for Jewish Existence* (Jerusalem: Magnes, 1981).

Benziman, Uzi and Atallah Mansour, *Sub-tenants: The Arab Israeli Citizens – Their Status and the Policy toward Them* (Jerusalem: Keter, 1992).

Boimel, Yair, *Blue White Shadow* (Tel Aviv: Pardess, 2007).

Cohen, Raꜥanan, *In the Tangle of Loyalties – Society and Politics in the Arab Sector* (Tel Aviv: Am Oved, 1986).

Dror, Yehezkel, *Improving Policy Making and Administration in Israel* (Tel Aviv: Sifriyat ha-Minhal, 1978).

Gal, Reuven, *The Perception of the Rights and Obligations of Arab Israeli Citizens as Reflected in the Idea of Civil Service* (Tel Aviv: Tel Aviv University, May 2008).

Gal-Nur, Yitzhak, et al., *The Committee for the Examination of the roles of the third sector in Israel and the policy taken towards – a summary report.* (Ben-Gurion University, the Israeli Institute for Research into the Third Sector, 2003).

Gera, Ramses (ed.), *The Book of Arab Society 7* (Jerusalem: The Van Leer Institute, 2015).

Haidar, Aziz, *The Collapse of the Local Arab Municipalities: A New Offer for Reconstructing* (Jerusalem: Van Leer Institution, 2010).

Hershko, Tsilla, *Between Paris and Jerusalem: Zionism and the Establishment of the State of Israel 1945–1949* (Tel Aviv: The Defense Ministry, 2000).

Horowitz, Einat, *"Love thy neighbor as thyself – Racism in the name of the Halacha: An incitement by Rabbis"* ([New York]: The Reform Center for Religion and State, November 2011).

Jabarin, Yussuf, *Strategies for the Development of Employment for Arabs in Israel: The Vision of Broadening the Arab Middle Class* (Haifa: The Shmuel Neeman Institute, 2007).

Jabarin, Yussef, and Iman Aghabariyyah, "Awaiting Education," in: *Dirasat* (The Arab Center for Legal and Political Affairs), (Nazareth, 2010).

Jiryiss, Ṣabri, *The Arabs in Israel* (Haifa: The ha-Mehaber publication, 1966).

Kalo, Hezi, "The development of the national leadership of the Israeli Arabs – trends and directions," A thesis presented to the National Security College (1993).

Landau, Yaakov M., *The Arabs in Israel: Political Studies* (Tel Aviv: Maʿarkhot, The Ministry of Defense, 1971).

Levin-Epstein, Noah, Majd el-Hajj & Mosheh Semyunov, *Arabs in the Work Market in Israel* (Jerusalem: The Florsheimer Institute for Policy Research, 1994).

Luz, Nimrod, *al-Haram al-Sharif in the Palestinian Arab Dialogue in Israel: A Collective Identity Memory and the Ways to Construct It* (Jerusalem: The Florsheimer Institute for Political Research, 2004).

Merom, Shirli, *The Importance of the Arab Language for the Integration and Advancement of the Arab Population in the Employment Market*, The Joint Organization Israel, (2012).

Morris, Benny, *The Birth of the Palestinian Refugee Problem 1947–1949* (Tel Aviv: Am Oved, 1986).

Nasser, Kais, *Housing Shortage and Illegal Building within the Arab Society in Israel: Current Obstructs and Recommendations for a Change* (Nazareth: *Dirasat Center*, 2011).

Ohana, Yuval Arnon, *The Arab Revolt in the Land of Israel 1936–1939* (Jerusalem: Ariel, 2013).

Peled, Yoav and Adi Ophir (eds.), *Israel: From a Mobilized State to a Civil Society?* (Tel Aviv and Jerusalem: Hakibbutz Hamehuad and the Van Leer Institute, 2001).

Reiter, Yitzhak, and Reuven Aharoni, *The Political World of the Israeli Arabs* (Beit Berl: The Center for the Study of Arab Society in Israel, 1992).

Rekhess, Eli, *Challenges for Rakah in the Arab Sector* (Tel Aviv, 1983).

Rekhess, Eli, *The Eleventh Knesset Elections in the Arab Sector* (The Dayan Center for Studies of the Middle East and Africa, Tel Aviv University, August 1984).

Rekhess, Eli, *Between Communism and Arab Nationalism: Rakah and the Arab Minority in Israel* (1965–1973), (Tel Aviv: Tel Aviv University, 1993).

Shiloh, Gideon, *The Arab Citizens of Israel in the Eyes of the Arab Countries and the PLO* (Jerusalem: The Harry Truman Institute of Research into the Middle East, series of research and studies, 1982).

Shtainer, Talia, *Breaking Inequality: Competing with Arab Discrimination in the Israeli Labor Market*, Policy paper 97 (Jerusalem: The Israel Democracy Institution, 2013).

Smooha, Sammy, *Don't Break the Rules – Measuring the Arab–Jewish Relations in Israel* (Haifa University and the Israeli Institute for Democracy, 2012).

Svirsky, Shlomo and Yael Hasson, *Transparent Citizen: Government's Policy towards the Bedouin in the Negev* (Tel Aviv: Adva Center, 2005).

Zidan, Elias and Asʿad Ghanem, "Contribution and Voluntarism in the Arab-

Palestinian Society in Israel," *The Israeli Center for Research into the Third Sector*) Beer Sheva, Ben-Gurion University, 2000).

Zuᶜbi, ᶜAbd al-ᶜAziz, *The Arab Citizens of Israel and Their Dilemma of Double Loyalty* (Maᶜalot, 1971).

Articles

English

Amara, Muhammad, "The Collective Identity of the Arabs in Israel in an Era of Peace," *Israel Affairs* 9 (2002), no. 1–2, pp. 249–262.

Bligh, Alexander, "Israel and the refugee problem: from exodus to resettlement 1948–52," *Middle Eastern Studies* 34 (1998), no. 1, pp. 123–147.

Bligh, Alexander," Political trends in the Israeli Arab population and its vote in parliamentary elections," *Israel Affairs* 19 (2013), no. 1, pp. 21–50.

Edwards, Bob and John D. McCarthy, "Chapter 6: Resources and Social Movement Mobilization", in: D. A. Snow, S. A. Soule, and H. Kriesi (eds.), *The Blackwell Companion to Social Movements* (Malden, MA: Blackwell Publishing, 2004), pp. 116–152.

Ghanem, Asᶜad, Nadim N. Rouhana and Oren Yiftachel, "Questioning 'Ethnic Democracy': A Response to Sammy Smooha," *Israel Studies* 3 (1998), no. 2, pp. 253–267.

Haklai, Oded. "Palestinian NGOs in Israel: A Campaign for Civic Equality or" Ethnic Civil Society"?" *Israel Studies* 9, (2004), no. 3, pp. 157–168.

Hitman, Gadi, "Israel's Arab leadership in the decade attending the October 2000 events." *Israel Affairs* 19 (2013), no. 1, 121–138.

Jiryis, Şabri. "The Arabs in Israel, 1973–79," *Journal of Palestine Studies* 8 (1979), no. 4, pp. 31–56.

Klandermans, Bert. "The social construction of protest and multiorganizational fields." *Frontiers in Social Movement Theory* (1992), pp. 77–103.

Nakhleh, Khalil, "Cultural Determination of Palestinian Collective Identity: The Case of the Arabs in Israel," *New Outlook* 18 (1975), no. 7, pp. 31–40.

Polletta, Francesca and James. M. Jasper, "Collective identity and social movements," *Annual Review of Sociology* 27 (2001), pp. 283–305.

Robinson, Shira, "Local Struggle, National Struggle: Palestinian Responses to the Kafr Qassem Massacre and its Aftermath, 1956–1966", *International Journal of Middle East Studies* 35 (2003), pp. 393–416.

Rouhana, Nadim N., "The Political Transformation of the Palestinians in Israel: from Acquiescence to Challenge," *Journal of Palestine Studies* 18 (1989), no. 3, pp. 38–59.

Saᶜdi, Ahmad, "Social Conceptions, Citizenship Rights and Protest: The Road to the October Events," *Orr Testimonies*, pp. 184–203.

Saouli, Adham, "Arab Organizations within the Israeli State," *Journal of Social, Political and Economic Studies* 26 (2001), no. 2, 443–460.

Hebrew

Abu Aşba, Khaled, "Young Arabs in Israel in the Whirlpool of Social-Cultural Change" in: Eli Rekhess & Arik Rodnitsky (eds.), *Young Arabs in Israel: Between Opportunity and Risk* (Tel Aviv: Tel Aviv University, The Dayan Center, 2008), pp. 19–23.

Abu Ras, Thabet, "Arab-Bedouin Population in Unrecognized Villages in the Negev: Between the Hammer of Praver and the Anvil of Goldberg", *Electronic Monthly of Adalah*, 81 (April 2011).

Abu Raya, Issam, "The Northern Branch of the Islamic Movement and the Israeli Establishment: A Security Confrontation and/or a Political and Ideological Confrontation" in: *Dilemmas of Identity* (Tel Aviv: The Dayan Center for Middle Eastern and African Studies, 1998), pp. 257–271.

Aharoni, Reuven and Yosef Ginat, "The Arab Citizens of Israel: From a Struggle for Equality to Political Separatism," in: David Mensheri (ed.), *Religion and State in the Middle East*, (Tel Aviv University: The Dayan Center for Middle Eastern and African Studies, 2006), pp. 278–315.

al-Hajj, Majed, "Arab voting trends for the *Knesset* in Israel," in Eli Rekhess (ed.), *The Arab Minority in Israel and the 17th Knesset Elections* (Tel Aviv: Tel Aviv University, The Dayan Center, 2006), pp. 17–21.

Amitai, Yossi, "The Arab Minority in Israel during the Military Government period: 1948–1966," in: Anita Shapira (ed.), *Independence – The First Fifty Years* (Jerusalem: The Zalman Shazar Centre, 1998).

Bastuni, Rustam, "The Arab Society in Israel," *The New Orient* 15 (1965), pp. 3–11.

Bastuni, Rustam, "Socialism and the Israeli Arabs," in Zeev Goldberg (ed.), *Western Socialism – Anthology* 16 (Beit Berl, 1971), pp. 65–71.

Belikof, Michal, "Government's resolutions regarding Arab Citizens: Development Plans 1999–2005", in: *Sikkuy Annual Report 2004–2005*.

Bishara, Azmi, "The Israeli Arab: A study in a mutilated political discourse." In: Ruth Gabizon and Dafna Hacker (eds.), *The Arab–Israeli Rift in Israel: An Anthology* (Jerusalem: The Israeli Institute of Democracy, 2000).

Boimel, Yair, "The Military Administration and its Cancellation Process 1958–1968," *The New East* 43 (2002), pp. 133–156.

Dahleh, Muhammad, "The Demand for Collective Rights to Arab Minority," in: Elie Rekhess and Sara Osatzcy-Lazar (eds.), *The Status of Arab Minority in Jewish Nation State* (Tel Aviv: Tel Aviv University, 2005), pp. 84–90.

Ghanem, Asʿad, "The Palestinian Minority in Israel: The Challenge of the Jewish State and its Ramifications," *Studies in the Revival of Israel*, 9 (1998), pp. 420–443.

Golan, Arnon, "The seizing of Arab lands by Jewish settlements in the War of Independence", *Cathedra* 63 (5752), pp. 122–154.

Haider, Aziz, "The boycott of elections by the Arab public: the perspective of a decade (1996–2006)," in Eli Rekhess (ed.), *The Arab Minority in Israel and the 17th Knesset Elections* (Tel Aviv: Tel Aviv University, The Dayan Center, 2006), pp. 89–92.

Jamal, Amal, "Avoiding participation: on the illusions of Arab politics in Israel" in: Asher Iran & Michal Shamir (eds.), *The 2001 Elections in Israel*, pp. 57–100.

Jamal, Amal, "Collective Rights for Original Minorities: Theoretical and Normative Views", in: Eli Rekhess and Sarah Osatsky-Lazar (eds.), *The Status of the Arab Minority in the Country of the Jewish Nation* (Tel Aviv University: The Ziv Centre, 2005), pp. 27–45.

Kayman, Charles, "After the Catastrophe: The Arabs in the State of Israel, 1948–1950," *Research and Review Notes*, booklet 10, (Haifa, 1984), pp. 5–91.

Khamaisi, Rasem, "The al-*Aqṣa* Intifada among the Palestinian Arabs in Israel: Processes, Motivations and Factors", in: *The Orr Testimonies* (Tel Aviv, Keter, 2003), pp. 50–86.

Lustik, Ian, *Arabs in the Jewish State* (Haifa: Mifras, 1985).

Oded, Yitzhak, "Land Losses among Israel's Arab Villagers," *New Outlook* 7, (1964), No. 7, pp. 10–25.

Regev, Avner, *Israeli Arabs: Political Issues* (Jerusalem: Jerusalem Institute for Israel Studies, 1989), pp. 28–32.

Rekhess, Eli, "The Arab in Israel and the Palestinians: Political Linkage and National Solidarity, 1967–1988, " *The New East* 32 (Jerusalem: Magnes, 1989), pp. 165–191.

Rekhess, Eli, "The policy principles towards the Arab population in Israel," in: Varda Pilavsky (ed.), *The Passage from the Yishuv to Statehood 1947–1949: Continuity and Change* (University of Haifa, The Herzl Institute for Zionist Research, 1990).

Rekhess, Eli and Doron Navot, "Equal Policy and Arab Politics: Paradigmatic and Pragmatic Obstructions," in: Shlomo Hasson and Michael Kraini (eds.), *The Arabs in Israel Facing Obstacles towards Equality* (Jerusalem: Florensheiner Institution for Policy, 2006), pp. 141–161.

Stendahl, Ori, *Between the Hammer and the Anvil* (Jerusalem: Academon, 1992).

Smooha, Sammy, "The existing policy and alternatives towards the Arabs in Israel," *Megamot* (September 1980), pp. 3–21.

Smooha, Sammy, "Approaches to Arab–Jewish relations and the October 2000 Riots," in Jewish–Arab Relations in Israel: Dream or Broken Dream?" *Studies in National Security* (2001), issue no. 1, pp. 17–32.

Tal, Nachman, "The Islamic Movement in Israel," *Strategic Bulletin* (February 2000), no. 4, pp. 8–12.

Vashitz, Yosef, "Majority and Minority," *Basha'ar*, (1966).

Yahye Yunis, Tajrid, "Political and Social Views and Positions of Palestinian-Arab Youths in Israel" in: Hagar Tsameret-Kercher (ed.), *Both This and That: Identity Contradictions in Young People in Israel* (The Friedrich Ebert Fund, 2010), pp. 287–328.

Yahye Yunis, Tajrid, "Changes in the research dialogue about Palestinian-Arab women in Israel" in: Uzi Rabi & Arik Rodnitsky (eds.), *Women in*

Arab Society in Israel (Tel Aviv University: The Dayan Center, 2011), pp. 12–16.

Yinon, Avraham. "Tawfik Ziad: We are the majority here," in: Aharon Layish (ed.), *The Arabs in Israel – Continuity and Change* (Jerusalem: Magnes Publications, 1981).

Index